History of Western Philosophy

CU00925953

# History of Western Philosophy

Nigel Tubbs
*University of Winchester, UK*

First published 2009 by
PALGRAVE MACMILLAN

Palgrave Macmillan in the UK is an imprint of Macmillan Publishers Limited, registered in England, company number 785998, of Houndmills, Basingstoke, Hampshire RG21 6XS.

Palgrave Macmillan in the US is a division of St Martin's Press LLC, 175 Fifth Avenue, New York, NY 10010.

Palgrave Macmillan is the global academic imprint of the above companies and has companies and representatives throughout the world.

Palgrave® and Macmillan® are registered trademarks in the United States, the United Kingdom, Europe and other countries

ISBN-13: 978-0-230-01938-6     hardback
ISBN-13: 978-0-230-01939-3     paperback

This book is printed on paper suitable for recycling and made from fully managed and sustained forest sources. Logging, pulping and manufacturing processes are expected to conform to the environmental regulations of the country of origin.

A catalogue record for this book is available from the British Library.

A catalog record for this book is available from the Library of Congress.

10   9   8   7   6   5   4   3   2   1
18   17   16   15   14   13   12   11   10   09

Printed and bound in Great Britain by
CPI Antony Rowe, Chippenham and Eastbourne

*the 'true world' ... [is] the history of an error*

Nietzsche, Twilight of the Idols

*should we not be concerned as to whether this fear of error is not just the error itself?*

Hegel, Phenomenology of Spirit

# Contents

# Preface

When I agreed with the publishers to write a *History of Western Philosophy* they hoped, I think, for an introductory text suitable for first year undergraduates. But in essence, such a book would only have been an introduction to other introductions to the history of Western philosophy. It would have tried to summarize the latter in ever more reductionist ways, replaying the same historical detail and the same shorthand versions of different periods and different writers. Instead, I have written a different kind of Introduction to the history of Western philosophy; an introduction, that is, to a different way of thinking about it.

I am introducing – perhaps reintroducing would be more accurate here – the idea that the history of Western philosophy is an autobiography of Western thought, a recollection of its own development, as of the child by the man. As it surveys this development it finds itself making all kinds of mistakes based on misunderstandings of itself in different ways at different times. But, as we know, those mistakes in our lives are formative. They make us what we are. The adult cannot eschew this development as something left far behind and overcome, for that is just another mistake that can be recollected, now, even as it is made. Rather, then, the more one examines one's autobiography, the more one finds out about who one is.

This is not just the benefit of hindsight. Hindsight suggests that one can see how one might have done things differently. But this is not the point of recollection. One recollects not to see how things might have been but to understand more clearly actually how they are.

The autobiography not only recollects the past, it educates the enquirer, the writer, in the present. And, perhaps most surprisingly, when recollection opens the enquirer to learning about the child as the father of the man, then the writer is also being opened to himself as living the life of learning. This openness is the concept of the future. True, the enquirer must presuppose himself to begin with, or else there is no beginning to the enquiry. But what he learns thereafter is that this presupposition of the enquirer, while unavoidable, is also one based in illusions. Here, the presupposition of the enquirer collapses under its own educational weight. In the recollection of his life he learns of himself formed in and from such learning. Indeed, he learns that he is only someone who learns and re-learns. This is a new truth – the truth of the learner who learns, by learning, of himself as a learner – and it is a new manifestation of the theory and practice of philosophical education.

The autobiography that I am presenting below is that of Western thought undertaking to follow the maxim of the Delphic Oracle, to Know Thyself. This thought is present to itself in different shapes – as freedom, as nature, and as logic – but together they are the one educational relation that constitutes the autobiographical work. Freedom, nature, and logic learn of the truth of themselves as learning. Those who are sceptical of the imperialism that is grounded in the whole idea of a history of Western philosophy miss the point. It is in the enquiry, in the learning, that the imperialism of the project is most open to its being negated and undermined. The history of Western philosophy, as Know Thyself, is a – perhaps *the* – most effective form of self-critique that the West has available to it. It cannot survive this critique without the formative change that comes from negating its positing of itself. What it learns and how it changes is the subject of the following account of the history of Western philosophy.

\* \* \* \* \*

If I can add a personal note now, I see ever more clearly the developing shape of my own thinking. I began my time in higher education as an undergraduate, a learner, who believed in the educative significance of sociology to disrupt natural consciousness with contingency, relativism, and dialectic. I then found that this education was called philosophy, or at least the philosophy that related to the European speculative tradition, and could be understood as the *contradiction of enlightenment*, or as *philosophy's higher education*. I worked in a few comprehensive schools in England and found a *new teacher* in the theory and practice of the learning learner. This theory and practice elicits a *philosophy of the teacher*. To draw out this higher education in Hegel in particular, I have argued for a different kind of Hegel, one that calls for an *education in Hegel*. Now, the *history of Western philosophy* presented below is this same theory of philosophical education writ large as the journey of Western thought to its recollection of itself in and as learning.

And, as at the end of each book, so at the end of this one, the next project has already made itself known: how to a teach present recollection? How to give voice to freedom and nature and logic as modern philosophical learning? My work with these questions will now form the basis of a new programme of studies at the University of Winchester, England, in Modern Liberal Arts.

# Acknowledgements

I offer my thanks to the University of Winchester for the time given to me for writing this book, and for the opportunities they continue to afford me for bringing theory and practice together. I thank, too, the Department of Education Studies for their support.

I recollect my due, as always, to Howard and Josh.

Julie and Will have complemented beautifully my isolation with their love and friendship. They have ensured that the history of Western philosophy has always been informed by *The Office*, *Frasier*, Nadal and Federer, and Springsteen with the Sessions Band.

Finally, I would like to dedicate this book to someone who lives the theory and practice of learning to be the learner, and does so very much in the public eye – to Rowan.

Chandler's Ford
March 2009.

# Introduction

What justification is there for writing another history of Western philosophy, and especially one that appears to repeat the same material in the same order that so many others have done before? Indeed, is not the very idea of a history of Western philosophy disreputable, outdated, and exhausted? Does it not ground itself in fantasies of totality and truth that are no longer appropriate or sound in a pluralist world? Is the history of Western philosophy not in fact the master narrative of all master narratives, and really only an apology for the imperialism of Western reason? Finally, is not the history of Western philosophy imbued with the arrogance of the idea that reason in Western civilization marks the highest form of social and political organization yet achieved on earth, and perhaps that mankind is capable of at all? Why, then, waste time and resources repeating a project that, in falling into such disrepute, is at best redundant and at worst dead?

The answer to these questions, probably not very different from any such apology, is that in what follows, we are offering the usual content of the history of Western philosophy but understood in an unusual way. We are concerned to look behind the familiar collection of the content of the history of Western philosophy to search for the *conditions of possibility* that sustain it. This means looking at what is going on behind the back of the content. It is to ask, what conditions are presupposed that have shaped this content into what we know as the history of Western philosophy?

## Conclusion

What emerges from our study is a tale of two relations – life and death, and metaphysics and social life – and two logics – Neoplatonic logic and aporetic logic, of which more later. The story we will tell is of the *education*

1

of the Western master about the certainties that he *posits* for himself and for his idea of truth. Philosophy will slowly erode these certainties until they collapse under the weight of their empty assertions.[1]

This story begins with the template of positing as it appears in Ancient Greece and is played out in the dialectic between Plato and Aristotle. This template then becomes concrete and divided in the emerging and struggling self-consciousness of Christian subjectivity. Truth here is posited in Neoplatonic principles where doubt, ambivalence and contradiction are marked as errors in relation to the undivided, unchangeable, and simple essence of the one.[2] However, these *cultures of error*, as we will come to know them, although alienated from the truth whose principles they espouse, nevertheless take culture, or education, very seriously. We will see in Augustine, Eriugena, and Aquinas, as well as in the Judaic philosophy of Maimonides, and the Islamic philosophy of al-Farabi and others, how closely related truth and ambivalence are in the concept of philosophical education. These cultures of error, including the rationalism of Descartes, pass into the modern mind in the Kantian revolution of the relation between thought and object, and in the Hegelian experience of this revolution. Here Neoplatonic logic collapses into the aporetic or recollective logic of the modern mind wherein, also, social relations and metaphysical relations come together, although not in any simple sense of unification. We then briefly explore some examples from the recent history of this aporetic logic in what is loosely called the Continental or European tradition, before, finally, discussing ways in which aporetic logic re-educates the master about three of his most trusted logical standpoints: self over other, man over God, and life over death. Such a presentation of the history of Western philosophy amounts to nothing less than a challenge to the West, and to its current standpoint in the bourgeois master, to 'Know Thyself' in the truth of the logic of its vulnerabilities.

The implications of this reading of the history of Western philosophy are far-reaching. It commends a vision of and for the West, and of philosophy within it, of personal, social, spiritual, and global life characterized by *learning*. It commends education *as truth* within the experience of some of the West's most intractable binary oppositions – self and other, East and West, rich and poor, master and slave, and life and death. This truth in education opens up Western reason not only to its own rational aporias, but to the spiritual significance of reason's complicity in these aporias. Philosophical education emerges here as the critical voice that challenges any and all standpoints that posit immunity for themselves from modern abstract reason and from its collapse into contradiction and negation. In addition, and this is its absolute significance as education, this critical voice learns of truth in this negation. Living with the implications of negation, and enduring these negative states, is precisely what has its truth in philosophical education. Learned as *recollection*,[3] the history of Western philosophy becomes a *present* negation. Learned of as a totality constituted by negation and education, these negative states are also in themselves open to the dialectic of truth and vulnerability. This openness is the recollective concept of the future.

The substance of our reading of the history of Western philosophy, then, is this: recollection teaches that the history of Western philosophy is the study of an error carried in thought and displayed when thought tries to comprehend the true. Thought is deemed to be in error because its comprehension is compound, contingent, and changeable in comparison to the true which is simple, self-sufficient, and unchangeable. Recollective logic in the modern mind offers a fundamental re-education about this relation of truth and thought. It offers the logic of aporia as recollective, and it offers this recollective learning as the modern logic of philosophical principles. This means, in turn, that we can present a recollected history of Western philosophy as both chronological content and the disruption of this chronology.

## First principles

The distinctiveness of our approach is illustrated by our seeking to uncover what it is that the shapes of thought that constitute the history of Western philosophy have taken for granted in presenting themselves. If the history of Western philosophy has been characterized as the logical search for first principles, then we are seeking the presuppositions of logic that drive and underpin such a search. We seek the logic of logic. This takes the history of Western philosophy into unfamiliar waters, and requires certain key terms and concepts to be understood in new ways in order to stay afloat. We will briefly rehearse this buoyancy now.

The history of Western philosophy is grounded in presuppositions of Neoplatonic logic that are rarely examined in their own right. These presuppositions are the conditions of the possibility of the principles by which thought works and by which it investigates itself, and which therein underpin the history of Western philosophy. The principles are those of non-contradiction, of first cause, and of the absurdity of infinite regression. Non-contradiction eschews negation as other than truth. It is, therefore, the ground of the logic in which the standpoint of infinite regression – where a cause needs to be explained by a cause *ad infinitum* – is seen to be *clearly* absurd and revealing of the necessity for a first cause. The absurdity of this infinite regression, and of the pernicious contradiction of lack of a first cause, was avoided by the *clearly* obvious necessity of God, or an unmoved mover, or a first principle.

We present later the case that what these principles presuppose and reproduce are certain fundamental relations – metaphysical, social, and natural – which, in turn, presuppose and reproduce the conditions of their own possibility. Such positing is *clearly* evident in the presupposition that infinite regression is *clearly* absurd. Through the educational concept of recollection, we will illustrate what it is that 'clearly' here takes so easily and incontrovertibly for granted. It will reveal how such positing has its appearances in the world in the fundamental relations of truth and error, independence and dependence, God and man, self and other, and master and slave. If you recognize these terms as of Hegelian inspiration, then you would be right. In turn these relations are manifestations of an absolute relation, that of life and death. Life and death, we will argue, are the pedagogy of the mind of God making itself known to the intellect.

In the presentation of the history of Western philosophy that follows, then, we are concerned to discover the ways in which logical principles posit these relations in particular ways at different times, ways that become the irrefutable bases of philosophic proof. We will follow this positing from its beginnings in Ancient Greece to Kant and Hegel, and beyond, where by means of positing, positing becomes aware of itself as groundless. This groundlessness becomes the aporetic logic and content, then, of the modern philosophical mind. What is learned here in the modern mind is the truth of positing, wherein philosophy is able to trace a genealogy of its thought back through the various shapes of its conditions of possibility to that of life and death. It is here that the history of Western philosophy is revealed as grounded in the positing of life as separate from death, and of groundlessness as separate from truth.

This positing is inevitable and unavoidable, for it is the pedagogy of the truth in its own aporetic logic. Life is that which posits itself as *what is*, and over and against *what is not*. To know this is to learn of life as its own self-determining illusion. This changes fundamentally how to comprehend the history of Western philosophy. Instead of recording the ways in which the logic of non-contradiction, of first cause, and of the absurdity of infinite regression have been wielded by philosophers in trials of rigour, robustness, and consistency, now we can look behind the scenes of these trials to their conditions of possibility in the illusions of life and its eschewing of negation and death as other. As such, the history of Western philosophy is transformed from the mere presupposition of life as the ground or master of logic, into the story of its suppression of death and of the logic of negation. We are now able to read the history of Western philosophy as the manifestation of life's misrecognition of its relation to death as it has shaped, and continues to shape, Western philosophy's notion of truth. It reveals the aporia of logic but learns, too, of the logic of aporia. It leaves the search for first principles grounded only in the illusions of assertion and positing, but learns that the groundlessness of positing has its principle in its negative character. This amounts to nothing less than the re-education of the West about how to understand itself.

## Recollection, not recognition

In order to emphasize the educational nature of this aporetic logic we will employ the notion of recollection, and invoke aporetic recollective logic as the form and content of the modern mind. This recollective logic has its ground in the groundlessness of positing, which is the same as to say, that it has its ground in the truth of death in life, of the slave in the master, of God in man, and of the other in the self. It is a logic known as positing by positing. *Clearly* this threatens to collapse into infinite regression if conditions need their own conditions, and so on. But recollection learns something different here than does Neoplatonism. As we will come to see, it learns of a logic of positing. This logic unfolds itself in thought's self-education as the condition of the possibility of Neoplatonic logic and principles. Such recollection of Neoplatonic logic is the modern subjective and substantial mind characterized by Kantian and Hegelian logic.

It would be simpler here to describe the relation between Neoplatonic logic and recollective logic in the educative terms of the *recognition of misrecognition*. This would mean that the content of the history of Western philosophy misrecognizes itself when it fails to know its own conditions of possibility, and that Neoplatonic logic is characterized by this misrecognition. This would also enable us to say that recollective logic recognizes this misrecognition and thus comprehends the mistakes that Neoplatonic logic has repeated. However, the education contained in the recognition of misrecognition is insufficient to describe the educational significance of recollective logic. The logic of the recognition of misrecognition is a simple logic where, in learning and understanding, truth overcomes error. But this only raises exactly the kind of philosophical question that characterizes our study of the history of Western philosophy, namely, what is presupposed in this positing of philosophical education as overcoming contradiction? The logic of recognition overcoming misrecognition is all too easily read as just another positing by life of mastery over the error of negation and contradiction. Recognition, and even the more refined concept of *re*-cognition, express a new knowing, but do not suggest with equal impact the preservation of what is misrecognized.

Somehow, recollective logic has to hold what it has learned about overcoming having its condition of possibility in positing, but without again obscuring this education behind another such positing, or mastery. But how is this possible? How can one recollect one's genealogy in the conditions of possibility, or in life and death, without again taking the side of life and using philosophical education as mastery over negative error? How can it criticize the positing of truth and error without positing truth and error in doing so? The answer is that it cannot. Here the two logics part company. Aporetic logic finds something of itself in the nothing, where Neoplatonic logic finds only error and demands that truth be other to this error. Recollective logic knows the groundlessness of the positing that is the condition of its own possibility, to be neither an overcoming nor a non-overcoming, but to be education. It knows the groundlessness of positing to be both formation and re-formation, an assertion and an education about assertion by assertion. Positing, re-formed by itself here in education, is the educational logic of recollection. And the name of the truth of this aporetic logic is learning.

This concept of learning is the truth that Neoplatonic logic ruled out as contrary to the truth of what is. Where such logic held that nothing can come from infinite regression or contradiction, and that God must contain neither of these, now the modern mind finds something in the nothing; it finds itself. It finds learning to be *what is*. Learning holds overcoming and non-overcoming as the one divided experience. It retrieves the negative that life has suppressed but does so without also suppressing the life that suppresses it. Learning is by its very nature complicit in itself.

## The three relations of philosophy

We will see many times below how, when thought tries to think truth in itself, it fails because it collapses into contradictions, not least into the contradiction of infinite regression. Thought expresses this error in and as three relations to the true. In the *natural* relation thought is error against the laws of the natural universe; in the *social* relation thought is error against freedom and in the *metaphysical* relation thought is error against the truth of the in-itself, or God. Each relation posits thought as error, in that it is separated from its object and unable to unite with it by knowing the object in itself. But these relations of posited error mask the very positing that is their condition of possibility, creating therein an illusion of an originary relation that is unknowable in itself. It is these illusions which have established themselves as the 'proper' content of the history of Western philosophy. But in such a history comprehended in recollection, it is the nature of these illusions and the positing they hide that is the focus of the enquiry.

There is not space in the present volume to trace all three relations in the history of Western philosophy. But neither is it possible to follow one without implication in the others. The present volume therefore employs the following strategy in response to this. We will, in the main, pursue the metaphysical as it appears in relation to the true, and in the way it posits a logic of first principles. We have to accept that this does not do justice either to nature or freedom in the story of the history of Western philosophy. This is addressed in small part in the *Appendix* to the text which presents a recollective reading of freedom in Hegel's philosophy of history. However, in examining the ancient mind we will include the natural and spiritual appearances of thought's relation to truth alongside the logical and metaphysical. Then, in the cultures of error of the mediaeval mind the natural and spiritual relations are subsumed within metaphysics. This reflects the actuality of the mediaeval world in the sense that the metaphysical dominates other relations, perhaps symbolized in the relation between the trivium and the quadrivium in mediaeval liberal arts. The natural relation re-asserts itself in Bacon's *Novum Organum*, where the object is given its own status and is freed from the mediaeval view that the world exists for man. Indeed, inductive logic here claims to be able to create or invent new particulars by itself.

Similarly, the social relation re-asserts itself in the modern mind. More accurately the social and metaphysical relations here recollect themselves in the aporetic logic they share. This modern mind is characterized by the Kantian experience of groundlessness and the Hegelian experience of this Kantian experience. We will explore this later in Part III. What we do not explore is the natural relation in the modern mind except as it appears in the illusions of life and death.[4]

The metaphysical relation expresses the relation of finite thought and experience to the true as one of error. As such, the term metaphysical already carries and hides the positing of its own condition of possibility. This refers to the positing of truth beyond mere thought in a realm *a priori* and not *a posteriori*, and therefore not dependent on human experience. This distinction has its actuality in three ways. The *a priori* is other than the *a posteriori*; the *a priori* is master over the *a posteriori*; and the *a priori* is something in itself and the *a posteriori* is nothing in itself. Thus, metaphysics is the positing of the distinctions of self and other, master and slave, and life and death. There is also here a staging of the metaphysical relation, where life and death beget master and slave, which beget self and other, which beget metaphysics. But, in the illusions of Western, modern, abstract, rational consciousness the staging appears in reverse. It appears that it is in metaphysics that we learn of the separation of the subject in itself from its being known, and of the priority of the *a priori* over experience. It is from this, then, that thought believes itself able to understand identity, priority, and the error of negation. It is in the light of recollection that the illusions of this staging are exposed.

This experience demonstrates how identity, priority, and the error of negation all posit the relation of life and death as *what is* over death as *what is not*. This positing, unknown to Neoplatonic metaphysics as positing, is the logic that shaped over 2000 years of the history of Western philosophy. It is in the modern mind that metaphysics learns of or recollects the conditions of its own possibility as posited, and learns too that its logic is aporetic and recollective. Here, as it were, everything changes. Recollection knows the logic of death in life, of the slave in the master, and of the other in the self. It knows too, of the recollective truth of the aporias of non-contradictory logic, of first cause, and of infinite regression. This is the challenge to Neoplatonic logic that emerges from the modern Kantian and Hegelian mind. We will return to this in Part III.

We must also note here, that if the logic of first cause is undermined, then one of the cornerstones of the logic of the existence of God is also removed. God known Neoplatonically is the posited necessity of a first cause. But if the logic of first cause is only an illusion of the appearance of the life and death relation, then God becomes only an effect of this illusion. However, and as we will return to in Chapter 7 below, recollection is not the death of God *per se,* only the death of God in a way that reveals his actuality. Nor, in the same way, does recollection take sides in the debate that so preoccupied Neoplatonic logic, as to whether the universe is eternal or created. Recollection seeks the conditions of the possibility that are posited in both claims. The need for a creator posits life needing a beginning from nothing, for otherwise, due to infinite regression, there is no cause for the universe. The case for infinity, on the other hand, posits creation as a contradiction of God's identity for it involves a decision, a change in God, who is posited as unchangeable.[5] Both sides of the argument are grounded in the positing of contradiction as error. When recollection knows the conditions of the possibility of the arguments for creation and infinity, and for God and first cause, to be the positing of life without death, it knows too that the groundlessness which Neoplatonism seeks to avoid, in fact grounds itself. This ground of groundlessness is the education that learning of its conditions of possibility in recollection re-forms the truth of the thought that thinks it. This, as we will see, is the condition of the possibility of the modern mind in the history of Western philosophy, and, therein, of our knowing God.

We will present this account of the history of Western philosophy below. This means we will concentrate on ways in which the illusion of thought as error plays a decisive role in the history of Western philosophy, as well as the ways in which different thinkers have tried to negotiate with error to find truth within it. We will see some remarkable examples of how error and negativity have been viewed as formative of the knowledge of the true. The history of Western philosophy has always carried its truth with it, but in its history some have worked harder than others to work with the conditions of its own possibility. For us to recollect this truth is also to pay tribute to the struggles and to the truth of those who are our recollection.

## The end of the history of Western philosophy

Famously, recollection was present at the beginning of the history of Western philosophy as one of the subjects Socrates spoke of just before his death. Two and a half thousand years later the history of Western philosophy can recollect the reports of its own death. It can take its beginning from the death of Socrates, and its end from the death of the concept of the history of Western philosophy. These reports of its death have not been exaggerated, only misunderstood. As death returns to educate the life of Western philosophy, so it recollects backwards, looking for ways in which negation and contradiction have been posited as error; it recollects itself presently as this recollection; and it recollects forwards as the past of a future that is now open to its own truth, to being recollected as learning. Here the modern mind retrieves life and death as the essence of philosophy, and as the source of the question of meaning. Putting life and death at the origin and at the end of the history of Western philosophy retrieves philosophy not just as the love of wisdom, but also as the fear of death that is the beginning of wisdom.[6]

# Part I  The Ancient Mind

# 1
# Naming the Beginning

## Socrates

The recollection of death in life, at the beginning of Western philosophy carries names from the Ancient world.[1] Heraclitus is the name of
a living universe that is eternally becoming and constantly changing.
Difference in the universe is only the universe in agreement with its
own *logos*, a universal reason that binds all things together in change
and flux, like the movement back and forth that is created when the
string of a bow is released.[2] Here life is defined without any loss of
itself to rest or being. Parmenides is the name of a living universe that
is eternally being, and is that from which movement comes. Here life
is defined without any loss of itself to movement and change. Both
beginnings are eternal, in eternal becoming and eternal being. A third
name – Anaxagoras – carries the relation of *nus* as the mind that knows
itself as being or becoming. But it is in a fourth name – Socrates – that
we know *nus* as the recollection of the life and death relation, that is,
as the dialectic of revel and repose together, never one without the
other. As the *Phaedo* reveals, Socrates relates to death and to life dialectically. The ambivalence in Socrates here is formative. On the one
hand he moves the identities of life and death into a revel and repose
where each is in the other. Death is in life in the recollection of the
soul, while life is in death in the transmigration and immortality of
the soul. On the other hand a hierarchy of values is posited when the
soul is contrasted with the body. Socrates praises the life of the philosopher who works for the death of the body and its material distractions
and temptations. *Nus* values itself most when it values the body least.
Socrates relativizes life and death in dialectical relation to each other
but he sees true negation in death alone. Thus, life knows its relative

13

truth in death as recollection, but knows its absolute truth in death to be without the body. Here Socrates lays down a philosophical principle that will underpin the history of Western philosophy for centuries to come. 'If we are ever to know anything absolutely, we must be free from the body and must behold the actual realities with the eye of the soul alone' (Plato, 1982, 231).[3] Why then, does the magisterial dialectic of Socrates yield the absolute to incorporeal thought rather than hold to the truth in life of the circle of recollection and transmigration? The answer is, because the dialectic of life and death is judged from the perspective of life. Life posits embodied-thought as error because of its dialectics, its oppositions, which are not the truth of what is simply in itself. The truth of the dialectic is posited as other than dialectic, and thought posits itself as error. Even Socrates cannot find a way in which the truth of loss in the dialectic can be absolute and pure in the embodied mind that it negates. The history of Western philosophy will retain this standpoint of thought positing its own oppositions as error as the foundation of Neoplatonic logic and principles.

Yet the Ancient world also has names for the relation that tries to think about itself as what is and what is not. The names of this struggle are Plato and Aristotle, who, in turn, explore the relation as metaphysical logic, as nature, and as spirit.

## Plato

Plato recognizes the truth as thoughts within the sphere of the intellect, and not in sensuous objects or mere perception. In the *Republic*, the cave is a metaphor for the relation between truth and thought. The prisoners in the cave come to see that the objects they have taken to be real are in fact only shadows of the real objects lit from behind by a fire. The philosopher comes to see that the objects perceived in the mind are in fact only particular images or shadows of the universal forms of the true, the good, and the beautiful. Plato reads the opposition of the being of Parmenides and non-being of Heraclitus – the dialectic of identity and unrest – together with the Eleatic dialectic of contradiction, and expresses therein the totality of *nus* as the concrete thought of truth and the universal truth of thought. This establishes the domain of the philosophical mind. Philosophy, as in the cave metaphor, is the dialectic of loss and return: loss in that the conditions of the possibility of a true thought lay beyond the experience of what is; and return in that the conditions of the possibility of truth per se recognize their own experience in what is. This is the principle of the intellect – that the truth of itself is in knowing itself. The misrecognition of this relation as error by the standpoint of truth taken as *what is*, defines future Neoplatonism.

This intellectual principle has three distinct relations in which its dialectic speaks its own impossible truth. *Logic* is pure dialectical form as content; *nature* is the dialectic of mind and the external world; and *spirit* is the dialectic of mind and the social world.

## Logic and metaphysics

Dialectical logic in Plato speaks of the way the conditions of the possibility of the thought of truth are likewise the conditions of the possibility of truth as thought. *Nus* is this circular logic as essence and existence. It is evident in some of the Socratic dialogues, although – and here is its actuality as aporia – this unity can only appear over and above the dialectic. Socrates often employs dialectic to relativize identity through opposition. For example, hot is defined relative to cold, large to small, and truth to man. But when the truth of this opposition appears, it is as a third partner somehow, over and above the dialectic. The *Sophist* shows Plato's aversion to siding with either revel or repose, but the *Protagoras* exhibits the unity of this revel and repose as a finger hovering above the participants. It points out how, in their discussion, each started and ended with opposing views but exchanged these views in the process. In the *Philebus* the relation of the divine and the concrete is the unity of finite pleasure and infinite wisdom, and in the *Parmenides* the unity of universal forms is assigned to the one and the many.

Modern subjective thought experiences the hovering finger of such unity as domination or external imposition. But for Plato this unity is the thought of truth and the truth of thought, a bond that fuses itself with that which is bound by it. It is where truth and thought share the one condition of possibility. The distinctions of inner and outer, master and slave, and truth and thought here do not carry the subjective significance of freedom that they do in modernity. This is why modern readings of Plato have no problem finding totalitarianism therein, for what he takes to be a shape of unity the modern mind sees as the opposition of freedom and non-freedom, or autonomy and heteronomy. In the *Republic*, for example, the philosopher-kings can be seen as an elite band of despots that govern without the consent of the people. We know that Plato wrote the *Republic* in order to counter the fragmentation and corruption of the *polis* into self-interested factions; but Plato did not believe that the *Republic* was replacing one corruption with another. That the modern mind reads (or could read) the *Republic* so differently is in itself evidence of the development of Western philosophy that we will be following below. What we can say is that in representing unity as a third to dialectical logic, Plato was able to hold on to an ambivalence of unity. It is precisely Plato's aim *not* to resolve the opposition of the dialectic but to let it speak as a whole.

## Nature

If logic is the thought of truth and the truth of thought as one form and content, Plato's philosophy of nature tries to comprehend unity in the dialectic of thought and matter or the external universe. In the *Timaeus* Plato gives voice to the common religious mythology wherein God is understood to find eternal matter existing as chaos. He forms this matter in an act of creation in his own image, that is, into intellect as life and, by way of the soul, also forms man in this same image. That God finds matter already existing shows the particular problem that nature creates for dialectical philosophy. How can the dialectic which is logically its own unity, account for something that pre-exists it? This will become one of the most important questions in the history of Western philosophy, namely that if God creates matter then God is subject to change and to chronological time, but if the universe is eternal then (and contrary to holy texts) God cannot have created it. As such, pre-existing matter pits creation and eternity against each other and, therefore, God against himself. In his *Lectures on the History of Philosophy*, Hegel warns that we should read any such abstract beginnings in Plato only as ordinary propositions and not as philosophical or dialectical propositions. He says that what we should look for in the *Timaeus*, as elsewhere in Plato, is the way in which such ordinary propositions serve only to facilitate the proper dialectical determinations. Hegel is suggesting here that ordinary propositions are childlike and naïve ways of beginning, but may help in bringing unphilosophical minds to dialectical determinations. The religious myths that Plato at times employs 'are not the philosophic doctrines which Plato seriously held' (1974, 74; 1970, 88), that is, those in which dialectic sustains its aporias without falling back on immediacies that ease its difficulties.

A less pragmatic explanation comes by way of reading Plato's philosophy of nature in terms of recollection. Plato's concern is to show the dialectical unity of nature in the intellect, or to show how God is in the material universe. He does this by way of the soul. The soul is the middle between the unchangeable and the corporeal. It is how God made material in the universe to be in his own image, and how he made himself knowable in and to the universe as its truth. Just as the soul recollects itself in life and death, so also the soul recollects itself in creation and eternity. Seen in this way, the opposition of creation and eternity is as logically consistent as the opposition of life and death, for both show how the soul recollects the conditions of its possibility in aporia.

This aporetic recollection is much more consistent than positing nature without intellect. To do so leaves nature as a fourth partner to unity in difference, outside of formative intellectual significance. This has special significance for modern thought, for Auschwitz can also be seen as a fourth city, beyond the logic of immediacy, mediation and recollection, beyond the dialectic of identity and other, and unaccountable for its 'nature' to any dialectical unrest. This fourth city is the triumph of otherness as natural and is beyond political accountability. Auschwitz, here, is a philosophy of nature that remains free from the realm of freedom.[4]

## Spirit

The third sphere wherein dialectic expresses unity is in spirit or the relation of intellect and the social and political world. The society that Plato describes in the *Republic* has its unity in difference in the dialectical relation wherein the conditions of the possibility of the universal are likewise the conditions of the possibility of the singular. Their unity, the unity of the one and the many, will be justice or the form of the good. But, in the same way that logic and nature had to identify the unity as a third to the relation of identity and unrest, and the divine and man, so the *Republic* also has to give a name to the unity. This unity we know as the philosopher-kings in the city, and as reason in the soul.

For Plato, such distinctions are only unity in its own shapes, whereas for modern subjectivity the philosopher-kings and rational duty are experienced not as expressions of unity but of domination and lack of freedom. For Plato, the philosopher-kings are the truth of the city, for they are the truth of the struggle between universal and particular, or the whole and its members, in their dialectical opposition. The philosopher-kings are the wisdom that comes from the intellect knowing itself dialectically in the opposition of universal and individual needs. This is the Platonic notion of *phronesis*. Similarly, the truth of the city shares the same dialectical structure as the truth of the soul. The soul is the truth of the unity of reason that knows itself in the dialectic of the needs of the self and the needs of others. The soul and the city are the same unity grounded in the real struggle between men for just social relations, or in the will. In the city this is the struggle that the philosopher-kings face in trying to live as the justice they seek for the society as a whole. They are required to give up personal wealth, families, and property so that their truth in and of universality is not compromised by any merely local or personal demands. In the soul this is the struggle that reason engages in against immediate desire. The important point here is that the unity is not an identity, unmoved and set in stone, nor, in the absence of such fixity, is it meaningless and empty. The struggle for justice in the city is in the truth that the philosopher-kings cannot remain outside the cave, but must return in order to work for justice. The struggle for reason in the soul concerns the spiritedness of its character. Reason needs courage in the face of disharmony in its struggle against desire that is always try-ing to corrupt it. These struggles, indeed, are educational struggles, for they form and re-form the character of the city and the soul. The unity in this educational struggle is overlooked when the philosopher-kings, or reason, are seen by modern subjectivity as merely imposition. This is to abstract the unity from its conditions of possibility in dialectic. Plato's fate, to be read this way, however, is already present in the raison *d'être* of the *Republic*, that the unity is already collapsing into parts that can no longer add up to the whole.

## Aristotle

If a case can be made in Plato for comprehending the unity of the intellect in the struggle between its extremes of the one and the many, of mind and material, and of thought and truth, and if this struggle is unity in the philosopher-king, then a case can also be made for Aristotle being the first of these philosopher-kings after Plato. His is the life that lives out the struggle of the self-relation of the intellect. He is the Platonist who tries to deal with the problems bequeathed by Plato, not least in the gap between metaphysical truth and its being experienced in the world. Even though at the beginning of *Physics* Aristotle makes it absolutely clear that in any field of study that has first principles knowledge must begin with those and work down to its elements, he nevertheless also acknowledges the difficulty of the difference that per-sists between the in-itself of principles and the for-us of its elements. Thus, as a student of Plato, Aristotle tries to work with the unity of thought and truth as it is experienced, that is, as the dialectic of identity and unrest. This means that his thought takes a different relationship to Plato at different times, but as a whole it reveals consistently how rest and unrest are interrupted and negated by each other.

Werner Jaeger's reconstruction of the chronology of Aristotle's work enables us to better understand the different stages of his develop-ment, and of how his relation to Plato changed over the years. Jaeger suggests three distinct periods in Aristotle's thinking and writing. In his earliest period Aristotle gives priority to the forms, retaining allegiance to Platonic metaphysics, to the soul's immortality, and to the Platonic theory of recollection as found in the *Phaedo*. The *Eudemus* and the *Protrepticus* both express this, as they do the centrality of *nus* as the presence of the divine in the body.

Aristotle's middle period is characterized as a religious stage, which at once looks backwards to the universal form and forwards to the idea of empirical science. The lost text, *On Philosophy*, is shown, by fragments from later writers, to be critical of the Platonic theory of universal forms.[5] From Cicero, we learn that Aristotle put forward his own version of the cave metaphor, wherein he tried to bring more closely together transcendental and inner emotion so that religion would be both universal form and its particular experience. He says,

> [s]uppose there were men who had always lived underground, in good and well-lighted dwellings, adorned with statues and pictures, and furnished with everything in which those who are thought happy abound. Suppose, however, that they had never gone above ground, but had learned by report and hearsay that there was a divine spirit and power. Suppose that then, at some time, the jaws of the earth opened, and they were able to escape and make their way from those hidden dwellings into those regions which we inhabit. When they suddenly saw earth and seas and skies, when they learned the grandeur of clouds and the power of winds, when they saw the sun and realized not only its grandeur and beauty but also its power, by which it fills the sky with light and makes the day; when, again, night darkened the lands and they saw the whole sky picked out and adorned with stars, and the varying light of the moon as it waxes and wanes, and the risings and settings of all these bodies, and their courses settled and immutable to all eternity; when they saw those things, most certainly would they have judged that there are gods and that these great works are the works of gods.
>
> (Aristotle, 1984b, 2392; fragment 12)[6]

This is characteristic of Aristotle's middle theological period. It sees the need to demonstrate the highest principles at work within the forms of nature. It brings the forms down to the human level and seeks to comprehend how they are experienced in the individual mind. 'Those who are being initiated are not required to grasp anything with the understanding, but to have a certain inner experience, and so to be put into a particular frame of mind' (Jaeger, 1962, 160).[7] This middle period also speaks of Aristotle's ambivalence as a Platonist who is becoming a Platonic Aristotelian. In his middle period this is a question of emphasis. Where Plato's cave-dwellers leave the cave for their transcendental education, Aristotle's underground-dwellers rise to the world of natural objects and this becomes the site of their transcendental education, one characterized by awe and wonder. Thus, Aristotle's cave, like Plato's, still holds that the relationship of the transcendental and the real, and of inner truth and outer truth, is in *nus* as the divine that is within and without.[8]

This ambivalence of Platonic Aristotelianism is emphasized in some of the earliest writings in the *Metaphysics*. In Chapter 10 of Book M, Aristotle notes that problems are raised for those who support the theory of universal forms *and* for those who do not. He states this as a dialectical problem of knowing the true. On the one hand, he says, if we – and here 'we' shows Aristotle speaking as a Platonist in the community of Platonists – keep material things separate from the universal substance 'how are we to conceive their elements and their principles?' (*Metaphysics*, 1086b, 20; 1984b, 1717). But, on the other hand, if we do not keep them apart, 'we shall destroy substance in the sense in which we Platonists understand it' (1962, 188).[9]

Aristotle is Platonic in stating Platonism's internal ambivalence. The original *Metaphysics*, says Jaeger, was written 'during the critical period in Assos when Aristotle was attacking the theory of the Ideas as a Platonist among Platonists' (1962, 189). It addressed the question of overwhelming importance: how to reconcile the sensible and the transcendental by rehabilitating rather than overcoming the theory of the ideas. Indeed, the dilemma of the separation of the sensible from the supersensible substance could only be a real dilemma 'for those who stand on Platonic ground' (1962, 188), and this is exactly true of the earliest Aristotelian metaphysics which grants the necessity of the contradiction that 'knowledge is universal and in a sense it is not' (*Metaphysics*, 1087a, 25; 1984b, 1718). From such irresolvable dilemmas, for Aristotle in particular, 'the conclusion is obvious: the contradictions can only be resolved by a new notion of substance' (1962, 188). Aristotle, in the early aporetic metaphysics, can only hint at the reconstruction of substance that he will later attempt.[10]

The late phase of Aristotelian philosophy emphasizes the necessity of empirical experience over speculation. In this sense Aristotle can be said to be working in an entirely new way. The Introduction to *On the Parts of the Animals* sets out this new empirical manifesto, arguing that there is no corner of the animal kingdom where one cannot find 'absence of haphazard and conduciveness of everything to an end' (645a, 23–5; 1984a, 1004). It is to the natural world in its smallest detail that Aristotle finally turns, seeking evidence of the universal in each particular, no matter how small or insignificant it might appear. This marks a dramatic shift of methodology from Platonic metaphysics and *nus* to empirical science. Emerging from underground, Aristotle now aligns himself with those whose religiosity comes from a sense of awe and wonder at the natural universe, and finds in empirical research a form of worship appropriate to that religiosity.[11] It prioritizes experience over speculation, the near at hand over the distant, and the humble animal over the mightiest planet. Jaeger says here that

> his empiricism is a not a mechanical amassing of dead material, but the morphological articulation of reality. He organizes and overcomes the manifold of appearances, which Plato simply passes over, by ascending from the smallest and most insignificant traces of organic form and order to more comprehensive unities. Thus he builds up out of experience the total picture of a world whose ultimate efficient and final cause is once more a highest form, the form of all forms, creative thought.... There is nothing in nature, even the most worthless and contemptible, that does not contain something wonderful within itself; and he whose eye with glad astonishment discovers it is akin to the spirit of Aristotle.
>
> (1962, 340–1)

The stages of Aristotle's development show his different relationships to his teacher. What they illustrate is that it was not his intention to overcome his teacher and replace his system. Rather he tries to work with all the problems left by Plato in ways that go beyond his teacher, unafraid of the contradictions this produced in his own work.[12] These contradictions, which he never overcame, are the dialectical logic of his work as a whole. It is within this whole that we now explore logic and metaphysics, nature, and spirit, with particular emphasis on the first. This is because Aristotelian logic establishes the principles of philosophical reason for many centuries to come.

## Logic and metaphysics

There are two shapes of logic in Aristotle, the abstract logic of the *Categories* and the books of the *Organon* in general,[13] and the metaphysical logic of the first principles. We will see that in fact they are two versions of the same fundamental principle that the truth of what is cannot be otherwise.

The *Posterior Analytics* argues that demonstration, or scientific/logical deduction, depends on understanding *simpliciter*, or the ordinary understanding that what an object is 'is its explanation, and that it is not possible for this to be otherwise' (I. 2. 71b, 11; 1984a, 115). Principles derived from this understanding are therefore the foundation of the deduction and demonstration of particular things. Induction works in reverse, from the particular to the general. The axioms work in both directions, for simple understanding is grounded in the object, and the object is defined according to the principles that emerge from simple understanding. The axiom, then, has a tautological grounding in that the thing yields the principle and the principle yields the thing. It does not attempt to think its own conditions of possibility within this tautology.

The positing of logic as instrument[14] does not only abstract logic from its conditions of possibility. It also bequeaths to the history of Western philosophy after Plato and Aristotle, the principles by which philosophy was to be practised, principles that easily separated logic from metaphysics, and left the metaphysical relation unknowable in and for itself for some 2000 years. In addition, where Aristotle says that one must be better convinced of the principles than of the conclusions arrived at through their application, he opens the way for interminable, abstract – sometimes called scholastic – debate. The key axioms that kept metaphysics from logic and God from thought for 2000 years were those that Aristotle found in the ordinary understanding: the principle of non-contradiction and its implications for reduction to infinity, and of the syllogism, where a middle term connects two premises by being either the subject or predicate of each premise.

Because metaphysics in the *Organon* is separate from logic, logic has no means by which to know its dialectic in and for itself. Aristotle's notion of dialectic is much more a method or rule of disputation and persuasion. Dialectic in itself is not a universal form and content, nor famously for him does it prove anything.[15] Restated in Platonic terms, the tautology of the axiom is where the conditions of the possibility of understanding *simpliciter* are likewise the conditions of the possibility of understanding objects. Where Plato finds unity in the struggle of this opposition, the Aristotelian *Organon* finds ambivalence. The *Posterior Analytics* argues that a principle of deduction is dependent on nothing, *and* that it is dependent on an object. This leads him to remark in the *Metaphysics* that 'the starting-point of demonstration is not demonstration' (IV. 1011a, 12–13; 1984b, 1596).

This ambivalence is the *experience* of the principle of deduction, and it threatens a regression into groundless absurdity. From the point of view of deduction this negation is an error against the certainty that what is cannot be other than itself. It is to metaphysics that Aristotle turns in order to redeem the indemonstrable principles of demonstration with a first principle. That he turns to metaphysics at all here is a recognition that the experience of ambivalence is a content in its own right. However, Aristotle does not grant the content of ambivalence a logic of its own. Instead, it is the logic of understanding *simpliciter*, that what is cannot be otherwise, that is granted metaphysical sovereignty over ambivalent experience. This shapes the thought of first principles in Western philosophy for more than 2000 years after Aristotle.

Thus, Aristotle's metaphysics of first principles is grounded in the truth of the logic of non-contradiction, the necessity of a first cause, and the obvious absurdity of infinite regression. The 'most certain of all principles' (*Metaphysics*, 1005b, 22; 1984b, 1588) is that of non-contradiction whereby 'it is impossible for any one to believe the same thing to be and not to be' (*Metaphysics*, 1005b, 24–5; 1984b, 1588). This means that infinite regression in demonstrating principles, a regression driven by contradiction and characterized by negativity, cannot be true. Therefore, there must be a first principle where regress ends, and which is the truth that trumps regress. There must also be a first cause which trumps the regress of cause and effect. The errors of regress mean that their truth must be found in what is, and not in what is not. Thus, from presupposing error, logic demands whatever is necessary to resolve this error, in this case the first principle and the first cause, which in themselves contain no privation of any kind. Infinite regress explains nothing, but its usefulness is in proving the logical need for God as the explanation of everything. We will see many times in the history of Western philosophy how negation and privation are taken as the proof of the necessity of God.

In line with the principle that what is, is itself, Aristotle views the first principle as invisible, indivisible, unchangeable, and eternal. The question of how this first principle can also be the principle of everything material that is changeable is one that greatly concerned Western philosophers. Aristotle's answer to this question includes the vitally important idea of actuality and its opposite, potentiality.

Actuality is grounded in the same logic that knows negation as error. The actual has priority over the potential because potential is merely negative unless it is realized. For Aristotle, to be able to do something is to do it. If it is not done then this contradicts what is, and is in error.

Thus potential only *is* when it is actual. The actual must precede any knowledge of potentiality. As such, actuality is the unity that appears in difference. 'Unity,' says Aristotle, 'has as many senses (as many as "is" has) but the proper one is that of actuality' (*De Anima*, 412b, 8–9; 1984a, 657). This is the same logic as knowing cause by effect, God by the universe, and principles by the real.

The actuality of a first principle, since it cannot contain privation or the potential to be other than it is, must be simple and pure potentiality. When Aristotle says in *De Anima* that 'actual knowledge is identical with its object' (430a, 20; 1984a, 684), this is a statement of understanding *simpliciter* – that what is cannot be otherwise – and a metaphysical statement about the logical necessity that what is actual has no negation or privation. Thus, actual knowledge is that which is known *and* is itself in being known. The 'and' here is the Aristotelian unity of the logic of non-contradiction and first cause. It is in the logic of actuality, then, that what is compound and contingent and changeable must be an error in relation to the pure actuality of the first principle. This includes reason, for reason has contrary possibilities within it that are made possible by choice and desire. Here is a logic that will command the history of Western philosophy. Since God or truth known in reason is necessarily compound, truth is unknowable to man in itself. God is truth, and man's thought of truth is error. God is essence and existence, cause and effect, and actual and potential in a way that man is incapable of understanding.

# Part II Cultures of Error

In Part II we explore the history of Western philosophy from Stoicism and Scepticism in the Ancient World to Descartes and the Rationalists of seventeenth-century Europe. We will see that this is a period dominated by Neoplatonic principles that are grounded in the one incontrovertible truth that God and absolute truth are unknowable in themselves to a finite philosophical mind that produces only contradictions and infinite regression. It is the period of an unhappy consciousness, unhappy because it is alienated from itself, and unaware that the source of this unhappiness is all its own work.

The phrase 'culture of error' describes the experience of the broken relation between truth and thought. As such, it carries its meaning in the chiasmus of culture of error and error of culture. The latter pertains to the Neoplatonic positing of thought that produces contradictions that are presupposed to be in error in relation to the simple essence of the true. The former discerns ways in which the true is learned about even in these contradictory experiences, and the ways in which contradiction and negation re-form and educate the mind that is experiencing them. As such, the culture of error speaks of the education carried in the error of culture. Both coexist in the unhappy philosophical consciousness for they constitute the relation of life and death. The error of culture marks the supremacy of life over death as what is not, or only negative. The culture of error is the persistence of death and negation in all of life's standpoints. We will see examples now of the ways in which death makes itself known as the culture of error within the error of Roman, Alexandrian, Christian, Islamic, Judaic, and Rationalist cultures.

# 2
# Hellenic and Alexandrian Philosophy

## Introduction

In this chapter we look briefly at examples of Neoplatonic, Hellenic, and Alexandrian philosophy. These are some of the earliest ways in which thought posits the experience of life and death as the truth of what is and what is not. They also mark the beginning of thought trying to understand its own principle within these shapes of life and death. The Hellenic philosophers sought to avoid negation and unrest, but the work of this avoidance accompanied the tranquillity they prized so highly. The Alexandrian philosophers began to think in triadic terms about ways in which error might be educative, and they therefore began to speak of error as culture.

## Stoicism

Stoicism is the shape that Western thought takes when, prior to subjectivity, it seeks independence as a mind of its own. This is where the template of the unity of revel and repose worked on by Plato and Aristotle, takes its first steps into the world as a consciousness that is an I, although not in the sense of a modern subjectivity. The Roman Stoic is the shape of consciousness that seeks independence from activity in which opposition or contradiction might occur. Stoic consciousness seeks purity as what is, against the error of its negation in movement and disturbance. Significantly its greatest challenge comes from the unrest of absolute negation, or death. When consciousness can remain untroubled and undisturbed by death, then it is deemed to be most perfectly itself.

Stoicism has its roots in the Cynics view of a natural rather than a social life, but really begins with Zeno of Citium in Cyprus (c. 331–261 BC), who is followed by Cleanthes (c. 331–232 BC) and Chrysippus (c. 282–206 BC).[1] If Zeno and the Greek Stoics retained a sense of dialectic in their discoursing, the Roman Stoics abandoned such sophistry for a more passive form of thinking, seeing no distinction between thought and the true nature of the universe. Roman Stoicism holds that rational thought is the expression of the highest form of thought, i.e., the *logos*, and that spirit (*pneuma*) is the highest form of matter. As the *logos* is 'pure' reason so the spirit is 'pure' matter. The stoical soul aims for purity in thought, for therein it will be one with the highest form of universal spirit, its ruling principle, or its true nature.

It is a principle of Stoicism that reason or nature or God should not be affected by heteronomous external elements but should enjoy an indifference towards them. The implications of this also form the fundamental principle of Stoic ethics. When the mind is focussed on external objects, including wealth, fame, and honour, then the mind is directed away from the true. This is powerfully set out by Epictetus (c. AD 50–130) in his *Handbook* of Stoicism which states 'do not seek to have events happen as you want them to, but instead want them to happen as they do happen, and your life will go well' (Epictetus, 1983, 13). Epictetus likens this to playing dice. The counters and the dice are indifferent he says, for who could know how they are going to behave? The player, like the Stoic, is called 'to use what does turn up with diligence and skill' (Epictetus, 2004, 70). Stoic happiness therefore means bringing one's desires into line with how the world is. Education, says Epictetus, 'is just this – learning to frame one's will in accord with events' (2004, 28), thus avoiding any negation or opposition within thought.

As such, Stoicism is the religion of life positing itself as what is and as what cannot be otherwise. Thought is true if it complies with what is, and it is in error if it opposes it or is disturbed by it. Thus the stoical mind, in the inner world of the soul, seeks peace and virtue in what is. This attitude towards the external offers a meaning of Stoicism familiar even to the modern usage of the term stoical.[2] Whatever happens in the world, these things are outside of human control and should produce in us no frustration, anger, or disappointment. What happens, happens. There is nothing to be done about it.[3] Mastery is achieved when the mind is no longer opposed by material circumstances, an opposition overcome by a mind that is immune to negativity and achieves pure tranquillity.

However, in actively pursuing passivity and indifference Stoicism opposes itself. This can be illustrated in two of its most influential exponents, Marcus Aurelius (121–80) and Seneca (c. 5–65).

The *Meditations* of Marcus Aurelius is a definitive statement of the struggle in consciousness for passivity and indifference. He believes that the universe is God, and that virtue therefore demands that consciousness be at one with the universe. This is to be achieved by being indifferent to its events and remaining undisturbed by them. To oppose events is to oppose God. Reason understands necessity; only the passions judge it. Therefore the passions need to be controlled by the rational mind, leading to perfect tranquillity and harmony with nature. He says in the *Meditations*,

> [t]o be a philosopher is to keep unsullied and unscathed the divine spirit within him, so that it may transcend all pleasure and all pain, take nothing in hand without purpose and nothing falsely or with dissimulation, depend not on other's actions or inactions, accept each and every dispensation as coming from the same Source as itself – and last and chief, wait with a good grace for death, as no more than a simple dissolving of the elements whereof each living thing is composed. If those elements themselves take no harm from their ceaseless forming and re-forming, why look with mistrust upon the change and dissolution of the whole? It is but Nature's way; and in the ways of Nature there is no evil to be found.
>
> (Aurelius, 1964, 51)

However, the real title of the book is *To Himself*, which carries rather better the nature of the inner conflict that characterizes its author. His struggle with Stoicism shows how the ideal of tranquillity evinces its own unrest and, in this sense, his stoicism is more a culture of error, a vocation to learn from struggle, than it is a statement of the tranquil mind. This struggle, as we will see later, is the basis for Scepticism.

Seneca was a native of Cordoba in Spain yet became one of the best known Latin writers from the time of the Roman Empire. He too advocates indifference as virtue, and argues that only the man who philosophizes can attain tranquillity in and freedom from the passions.

However, in his letter to his mother regarding his own exile, he too reveals an opposition at the heart of Stoicism, one reflective of the struggles of the *Meditations*. If he is to help his mother in her time of distress he says that he must reopen wounds that have healed. 'I shall offer to the mind all its sorrows, all its mourning garments: this will not be a gentle prescription for healing, but cautery and the knife' (Seneca, 1997, 35). Stoic principles see unlimited grief at ill fortune as 'foolish self-indulgence' (1997, 59) while no grief at all is inhuman. Thus it is to the struggles of reason, philosophy, and the liberal arts that his mother must return if she is to overcome the sadness she feels. She must realize that the cause of her sadness lies not with Seneca but with her judgements of the events. It is the judgement that must be conquered because 'the grief that has been conquered by reason is calmed forever' (1997, 61). But Stoicism here is healing wounds that it also keeps open, for philosophy divests 'from its anguish a heart whose grief springs from love' (1997, 64).

Death in life is also a negative wound that philosophy must heal while keeping it open. The natural event of death is unavoidable. But the mind can avoid its negative implications by accepting its necessity and being untroubled by it. Stoicism, in the face of death, is the ultimate triumph, for it overcomes absolute negation with absolute purity. In this ideal, Stoicism claims indifference to negation and unrest, and to that which threatens what is with what is not. The actuality of this master is the person in Roman law. The master and the Stoic are the one principle of independent identity, able to avoid the vulnerability of negation by death in natural relations and by the slave in social relations.

## Epicureanism

Epicureanism, from the canon of Epicurus (born c. 341 BC) sets itself against what it perceives to be the dogmatism of Stoicism. If Stoicism is the dogma of the mind as above negation, then Epicureanism is the dogma of the superiority of feeling over thinking. Epicurus, in his *Letter to Menoeceus*, says that every criterion of the good life must be judged by 'the criterion of feeling' (Epicurus, 1994, 30). A later Epicurean, Lucretius, adds that 'the conception of truth was originally created by the senses, and that the senses cannot be refuted' (1994, 65).

Regarding the physical universe, Epicurus took the line of Leucippus and Democritus that the universe consisted of indestructible atoms that were formed accidentally by a supernatural will. This meant that Epicureanism formed a powerful empirical critique, particularly to the superstitions of the Roman world. Nevertheless, in general terms Epicureanism, like Stoicism, saw the good life to lie in tranquillity of the soul, a tranquilly that could be achieved through pleasurable sensations. Thus the wise man was most likely to achieve this tranquillity as he could use his powers of reasoning to shape a life most likely to realize those pleasurable sensations. It is an 'unwavering contemplation' (1994, 30) of the causes of pain and pleasure that will lead to the blessed life, says Epicurus, even if our reasoning determines that short-term pain is necessary for longer term and greater pleasure. Since pleasure was intrinsically good, the pleasurable life is also the good life. However, and against ancient prejudices and suspicions, Epicurus makes it clear that pleasure cannot be derived from our indulgence or ignorance, but only from 'sober calculation which searches out the reasons for every choice and avoidance and drives out the opinions which are the source of the greatest turmoil for men's souls' (1994, 31). However, in practical life, this means that Epicureanism really fell back into the standpoint of the Stoics, for in both philosophies the tranquillity of the soul was to be achieved by using reason against negative unrest to discern the good and just life. This is clearest in the attitude of Epicurus towards death. Like Marcus Aurelius and Seneca, he argued that death should not be a cause of anxiety to the reasoning mind, because death is not present to the man who is alive, and is only present to the man who is not alive. Since we cannot perceive any unpleasantness in our lives before birth, so, there is no reason to posit any such unpleasantness after life. Thus, even though sensation was the guide to the good for each individual Epicurean, the good remained a rational end over and above current unrest and opposition.

## Scepticism

Scepticism becomes perhaps the most powerful philosophical perspective in Plato's Academy after Plato's death in 348/7 BC when, in the middle of the third century, Arcesilaus is made the leader of what became known as the New Academy.[4] In an important sense, Scepticism is a significant philosophical advance on both Stoicism and Epicureanism. Rather than siding with the dogmas of either peace or sensation, the sceptical outlook opposed both of them as holding to principles of the universal that were, at best, merely arbitrary. Arcesilaus opposed the Stoics in particular, arguing that if an individual's own thought is made the principle of the true, then the principle must undermine itself *as a principle*. This is demonstrated in the dialogue *Hermotimus*, written in a satirical vein by Lucian (born c. AD 125). Lycinus is able to confound his Stoic opponent by revealing the arbitrary nature of choosing any of the available philosophies as true against all of the others. The sceptic, says Lycinus, must 'believe them all, or disbelieve impartially' (Marcus Aurelius, 1945, 187). His principle must be 'sober and doubt all things' (1945, 198) because the assertion of truth in one philosophy is as arbitrary as the assertion of truth in any other. When Hermotimus has felt the full force of this scepticism he sees his treasured Stoicism crumble to dust and recognizes that he has been wasting his money and his life in studying it as the true philosophy.

Carneades (c. 214–129 BC) opposes Stoicism as a dogma that avoided the obvious truth that 'opposed to every account there is an equal account' (Sextus Empiricus, 2000, 51).[5] Thought undermines or negates or opposes all claims to universality, even those made in its own name. At the heart of Scepticism, then, there is the recognition that truth falls victim to the infinite reduction of its proof to absurdity.

But Scepticism is a philosophy of negation rather than one against it and in this sense marks the beginning in the history of Western philosophy of what might be called the subjective reflective standpoint. It is where the aporia of thought's groundlessness is realized every time thought tries and fails to establish principles within it. Thought here knows truth only in opposition. Ancient Scepticism tried to work around this. In the 'tropes' from Sextus Empiricus we see both the relativity of existing objects, and the call for discretion in the suspension of judgement, a discretion that resembled Stoicism in being free from passion, negation, and unrest and characterized by tranquillity. However, thought will face its negative universality in a more powerful way in the dualism of finite thought and infinite truth expressed as Christian subjectivity. This will mark the time when negative experience separates completely from truth and stands in need of a subjectivity that somehow can retrieve their relationship.

## Nature and mind

We can also note here how the spheres of nature and mind separate respectively into life as what is and thought as what is not. Those prioritizing a philosophy of nature are first, the Cynics and Cyrenaics, who argue for nature over social custom and convention, and for a natural simplicity that would bring about the pleasurable life; second, the Atomists Leucippus and Democritus who argue for the truth of the world as composed of an infinity of invisible atoms. This was a development of the particle theory of Empedocles and of the illogicality of motion argued for by Zeno of Elea (himself a disciple of Parmenides); and third, of Epicurus who argued for an empirical truth of an objective world that was correctly known through sense perception and to which no higher purpose or *telos* could be attached.[6] Those prioritizing a philosophy of mind are first, Anaxagoras, who is credited with being the first in Athens to argue for intelligence or *nus* as the first principle of the universe; second, various Sophists including Protagoras, who explores the nature of human existence rather than material existence; third, Stoicism, especially that of Marcus Aurelius and Seneca who both hold to the metaphysical truth of an intelligent, even rational Creator; and fourth, Scepticism, which is able to undermine any empirical or philosophical truth by the power of thought and which, as a result, finds tranquillity in the suspension of judgement. Both Stoicism and Scepticism hold to the priority of thought, of subjectivity and of the *logos* over an external or material reality, and to the good as the tranquillity of the soul.

It is not the case, however, that this division between nature and spirit is consistently reflected also in the sphere of practical ethics. For example, even though Epicurus argues for the feeling of happiness and the sense-perception of objects as the criteria of the true, it is still the wise man, the philosophical man, who will achieve tranquillity of the soul through reason. It is by reason alone, he says, that gods may be known. The same is true of the Stoics. Seneca holds that tranquillity, even though it requires subjective indifference to the material world, is nevertheless found only in the wise philosopher whose reasoning will match the order and peace of the universe, and will in turn ensure his actions in the world are just, holy, and true. Both Epicurus and the Stoics require a *thinking* of the universal and are opened up to the contradictions of what is. Scepticism is the thought of this openness but, as yet, not open to itself as its own logic and content, or as a culture of error.[7]

## Alexandrian philosophy

In the Neoplatonism within the Alexandrian Empire, cultures of error begin to define themselves. When Greek city-states unified under Philip II, father of Alexander the Great, Greek culture spread across the Alexandrian Empire, to Rome in the west, Alexandria in the south, and Antioch in the east. This resulted in philosophical cultures and conversations across a wide geographical expanse. In turn, philosophy was also to become the meeting place for Judaism, Christianity, and Islam. This period of shared epistemological concerns lasted for over 1000 years.

The Alexandrian library, at one time the largest in the world, became home to many Greek philosophical texts (which would, in turn, be reintroduced into the Western world by way of these Greek copies and Arabic translations) and to the Alexandrian school of Neoplatonism in which scholars learned their Greek philosophy and took it with them wherever they traveled. We will look at three examples now. The first is Philo of Alexandria (c. 25 BC–AD 40) where Neoplatonism meets with the Jewish mind; the second is Plotinus (204–70) who took his Neoplatonism to Rome; and the third is Proclus (c. 412–85) who, in moving from Alexandria to Athens, became head of Plato's Academy until his death.

In an important sense Alexandrian Neoplatonism expresses more clearly some of the structural contradictions of the Stoic and Sceptic consciousness which, in different ways, sought independence in thought immune from negativity. Passivity in Stoicism was pursued actively, and this contradiction became the principle of Scepticism. But for the conscious 'I', contradiction is error, for it reduces what is to what is not. In Hellenic Neolatonism this consciousness feels the force of its being grounded in error, and its response is the logically necessary one of positing truth beyond thought altogether. Subjectivity is not concrete in this culture of error because consciousness is yet to know error as self-determining. Nevertheless, this Neoplatonic philosophy plays out the relation of what is and what is not in ways that begin to exceed the Stoical and Sceptical mind. In driving truth beyond thought, the struggle for the truth of error becomes increasingly re-formative.

## Philo of Alexandria

In the work of Philo, sometimes referred to as Philo the Jew, there can be found several important features of Neoplatonism.[8] First, it is the *logos* that is deemed to mediate between finite and infinite consciousness, and is the means by which the pure thought of God as unknowable, as beyond human experience, is related to the philosophical reason of the wise man who may come to know the existence of God, perhaps intuiting it in a form of ecstasy. In this Neoplatonism man can know that God exists, 'but beyond the fact of his existence, we can understand nothing' (Philo, 2006, 163).[9] The proof of the *logos* as mediation is the soul, for 'how could the soul have perceived God if he had not inspired it, and touched it according to his power?' (2006, 29). He argues that the *logos* as the living word of God, is to be seen as ideas sent by God about the Creator to man so that He might be known. Reason is therefore a gift to man, given so that he 'should be able to praise' (2006, 201) his own creation. This praise, in speech, is changeable and always moving for it is in the human mind. God as pure thought is unmoved and unchanging.

Secondly, Philo understands the wise man, the man of reason, and of the *logos*, to be nearest to God. This requires constant study and discipline, and Philo writes a great deal about how drunkenness and other appetites of the sensuous body, will corrupt the eyes of the soul and prevent it from ever gaining the wisdom of God's own work in the form of ideas. Where the conscious 'I' of Stoicism and Scepticism saw tranquillity as pertaining to body and soul, now Philo holds them in total opposition and, indeed, at war with each other. For example, he argues that the man who puts pleasure above the education of the soul in and by the *logos* is variously 'lawless, savage, ill-tempered ... foolish, full of evil acts, unteachable' (2006, 98). He offers a list of some 152 vices attending such a man. The cause of ignorance, he says, 'is the flesh' ( 2006, 154). The appetites of the flesh are often untameable and always irrational, 'but the pleasure of the soul and of the whole man is the mind of the universe, namely God' (2006, 155). The opposition of embodied thought as error and disembodied thought as true carries Aristotle's logic of truth as what is, and error as what is not. Since embodied thought, being compound and negative, is error, the true must be free from such negation.

Thirdly, Philo says much about the *logos* acting as man's instruction and education regarding the existence of God and the soul carried by the body which, in God's image, should seek to be virtuous. Ignorance is a distance from the divine that cannot of itself be overcome. Only learning and education can open the mind and the soul to receive the ideas that God sends as his presence. God made a race 'capable of receiving all learning' (2006, 202) and, as such, education in and through the *logos* is God's work. The principle virtue of all learners, whether of a human or divine teacher, 'is to endeavour to imitate their perfect master, as far as those who are imperfect can imitate a perfect man' (2006, 102). Philo finds education in error as a gift from God. Plotinus and Proclus extend this idea.

## Plotinus

Alexandrian Neoplatonism has Plotinus as perhaps its foremost representative. His thoughts are recorded in the six *Enneads* selected and put together by his pupil Porphyry, who also wrote of the life of his master.

Plotinus offers a triadic metaphysics of the divinity as one, one-many, and one and many, that is grounded in Aristotle's distinction between the simple and the compound. In stretching the gulf between them, Plotinus also works harder on the education possible between them. The highest being in Plotinus is the supreme, or the first principle, or the first cause. It cannot be conceived using any attributes assigned to it by human thought that might confound its supremacy or reduce it to a compound or a composite. It will, he says, 'debar all telling and knowing except that it may be described as transcending Being' (Plotinus, 1991, 387). 'Untouched by multiplicity, it will be wholly self-sufficing, an absolute First' (1991, 387). It exists before any of the qualities by which it might be known to us and is without shape, without even the shape of an idea. It cannot be seen as at rest, for that would be to compare it with movement and it brooks no comparison. It is 'more authentically one than God' (1991, 542) and 'utterly a self-existent ... utterly without need' (1991, 542). It has no need even of being known and thus, Plotinus admits, we are 'sometimes baffled by the enigma in which it dwells' (1991, 539).

This bafflement is illustrated when considering how the one cannot be being, but can be that which generates being. How can the one remain an unknowable transcendental unity *and* somehow produce the differentiation of the manifold of all living things? How can it be completely itself *and* be the origin of all things different from it? Plotinus answers this with the second element of his triadic metaphysics, the one-many. He argues that the one overflows itself without losing anything of itself in doing so. This overflowing is the exuberance of the one. The one is not differentiated here, it is rather a 'circumradiation' (1991, 354), that is, its overflowing is as the light from the sun. What is created in the surplus is the *vision* of the one, or the principle by which it can be contemplated, but not known. He calls this vision of the one, the intellectual principle or the divine intelligence. But the only way it can be known by the human mind is for a complete eradication of any dependence upon the body so that pure thought might find its home in itself, in the intellectual principle. Should this mystical union occur, it will represent the virtue of purification from all matter. It will be beauty in the likeness of the supreme, beyond even the intellectual, to 'the entire content of the Good' (1991, 427).[10]

The third element of Plotinus's metaphysics is the life-principle, or the *logos*, and it is here that the relation to the one becomes that of philosophical education in the one and the many. The home of the *logos* is the soul. Since there is nothing in the material world that endures or can be called self-completing, it follows that the principle of being must lie elsewhere. Equally, since the soul cannot produce itself, nor bring itself to an end, the principle of its infinity must also lie elsewhere. Put together, this leads Plotinus to argue that the idea of objects has a principle beyond their particular manifestation, and that the principle of ideas is the intellectual principle. This increases the importance attached to the intellectual principle for it is now the conduit that can relate the individual soul to the supreme. The intellectual principle looks both upwards to the one and downwards to the soul and the material world.

At its lowest point the soul operates through the senses and is dominated by bodily needs and appetites. Plotinus separates himself here from the Aristotelian view that the soul is the body's actuality (entelechy). Indeed, the body for Plotinus is a hindrance to the development of the soul, and he keeps a strict separation between body and soul. A soul that lives in the body in the world of matter is ugly compared to the beauty of the soul that breaks its attachment to the sensible. When the soul lives the life of reason then it has cleared itself of the body's corruption of reason. It has become 'emancipated from all the passions' (1991, 51) and is in communion with the ideal form.[11]

In Plotinus, then, the logic of non-contradiction that separates the one from man does not rule out a mystical union between them in an ecstatic journey of self-exploration. The individual soul is lonely and isolated, partial and self-centred. It is 'a deserter from the totality' (1991, 338) because it is not living in the intellectual. But as error, the soul desired truth. As such, the soul is the principle of the intellectual cosmos yearning to return to its truth in the one. The maxim of this journey is one of self-exploration. It is to strive to bring back the God in the self to the divine in the universe. This return to the one is through the inner workings of the soul, and is the attempt to leave the world of sense and live solely in the mind. 'Withdraw into yourself and look' (1991, 54) and seek to shape the self into the image of the perfect goodness. Thus, 'cleared of all evil in our intention towards The Good, we must ascend to the Principle within ourselves; from many, we must become one; only so do we attain to knowledge of that which is Principle and Unity' (1991, 538). But the wisdom of the highest or the supreme transcends even this knowledge, and is knowable only mystically, in a union that is not dependent upon any form or representation, or on any secondary source. However, there is an emerging culture of error here in Plotinus, for error is seen to have educative significance regarding the true and the one.

## Proclus

The final example of a non-Christian Neoplatonic culture of error is that of Proclus. While Plotinus and Proclus both agree on the total ineffability of the one – Proclus says, 'we should celebrate in silence this ineffable nature, and this perfectly causeless cause which is prior to all causes' (Proclus, 1995, 162) – they differ in how they see the relation between the one and the many. The trinity of one, one-many, and one and many in Plotinus is held together by the intellectual principle. Negation is held to be error, and is overcome by that which is posited as pure and simple positivity, or what is. But Proclus has a more philosophically sophisticated triadic model. Where Plotinus in the end reduces the culture of error to the dualism of either truth or error, Proclus tries to hold error and truth together negatively in a third that is at one and the same time not one and not many. This realizes an immediate and abstract model of subjectivity for it allows for the opposition of the one and the many to determine itself negatively in relation to each other. That this union might be negative is a different response to the culture of error than in Plotinus or Philo. It acknowledges that consciousness might be a third partner in the relation of the one and the many, a third, that is, where thought as error is re-formed in knowing that *what is not* might be the truth of what is, or of both the conscious I and the pure divine consciousness. Here the unhappy consciousness of the culture of error goes as far as it can without this third coming to know itself as self-determined, or as subjectivity. This challenge, as we will see now, is taken up by Christian cultures of error.

## Conclusion

Stoicism and Scepticism are the shapes taken by thought as it begins to think itself, and develop a mind of its own as error. But they are not yet the question of subjective freedom. They are the shapes of thought that hold themselves sovereign in an indifference to the negations and contradictions of the world. Stoicism passively avoids subjectivity in its indifference to the vexations of the world that would oppose the pure essentiality of thought. The Stoic can be free only in the sense that he achieves equanimity with death and negative unrest. Scepticism avoids subjectivity by actively rejecting any standpoint for itself that the world might oppose. The Sceptic can be free only in the sense that he achieves death – the death of unrest – in life. There is no subjectivity in indifference, precisely because subjectivity is to be in difference. The Roman philosophies of Stoicism and Scepticism are cultures of error in that the Roman person has the world as error in relation to pure thought. But Scepticism already contains the negative significance of being that that re-forms and educates thought with regard to its being subjectivity. It will come to doubt itself, opening up an abyss of groundlessness wherein thought is universally error and truth is universally beyond thought.

   Neoplatonism in Alexandria moves thought ever nearer to itself as a culture of error by developing the opposition between thought and truth in ways that were only implicit in Roman Scepticism. This is the work of the unhappy consciousness, which re-forms Scepticism by means of its own self-contradictory and self-negating standpoint. Scepticism, sceptical of itself, begins to speak of a notion of subjectivity that is the groundlessness of thought known as and to itself. It is, however, Western Neoplatonic Christianity that takes up the challenge of this unhappy consciousness as a culture of error, seeking to learn how its being re-formed by its own aporias may also be an education regarding truth in the error of the culture of finite thought.

# 3
# Mediaeval Christian Philosophy

## Introduction

In this chapter we illustrate how Neoplatonic Christian philosophies can be seen as cultures of error. We look in detail at Augustine (354–430), Eriugena (c. 800–77), and Aquinas (1225–74), and draw more briefly on the early Christian philosophy of Origen (185–254), Boethius (c. 480–524/5), and Pseudo-Dionysius (c. 5th century), and the later work of Duns Scotus (1265/6–1308). For these men philosophy was to be used with theology in the service of knowing God, with priority generally given to theology because reason was deemed incapable of the understanding that is possible in faith. The philosophical tools available to them were Platonic and Aristotelian.

The most important way in which early and mediaeval Christian philosophy differs from Ancient and Hellenic philosophy is that it is grounded in the emerging notion of Western subjectivity. As such, God is known by a subjectivity that does not know its own truth. In this way early and mediaeval Christianity is grounded in the belief that the culture of thought is *error* in relation to truth. But such subjectivity is also a *culture* of error. Augustine, Eriugena, and Aquinas, for example, in different ways seek to comprehend the educative significance of error in knowing God. They each try to learn of the re-forming of subjectivity by error so that it can learn of truth from within itself. This learning essentially involves the soul in a journey from man to God by way of reason. However, as we will see, in early and mediaeval subjective Christianity thought is ultimately posited as error, contradiction is eschewed as insubstantial, and subjectivity remains without a notion of self-determination as freedom.

This means that in these Christian cultures of error negation is how God is known and not known. This aporia is the self-determining experience of subjectivity and will become self-determined as freedom. But before that, these Christian cultures of error posit *what is* as simple truth, *what is not* as compound error, and God as what is, and as unknowable. Its Neoplatonism is held to in the principles of non-contradiction, first cause, and the absurdity of infinite regression. It is to examples of this Neoplatonism in Christianity that we now turn.

## Origen

Origen provides an early example of a Christian culture of error. His argument for the necessity of a journey from error to truth involves moving from the corporeal to the incorporeal, the visible to the invisible, body to soul, and the material to the intellectual. He demands that the soul undertake this as a pilgrimage to God. This spiritual education of man has three stages. The first stage purifies the soul; the second clears the mind of all that is corruptible and changeable in contemplation of first principles and causes; the third is where the soul is 'led up to the contemplation of the Godhead by a genuine and spiritual love' (Origen, 1979, 234). These, in turn, he sees as a moral, natural/logical, and spiritual education having their origin prior to the Greeks in the three books of Solomon in the Scriptures. A similar educational trinity is found by Origen in Abraham, who teaches moral obedience, Isaac, who pursues meaning around him, and Jacob, who contemplates divine matters. The exodus of the holy fathers into Egypt is also symbolic of this educational journey.

Origen finds educational significance in a 'double line of interpretation' (1979, 253). Scripture contains ambiguities because God has ensured 'stumbling blocks or interruptions' (1979, 187) so that the divine can disrupt earthly understanding. Even though words are incapable of expressing God directly, nevertheless they carry the *logos* in their ambiguity. Temptation shares this pedagogical function, ensuring men cannot avoid knowledge of evil. Man, at best, can imitate God but his truth 'surpasses every sense of our understanding' (1979, 206).

## Boethius

The culture of error in Boethius can be found where finite knowledge and appetites are deemed to be error, and where God's providence has ensured sufficient means for man's higher education. This is illustrated in *The Consolation of Philosophy* (AD 524) which describes how Boethius is visited by Lady Philosophy who finds in him a sickness of spirit at his situation. She reminds him of the good in God and in the order of the universe that God has created, noting that earthly conditions are as error in comparison to true happiness. This true happiness is to be found in a self-sufficiency where abilities are commensurate with needs. Such self-sufficiency is an image of God in his unity and substance. Evil men are seen as too weak to achieve this and they fall away from the good. It is part of God's providence, however, to have allowed evil in the world because it offers the opportunities for doing good. When Boethius asks whether free will can exist within such providence Philosophy replies that the concern about such a contradiction has its roots in the limitations of man's temporal knowledge. Such knowledge is as error compared to the perfection of God's knowledge in which past, present, and future are one eternal present, and where it is possible for the free will of man to be known eternally by God. Both error and its re-formation in higher understanding are heralded by philosophy here.

### Pseudo-Dionysius[1]

For Pseudo-Dionysius a *vita negativa* can realize an ecstatic union with God. But even here 'all human thinking is a sort of error' (Pseudo-Dionysius, 1987, 105) in comparison to God's perfection. Evil is pedagogical in that it teaches of the good. Even in the evil man there is 'a distorted echo of real love and of real unity' (1987, 87). Names too express God only negatively. The 'good' and the 'one' come closest to his reality but no word or name 'can lay hold of him' (1987, 109) for God is 'beyond-being' (1987, 85) and 'beyond all intellect ... and all knowledge' (1987, 63). He is a simple unity unknown to compound thought. The ineffectiveness of names is itself a pedagogical incentive to seek the perfect.

This incentive is manifested in the providence and ordinance of the hierarchy of superior and inferior. The good descends to earth so that the inferior may learn of and desire to ascend to the higher. This is a circle effecting a negative education in that the self 'plunges into the truly mysterious darkness of unknowing' (1987, 137). Yet error has priority over culture in this educational circle for he notes that if only we were not corrupted by negation we would be able to see 'that which lies beyond all vision and knowledge' (1987, 138) and, beyond the ascent to God, to be 'at one with him who is indescribable' (1987, 139).

### Augustine

In Augustine we have one of the richest cultures of error of any Christian writer. Holding thought ultimately to be error in relation to the true, he nevertheless develops a sophisticated negative educational philosophy within the oppositions and contradictions he experiences. This section on Augustine is divided into three parts. First we look at oppositions from the *City of God*, then, drawing first on his early work and then on the *Confessions*, at how the error of finite philosophical thinking can be seen as a culture of subjective re-formation.

*Oppositions in the* City of God

Augustine distinguishes between the earthly city and the holy city. The former is ruled by desires of the flesh and is present only in ordinary time. The city of God, however, is only ever on pilgrimage on earth, drawing its standards not from man but from the spirit. It is also the destination of the righteous after death, promising an eternal existence independent of time. Sin is the source of the opposition between the two cities, for it changes human nature from obedience to God to the satisfaction of man's own desires. It is important for Augustine to show that God did not create evil, but created the capacity for evil in giving man free will. There is no cause of evil, just a lack of goodness, 'a falling away from good' (Augustine, 1972, 482). Corruption is not the cause of the first sin, but rather its effect, which sees the earthly city ruled by the finite pleasures of lust and self-love. The city of God is present on earth in the struggle of the spirit against the flesh. Only in the world beyond death will this contradiction be at an end, where there will be no conflict in the soul and no vices, and where for eternity the soul will hold sway over the body.

God created the city of man so that man would learn, in contradiction, of the difference between himself and God. The earthly city has an educative purpose or 'double significance' (1972, 598) in commending its opposite, the heavenly city. God, says Augustine, 'enrich[es] the course of the world history by the [use of] antithesis' (1972, 449). As such, the city of God is only ever present to us in the antitheses that God provides for our education, and provides also the rational soul which, faced with antitheses, strives for unity.[2]

The most important antithesis is that God allowed sin so that man might know good. God knew that good existed only in relation to evil.[3] Adam was not good because in paradise there was no evil. Ignorance here is not bliss, because it is in sin that man seeks future redemption. Thus, 'any man in the extreme of bodily suffering is happier than the first-created' (1972, 444).[4]

Two other important oppositions are those of life and death, and war and peace. Augustine speaks of two deaths; the death of the body where the soul departs, and the death of the soul if God departs from it. There can be no resurrection of the body for the eternal soul unless, first, that body has died. Death here becomes the path to God and to eternal life. It means that through the resurrection of Christ, God ensured that death, 'which all agree to be the contrary of life, has become the means by which men pass into life' (1972, 514). The greatest and worst of all deaths is the death that never dies. The greatest and best of deaths is that of death itself, from which comes eternal bliss. In this antithesis life is death – death of innocence – and death is life – life of eternity. The opposition is vital here, for without life *as death*, death *as life* would never be known.[5] Augustine also argues that good can emerge from war. God had intended for men to be linked together by a 'bond of peace' (1972, 547). However, the earthly city 'is generally divided against itself by litigation, by wars, by battles, by the pursuit of victories that bring death with them or at best are doomed to death' (1972, 599). The bond of peace is fought by means of war. There can, however, be a just war, if its goal is peace and justice, and is fought for the holy city, whose supreme end is peace.

War and peace also describe the opposition on earth between soul and body. The peace of the soul requires the desires of the body to be subordinate 'to the peace of the rational soul' (1972, 873). For Augustine, this peace is embedded in the idea of divine *order* as it appears on earth, and at times it comes very close to the Stoic notion of tranquillity.[6]

In each of these oppositions error is educative of man about God. Antithesis, as such, is a gift of divine order to man and to nature. The culture of error here is clear and unmistakeable. Conflict and opposition are the site of peace. Truth is found in the relation of life and death, and master and slave, and truth and error, and not in one partner or the other. The pilgrimage of peace on earth is present in opposition to itself. Faith and love believe in truth beyond conflict which cannot be seen or known in itself on earth.

These elements of the culture of error are present in Augustine's model of the trinity. The final chapter of *On The Trinity* emphasizes the error that pertains to the finite representation of the infinite perfection of God. 'We are like God inasmuch as we know Him, but we are not like Him to the extent of being His equal, because we do not know Him as He Himself knows Himself' (Augustine, 2002a, 37). Always our temporal knowledge of God will be less than God is, 'for the mind is creature, but God is Creator' (2002a, 37). This will be the case until the death of death when the body will be returned to the purified soul, and, no longer in conflict with it, a body happily subject to the soul, and 'this happiness shall remain forever' (2002a, 215).

But the *culture* of error is emphasized here. It is from within the positing of knowing God as impossible, and the aporias that this presents the human mind, that Augustine finds God on earth. 'We must believe before we understand' (2002a, 12) he says, because God's gift to man, through antithesis, is the means to know and love in advance what is not known. Faith in God is the way that leads to God. An example that Augustine gives here is of the idea of the just man. When one looks inwardly into his soul he can find there the truth of the just man even though he is not (yet) such a man. The just man is the beauty of the soul, and the soul therefore can educate man from within himself about justice in such a way that he can love it and strive for it *as his own truth.* Thus, he wills the just man as he wills himself. Augustine argues here that as the soul teaches man to love the just man in him, so too this educates man to love his neighbour, for to treat another unjustly would be to love the unjust in man himself. The soul provides here the means by which God can be known as the perfect in each man. To love the just man is to love the perfect. This love is God's work enabling man to love what is not present. It is therefore also the negative educational work of the eternal on earth. To seek God is already to love the soul, and to seek again is to love the love that is God in the soul.

Here Augustine distinguishes himself from the Neoplatonic philosophers who, he believes, miss the significance of faith. Lacking faith they are at best 'bravely miserable' (2002a, 115). They know what they aim for but they do not know how to get there. It is not by human reasoning alone that one can come to know God but also by the faith in what the soul teaches about love, happiness, and immortality. To love love, justice, and happiness is to enjoy faith in and knowledge of God's wisdom. From reason comes the wisdom that the soul is from God, and from faith comes the love that is eternal and immortal. Wisdom at its highest is worship.

*Order of education*

For Augustine, then, divine order is in the social and natural orders. But in his earlier works he expounds on this antithetical order of experience as a model of education in human experience, the theory and practice of which are both found in Augustine's life. In the *City of God* he notes that there is a 'process of education, through the epochs of a people's history, as through the successive stages of a man's life, designed to raise them from the temporal and the visible to an apprehension of the eternal and the invisible' (1972, 392). It is to these stages as the order of antithetical education that we now turn.

His earliest works criticize the Sceptics who held that wisdom and truth were unattainable. Despite having not apprehended the nature of human wisdom by the time he was 33, Augustine says in *Against the Academicians* that 'I do not think I ought to despair of ever attaining wisdom' (Augustine, 1957, 82). At this time he holds to Neoplatonism and Christianity as able to co-operate in the one truth of God. He is prescient when, in AD 386, against the Academy, he advises 'let us be prepared for some kind of a dilemma' (1957, 73). Around the same time, in *On Divine Providence*, Augustine introduces a theme that is to be the central point around which his theology and philosophy will revolve. This theme is announced by one of his pupils, Licentius, in a moment of dialectical revelation: 'everything is comprised in order' (Augustine, 1942, 39) including *antithesis*, for, he reasons, how could anything be known except in distinction from that which it is not. Thus, Licentius can explain the necessity of evil in the world through the benevolence of God. As such, he concludes, 'the beauty of all things is in a manner configured, as it were, from antitheses, that is, from opposites' (1942, 37).

Many of Augustine's early texts explore the implications of this. *De Ordine* finds order in the opposition of divine and human authority, and in the demand that the learner obey those things taught to him which he is yet to comprehend.[7] The *Soliloquies* explore the educative tension where things are true 'precisely because they are in some way false' (Augustine, 2000, 74). *On Free Choice of the Will* argues for the educational necessity of sin, for in the humility that accompanies sin man is led 'in the secure paths to divine mercy along the road to wisdom' (Augustine, 1993, 74). He is clear that it would *not* be better if sinful souls had never existed; 'a weeping man is better than a happy worm' he says in *Of True Religion* (Augustine, 1959, 74). The struggles of the soul with sin are what point us towards God.

In many ways, *On the Magnitude of the Soul* is the culmination of Augustine's early works. It is here that he sets out his seven stages of the soul's education. These stages are animation, sensation, art, virtue, tranquillity, approach, and contemplation.[8] Augustine's work to this point has been driven by the idea that the soul exists negatively and without physical magnitude. Now we can read the stages of the soul's education as the journey, via antithesis, from the physical to the metaphysical. Here divine education is given form and content by the order in which the soul is revealed to itself.

The seven stages of the soul's education may be read as follows: *animatio* is the movement by which life orders itself; *sensus* is the ordering of this order in and through the senses of the body; *ars* is the ordering of this experience as knowledge arrived at, in, and through thought. It is specifically a human achievement; *virtus* is the re-ordering of the order of the first three stages. It is a re-ordering through antithesis of physical order in the body to metaphysical order in the intellect, an order which reveals the justice of divine ordinance; *tranquillitas* is the peace of a re-ordering known as its own principle, the peace of truth in antithesis; *ingressio* is the tranquil soul that can now approach the order of antithesis as providence, as divine education; and the final stage, *contemplatio*, is ordinance and providence as the thought of the unmoved mover, or as God himself.

The order of the universe structures man's immediate sensual education, while the order of God re-orders that immediate ordering according to the divine principle of the intellect. Thus life, sensation, and tradition are negated in and by the soul, a negation which itself has substance as the last three stages, that is, as ethics, religion, and the divine. Seen in this way Augustine's educational model plays out the move from external to internal, from corporeal to non-corporeal, from physical to metaphysical, and from self to God, as one of re-ordering, or of the educative re-forming of the soul.

The fourth stage is crucial here for it is the middle where these oppositions relate to each other as oppositions. Virtue is essentially the struggle between God and man, a struggle where each seeks to re-order the other. We will now explore a little of this struggle and re-formative education in Augustine's own life.

### *Confessions*

It is not hard to trace the first three stages of the development of the soul in Augustine's early life. Animation or life came with birth, enabling the effective communication of immediate needs, and the expression of dissatisfaction if these needs were not met. Here the soul 'gives life' (Augustine, 2002b, 137) in such a way as to preserve 'the apt arrangement and proportion of the body' (2002b, 137).

In the second stage the soul orders sensation gained through the senses. It learns to find such experiences through movement and is attracted to the pleasurable and repelled by the unpleasant. Habit grows towards the desirable sensations and in this the soul requires memory in order to achieve harmony for itself in its environment and habitat. Prior to the moral ordering of these sensations the soul seeks pleasure for the self. For Augustine this meant pleasure in disorder, in disobedience, and in vice. He describes pleasure in both self-destruction and in disorder. 'I became to myself', he says in the *Confessions*, 'a region of destitution' (1991, 34).

In the third stage the soul learns to order what it stores in its memory, and to do so using its power as reason and thought. Here the soul rises to the regimen of human achievement in its arts. For Augustine this corresponds to his growing desire for wisdom, something generated from reading Cicero's *Hortensius*. While this desire will eventually lead to the re-ordering of Augustine's soul, it is nevertheless manifest in the arts that Augustine practises in his trade as professor of rhetoric. On many occasions he will look back at this work as revealing merely an interest in earthly rewards and status, and as antithetical to the genuine search for wisdom. It is a stage where the soul is still determined by the interests of the flesh and not of the mind. Augustine becomes miserable in the sadness and distress of his soul, and seeks to recognize how God was at work in such despair.

The most important stage of the soul's development from an educational point of view is the fourth stage, which Augustine refers to as virtue, but which we have described as the re-ordering of the order that is established in the first three stages. The re-ordering is of the order of the body to the order of the mind, and the order of the self to the order of God. Augustine is able to cite here, two main catalysts for this re-ordering. Both are of philosophical significance. The first he admits to being his principal error that he 'did not think anything existed which is not material' (1991, 85). As such, he did not know how to conceive of the mind except as something physical and with magnitude. In the tensions he was feeling between teaching the arts of rhetoric and the distress of his soul, the prejudice toward the material prevented its being re-ordered. As such, at this time, Augustine confesses to God that 'I was seeking for you outside myself, and I failed to find the God of my heart' (1991, 90).[9] In learning Manicheanism Augustine admits that he knew God to be unchangeable but did not yet know how to know or conceive of this unchangeability. He still had no idea 'how there could be spiritual substance' (1991, 93) for he was still 'unable to think any substance possible other than that which the eyes would normally perceive.... I thought that anything from which space was abstracted was non-existent' (1991, 111).

The second catalyst for the fourth stage of the soul's development concerns the freedom of the will and the question as to why God, if he was all powerful and all good, would allow evil to exist? Reasoning brought Augustine to the conclusion that the things which are vulnerable to corruption, sin, and evil must themselves also be good, for 'if there were no good in them, there would be nothing capable of being corrupted' (1991, 124). Augustine reasons that evil cannot exist without the prior existence of its opposite, for evil, as corruption, is dependent upon the good being available for corruption. This carries a revelatory import for Augustine, for now he is able to conceive a universe created as good by a God that was universally good, where sin can also exist without compromising God. But the most important aspect of this education was that what opposed the good in fact was the strongest evidence of the existence of God. Suddenly, here, God's ordinance and providence were seen by Augustine to include oppositions by which their truth would be revealed.

In putting these two revelations together, the form and content of the stage where the soul re-orders itself becomes clear. First, in Plotinus's advice to let the soul study itself[10] Augustine comes to understand why the word, the prophets, and Christ himself demand 'return' to the self. This is the way that the soul and its activity in reason and thought, find in itself a non-material existence, one that can think ideas of the largest magnitude without, itself, having any magnitude at all. Second, that which troubles the soul, the external world, and its distractions, are now understood within 'the totality' (1991, 125), meaning that they are understood as educative of the soul regarding God's ordinance and providence. It is in the combination of thought without magnitude and the sinful will being offered an educational path to God, that the soul can find God in itself. Once the educative ways of God became clear to Augustine, everything for him was re-ordered, and from within this re-ordering the remaining stages fell into their allotted place. He recognized that in learning about free will and spiritual substance he had turned toward himself, returned into himself, such that his soul could now discover its own truth from within its own resources. Stage four here means 'I was being turned around' (1991, 94), that is, the order of the self, of the senses, and of the arts was being re-ordered around the spiritual. In his own words:

> Step by step I ascended from bodies to the soul which perceives through the body and from there to its inward force.... From there again I ascended to the power of reasoning to which is to be attributed the power of judging the deliverances of the bodily senses. This power, which in myself I found to be mutable, raised itself to the level of its own intelligence, and led my thinking out of the ruts of habit. It withdrew itself from the contradictory swarms of imaginative fantasises, so as to discover the light by which it was flooded ... [and] in the flash of a trembling glance it attained to that which is.
>
> (1991, 127)

However, Augustine notes even here that his weaknesses reasserted themselves and denied him an unchangeable knowledge of the unchangeable. Nevertheless, if stage four is a re-ordering of the ordering of the body, its senses and its experiences, stages five, six, and seven are implicit in this re-ordering. From the soul's immaterial thought of the will's freedom to sin (as the true thought of God) comes stage five, the tranquillity of knowing God's order in all things, and particularly in the ambiguities and struggles of contradictory oppositions in reasoning; and stage six, the approach of this re-ordering to the providence of God. These two stages are the purification of the soul for they involve the re-ordering of the self, a re-ordering of the soul according to eternal standards and away from earthly and bodily standards. Thus in these stages of re-ordering and purification Augustine says he knows of God 'that in you all things are finite, not in the sense that the space they occupy is bounded but in the sense that you hold all things in your hand by your truth ... And I saw that each thing is harmonious not only with its place but with its time' (1991, 126). The final stage, stage seven, where the mind contemplates the will of providence and ordinance as the unchangeable itself, is, as we have seen, only a fleeting moment. Who, asks Augustine, 'can lay hold on the heart and give it fixity, so that for some little moment it may be stable, and for a fraction of time may grasp the splendour of a constant eternity?' (1991, 228).

This final stage is therefore no final stage. The last four books of the *Confessions* yearn to know 'where in my consciousness, Lord, do you dwell?' (1991, 200). What we learn here is that the fourth stage of the education, the re-ordering of order, becomes the subjectivity in which order and re-order struggle against each other. Subjectivity is the experience of their antithesis. The last books of the *Confessions* do not end with tranquillity but with the opposition between order and its re-ordering, seen when Augustine asks, 'where then did I find you to be able to learn of you?' (1991, 201). The dilemma is in the aporia of recollection. If God is stored in the memory then it is an image of something known or seen, but there can be no image of that which has no magnitude. If God is not stored in the memory then he has never been known, and if the soul finds God outside of the memory, how then 'shall I find you if I am not mindful of you?' (1991, 195). This aporia characterizes the last four books of the *Confessions*. Indeed, the urgency of the dilemmas presented there by Augustine far outweigh those of the soul's 'first' development, that is, the previous books of the *Confessions*. Something important is being confessed here. It seems that the mind that knows God is more troubled than the mind that seeks God for the first time. To comprehend this now, we must turn to the comments in the *Confessions* that deal specifically with Christ.

Philosophy could only take Augustine as far as a repetition of the antinomy of knowing the absolute. But Augustine finds this weakness before the truth as exactly the significance of Christ, a weakness he finds in himself, and expressed in the, at times, desperate confessing of the last four books of the *Confessions*. I sought a way to enjoy my knowledge of God, he says, but 'I did not find it until I embraced "the mediator between God and man, the man Christ Jesus"' (1991, 128). This is because in the development of the soul, it grows stronger only as the self grows weaker in that the turn to God requires the turn away from the self. This weakness, Augustine tells us, is precisely what Christ's weakness is meant to teach us. Between the pride of the self and the piety of the soul there is the meaning of the struggle, the hope, and the faith that Christ provides. But Augustine arrives at this understanding only after overcoming another error in his reasoning. He admits at first to seeing Christ as a 'man of excellent wisdom' (1991, 128) and as having 'great authority as a teacher' (1991, 128). This is the philosophical Christ. But in retrospect, Augustine also admits that 'the mystery of the Word made flesh I had not begun to guess' (1991, 128). He acknowledges the humanity of Christ but not the significance of his 'personal embodiment of the Truth' (1991, 129). It is his philosophical side that holds Augustine back here. Reason tells him that God is unchangeable, infinite without magnitude, and goodness. But philosophy does not help him with the anxiety that characterizes his relation to God. This relation is what is embodied in Christ, in all its weaknesses and vulnerabilities, and this is precisely what Christ is on earth to teach. The intellectual conversion to God can only reproduce the need for a personal relation to God. But Augustine found no piety or humility in the philosophical books. It is only when he reads the Scriptures, and particularly Paul, that he finds not just the existence of God but the relation to God discussed and acknowledged. Thus, says Augustine, in the Scriptures, 'all the truth I had read in the Platonists was stated here together with the commendation of your grace' (1991, 130–1). He now sees the Platonists as those who knew what truth is but not how to get there. Platonist pride gives way to the strength of Christian weakness.

We come, then, to the famous moment of Augustine's conversion from a Platonic good to a Christian way of living with the good. Still the battle rages within Augustine, between the body and the soul, the carnal and the spiritual. The one will takes up position against itself, as two wills, one willing to rise to the truth, the other willing to descend to the earthly and the material. Augustine knows this struggle to be himself, to be the one will divided against itself. This has been the engine of development of the *Confessions*, it is what confession consists in. 'It was I' (1991, 148), he says, and it was the presence of sin. It was also where the battle between becoming a Christian or remaining a philosophical believer was being fought. 'Inwardly I said to myself: Let it be now, let it be now. And by this phrase I was already moving towards a decision; I had almost taken it; and then I did not do so' (1991, 150). The rest of the story is well-known. Asking God again, 'why not now?', Augustine hears a child repeating 'pick up and read me' (*tolle lege*). Hearing this as a message from God Augustine opened the Bible and found himself reading Romans 13: 13–14, telling him to turn from lust to Christ. At once, 'it was as if a light of relief from all anxiety flooded into my heart. All the shadows of doubt were dispelled' (1991, 153). This is a peace, as he says, but not the kind of peace envisaged in the seventh stage of the soul's development. This is the peace of weakness, of the pilgrim of the city of God on earth; it is not a peace that overcomes the war or struggle within the self, or even reconciles the two wills. It is a peace *in* the inner war, an understanding of love in weakness and struggle. It is not the overcoming of the struggle between body and soul, but its mediation, in and through Christ who embodied the holy city in the earthly city and suffered that relation as himself.

## Eriugena

John Scotus Eriugena completed his *Periphyseon*, or *Division of Nature*, c. 867. The Christian culture of error expressed in the work is a sophisticated philosophical system of loss and return, which invokes negation and contradiction as key educational concepts capable of re-forming thought's unavoidable error in relation to the true. What is perhaps most remarkable is just how rich Eriugena finds the nothing or negativity to be. That the work pertains to the error of the culture of finite philosophical thought is clear at the beginning of the work where Eriugena notes that the most fundamental division in nature is that between what is knowable and unknowable to the mind. That it is also a culture of error is clear from the educational significance Eriugena assigns to God being nothing, that is, beyond being and non-being. He argues that when finite thought is in error in relation to God's truth, this is when man knows God most comprehensively. He argues not only for the divine educational significance of contraries and oppositions, but also for a view of nature as carrying error as truth.

*The division of nature*

From the primary division of nature as the genus of the knowable and the unknowable, Eriugena cites a fourfold division of this genus into species. These are: that which creates but is not created; that which is created and also creates; that which is created and does not create; and that which neither creates nor is created.[11] Each of the five books of the *Periphyseon* is devoted to one or more of these divisions of universal nature. In sum he sees the relationship between these four species of nature to be the whole of beginning and end, and of cause and effect. He says of the relations within this whole that

> [d]ivine Goodness and Essence and Life and Wisdom and everything which is in the source of all things [that which creates but is not created] first flow down into the primordial causes and make them to be [that which is created but also creates], then through the primordial causes they descend [and distribute] in an ineffable way through the orders of the universe that accommodate them, flowing forth continuously through the higher to the lower [that which is created and does not create]; and return back again to their source through the most secret channels of nature by a most hidden course.
>
> (Eriugena, 1987, 249)

In this process there is to be found everything that is and everything that is not.

Even though the enquiry is posited on the thought that nothing in the division of nature will avoid or reform the fundamental division of the knowable and the unknowable, Eriugena registers the ways in which this presupposition appears to the mind in the form of contraries, that is, as five modes of being and not being. These five modes are the oppositions of knowable and unknowable, higher and lower, actual and potential, immutable and changeable, and finally, in human nature, the order of sin and redemption. Eriugena acknowledges the education that is carried in the principle of negation and affirmation in the hierarchy of the order of higher and lower. We will return to this shortly.

This twofold division of nature requires a relation if they are to be known. Here Eriugena argues for theophanies. These are manifestations of God that make him intelligible. They are that by which 'it is made known that God exists' (1987, 593). As such, and characteristic of Neoplatonic Christianity, the soul can come to know *that* God is but not *what* God is. Even the righteous on earth can never see God in himself, although God has made it possible that he can be represented. In a mystical vein, Eriugena here points out that although 'God in Himself is visible to no creature whatsoever' (1987, 577), nevertheless in the most exalted theophanies and contemplations, God 'is seen and shall be seen' (1987, 577). These he calls the theophanies of theophanies. He also argues that those who comprehend a theophany in some way become or are transformed into what they have comprehended.

### The first three divisions of nature

The first division of nature concerns that which creates but is not created. God is not created by anything superior to him, but when he creates he also creates himself, for there is no division, no error, between his will and his being. This truth can be symbolized in finite understanding, but even here God's truth must exceed any positive determination that man cares to ascribe to him. Only negation, or that God is not a something, is affirmed here. He is always 'more than that which is said or understood of Him' (1987, 114). He is more than any predicate, for his truth is 'beyond language and understanding' (1987, 73). In the idea that God is more than what is said of God it is only negation, or what he is not, that is affirmed. This leads Eriugena to argue that God enjoys divine ignorance of himself. He cannot know himself positively or indeed negatively. This inability only looks like a weakness when judged according to a finite comprehension of what ignorance means. For God it is 'the highest and truest wisdom' (1987, 201) because he knows and understands that in his essence there is 'none of the things which are and are not, because He surpasses all essence' (1987, 208). Eriugena is keen to purge God of all thoughts of himself since it is a thought of something that is inescapably error. God too, would be in error if he knew himself positively. At this stage, Eriugena seems to hold that if God knew himself positively it would involve a privation, since the culture of finite thought is always error regarding the truth of what is.

The second division of nature, yields the primordial forms which are created and create. These are created by God to flow down to the primordial causes that will themselves create multiple forms of existing things. They are those 'species or forms in which the immutable reasons of things that were to be made were created before (the things themselves) existed' (1987, 129).

The third division of nature is created but does not create. It concerns the effects of the primordial causes. These earthly corporeal objects are the lowest in the hierarchy of divine nature because creation stops with them. There is no further for nature to descend than here. However, this third division provides one of the most philosophically significant discussions in the *Periphyseon*, namely, how the creature who inhabits this lowest level can know or understand his creator. Eriugena notes that it is from God's goodness that things which are not are called into existence and brought to essence, but that things that are not are also nearer to the good for they are not confined by 'differences and properties within some fixed and definite substance' (1987, 244). This speaks of an order in the primordial causes, that there is one type of goodness in things that are, and another in things that are not. But the most basic tenet of this division of nature is the division of what is knowable and unknowable. How, then, are those bodies at the lowest level of nature ever to know the goodness that is in their creation? It is in these theophanies that what is understood is unintelligible, what is manifest is hidden, and what is comprehended is incomprehensible. Thought, here, posits itself as error, such that 'it is impossible for the Essence of Father, Son, or Holy Spirit, and (their) Substance(s) to be revealed to the creature directly as they are' (1987, 159).

This question of God creating out of nothing takes us to the heart of Eriugena's negative logic and reveals how the third division of nature, that which is created but cannot create, is related to and in the mind of God, such that what is created is both eternal and made. Eriugena's view here can be understood as one that knows what is posited having its actuality in negation.

### Negative education

In assessing the question of creation *ex nihilo* Eriugena accepts a logic of contradiction. If all things were made from nothing, yet are eternal in the world of God, then reason must concede that there was not a time when they were not *and* a time when they were not. The former is neither existence nor non-existence and is eternal and unfathomable. The latter is educative, for the opposite of nothing is not something. The nothing has no opposite. But the nothing can negate itself *as creation*. In Eriugena the nothing can only be known as not itself, and when the nothing is not even itself, this is its truth. Little wonder then, that Eriugena constantly reminds us that 'the power of negation is stronger than that of affirmation for investigating the sublimity and incomprehensibility of the Divine Nature' (1987, 312).

Of course the real philosophical significance of the double negative cannot be realized by thought that posits itself as error and does not see the truth of this negation in and for itself. It is a truth that is not (yet) open to this unhappy self-divided and self-alienated consciousness.

Eriugena can only see the truth of the nothing as incomprehensible, and not as self-determining. Thus, he says here, 'so long as it is understood to be incomprehensible by reason of its transcendence', (1987, 308) then it cannot unreasonably be called nothing. But when it proceeds out of nothing into something, descends from beyond essence into essence, then it is only a theophany. Thus Eriugena says 'the further the order of things descends downwards, the more manifestly does it reveal itself to the eyes of those who contemplate it, and therefore the forms and species of sensible things receive the name of "manifest theophanies"' (1987, 308). As such, the representation of nothing in the form of something is all that is open to consciousness. Eriugena takes this to be a negative conclusion, that the nothing cannot be known. Yet his own logic of the negative, indeed, of the double negative, has already revealed a re-education in respect of the nothing. He has shown how the nothing is itself when it is not, and that this is as true in eternity – where there is not a time when the nothing is not – as it is in finitude – where there is presently and historically a time when the nothing, also, is not. Here is to be found the significance of the error of culture as a culture of error. In theophany the positing of the thought of God as merely finite error re-forms the relation between nothing and something, or between known and unknown, such that the negative finite not knowing of God is also the negative infinite not knowing of God by himself. In Eriugena's culture of error here only the negative can be for us as it is also for itself.

In God, for whom 'both being and commanding all things to be are the same thing', (1987, 313) creation is a unity, not an opposition. The descent of divine goodness to earth is only a descent 'from itself into itself' (1987, 308). This self-determination of nothing so that it is and is not itself is the creative will of God. The paradox of the will of God is that for God to be truly himself as uncreated he must create himself. His will, therefore, requires this paradoxical self-(un)creation. We, in the finite and the temporal, are the *effects* of God's paradox. We are created out of his 'un'-creation of himself as that which creates and is created. We are, as it were, the will of divine goodness.

But, it is not enough to state the relationship between the creator and the created as easily reconciled in this philosophical knowledge that man is the contingency of God's goodness. This contingency is unable to return to goodness on its own due to its determination in and by sin. Sin here means the shape of subjectivity that takes itself to be separated from God and to be in error. The fact that every created being 'was always a created being' (1987, 581) does not mean that the infinite is present in time truly and completely. Thus there arises the need for a form of subjectivity whose sin is not error but the truth of error. This subjectivity is Christ. Christ comes to earth to 'save the effects of the causes' (1987, 585) else 'the principles of the Causes would perish: for no Cause could survive the destruction of the effects of their Causes' (1987, 585). Where, for Aristotle, effect precedes cause as actuality precedes potentiality, the Christian Eriugena knows Christ as their broken relation.

### The fourth division of nature

As with the first division, there is a paradoxical nature to the fourth division, which Eriugena describes as neither created nor creative. He says that things made from nothing will return to nothing 'when every substance shall be purged of its corruptible accidents and freed from all things which do not pertain to the state of its proper nature, its indissoluble simplicity' (1987, 289–90). This, he argues, will be the division of nature that is neither created nor creative; 'not created because it is created by none, nor creative because here it no longer creates, for all things have been converted into their eternal reasons in which they shall and do remain eternally, and cease also to be called by the name of creature' (1987, 317).

Here, however, he must account for the way the first division, that which is not created but creates, returns to itself as what is neither created nor creative. Eriugena reasons that in the return to itself God cannot create, for He is already all creation, and cannot therefore be created. At the very end of Book V he states that the first and the fourth divisions of nature are the only ones that can be predicated of God. The first contemplates the beginning that is uncreated but creates, while the fourth is the end to which creation aims when all that is created is consummated in and as the creator. In this latter, God is neither created nor creating for when all things have found their rest in their true end 'it can no longer be said of It that It creates anything. For what should it be creating when It Itself shall be all in all, and shall manifest Itself in nothing save itself?' (1987, 711).

Book V explores how God and creation are within the logic of return and the educational significance of such return. In sum, for Eriugena 'all things are from Him and to Him all things return: for He is the Beginning and the End' (1987, 562). However, the Book itself begins by confirming that it is by contemplation that man may return to the eternal bliss from which he was removed by sin. The cherubim are evidence that God intended humanity to have a means by which to regain its former felicity. Eriugena draws evidence for return from the natural laws of the planets and the oceans. Every creature, he says, seeks peace in trying to return to its origin, that is, to itself. Similarly, the components of the Liberal Arts[12] see the rational mind as seeking to return to its principles in which they will find the end, the purpose, and therefore also the beginning of their activity. Every end returns (and is to return) to its beginning. Eriugena notes that *telos* for the Greeks did not differentiate between beginning and end. Now, if both physical and rational nature seek to return to their principles, so the same will be the case for human nature whose principle is the word of God.

Eriugena marks the time of return as after death and on the day of judgement. He describes five stages of this return. The first is the death of the body, then the retrieval of the body, which is followed by transmutations of body into soul, soul into cause and of causes into God. It is, he says, the 'common end of all created things to return, by a kind of dying, into the Causes which subsist in God' (1987, 568). Similar to Augustine, Eriugena questions whether death should really be the term used to describe the dissolution of the earthly body since, in truth, this death is more the death of death itself and the beginning of the soul's resurrection. Earthly dying is 'liberation from death' (1987, 540), where transitory bodily substance is changed into eternal spiritual substance on the day of resurrection. This is to be understood as return because, says Eriugena, we would be right to suppose that 'the whole of human nature, soul and body, was at first created immortal and incorruptible' (1987, 551).

The principle of return here is always that 'the lower nature is transformed into the higher' (1987, 563), and Eriugena is in no doubt about the educational significance that accompanies this ascent. He states that if we are 'unwilling to learn and know about ourselves, that means that we have no desire to return to that which is above ourselves, namely our proper cause' (1987, 619). He also brings the education that inheres in the negative to the fore when he says that while we may not understand *how* God works, we can at least speculate on why he does what he does. In doing so, Eriugena shares the Augustinian view that God needed to create oppositions and contraries so that the best in the universe would shine clearly against the worst. He lists the following such opposites: wisdom and foolishness, knowledge and ignorance, life and death, light and dark, righteousness and damnation, and good will and evil will. As for Augustine, the existence here of evil and other vices fulfils the pedagogical role of educating man regarding the truth of his oppositions. Truth shines more brightly when compared to its opposite. 'What', asks

Eriugena, 'is more desirable than that the immeasurable glory both of the Universe and its Creator should be manifested by the contrast of opposites?' (1987, 633). This is the ground in Eriugena of both the error of the culture of finite thought and the culture of this error.

Thus, and despite the fact that Eriugena has described a system of knowing and not knowing in which God is manifest according to his own truth, it is still a culture of error in that the system that educates the finite mind is not also the free self-determination of the finite mind. Just as it can be known from his creation *that* God exists but not also *what* he is, so, in the image of God, the finite mind can know *that* it is, but not *what* it is. For the man of wisdom, therefore, it is the case that 'the human mind is more honoured in its ignorance than in its knowledge; for the ignorance in it of what it is is more praiseworthy than the knowledge that it is, just as the negation of God accords better with the praise of His nature than the affirmation and it shows greater wisdom not to know than to know that Nature of Which ignorance is the true wisdom and Which is known all the better for not being known' (1987, 417–18). This again states the error of culture and the culture of error that characterizes Eriugena's thought in the *Periphyseon*.

## Aquinas

In Aquinas the culture of error is found in his struggles to think the logic and significance of ambivalence in trying to think the true. This is the case in his early, more philosophical works as it is in the *Summa Contra Gentiles* and the *Summa Theologica*. We will look briefly now at some of these ambivalences.

### Early ambivalence

In his early work (1252–9) Aquinas struggles with equivocation between pairs of opposites. Matter and form, for example, in *On Being and Essence* can be seen as the cause of each other, and essence 'whereby a thing is denominated a being cannot be form alone, nor matter alone, but is both' (Aquinas, 1998, 33). Even simple substances, forms without matter, have a 'tinge of potentiality' (1998, 42) in that being known to themselves is a part of their essence. There is compound even within the simple. Only the one has existence without 'the addition of some difference' (1998, 42).

He finds this same equivocation between other pairs of opposites. Theology needs philosophy even though theology is the higher science.

Reason can lead man to the need for first principles through the logic of non-contradiction, first cause, and the absurdity of infinite regression which, in revealing its inadequacies delivers the need for faith. The active intellect both unites and separates God and man. The soul is immaterial and embodied. Finally, the intellect is still not 'truth [ ] in the proper sense' (1998, 174) even where object and thought conform to each other.

If ambivalence confirms the possible culture of error in Aquinas, his adherence to Neoplatonic logic confirms too the error of the culture of finite thought. Again, in *On Being and Essence* he states:

> [B]ecause whatever is from another is reduced to what is *per se* as to its first cause, there must be some thing which is the cause of the being of all things by the fact that it is existence alone, otherwise there would be an infinite regress in causes, since everything which is not existence alone has a cause of its existence.... It is evident then that an intelligence is form and existence, and that it has existence from the first being who is existence alone, and that this is the first cause, God.
>
> (1998, 42–3)

We will now see how he approaches ambivalence in his two larger works.

### Summa Contra Gentiles

Written between 1259–64, the *Summa Contra Gentiles* is grounded in Neoplatonic logic and principles. For example, Aquinas notes that since man is dependent upon his senses for his knowledge, he cannot know God fully because God exceeds the senses and therefore the power of human reason. Also, he reiterates the Neoplatonic truth that

> there is naturally present in all men the desire to know the causes of whatever things are observed. Hence, because of wondering about things that were seen but whose causes were hidden, men first began to think philosophically; when they found the cause, they were satisfied. But the search did not stop until it reached the first cause, for 'then do we think that we know perfectly, when we know the first cause.'[13] Therefore, man naturally desires, as his ultimate end, to know the first cause. But the first cause of all things is God. Therefore, the ultimate end of man is to know God.
>
> (Aquinas, 1975c, 101)

Since there can be no infinite regress of cause and effect, so there must exist 'a first efficient cause. This is God' (Aquinas, 1975a, 95). God must be eternal, unmoved and unchanging, and have no potentiality. It is impossible for God to oppose himself and he has no opposites or contraries. He cannot, for example, create something that is being and non-being, or a man who is seeing and blind, or a man without a soul. The end or goal of essence is towards what it is, and 'nothing tends toward its contrary' (1975c, 49). 'Truth', says Aquinas, 'cannot be truth's contrary' (Aquinas, 1975e, 62), and 'everything that is multiform, mutable, and capable of defect must be reducible to a source in something that is uniform, immutable and capable of no defect' (Aquinas, 1975d, 40). It is also a principle that God cannot will that 'affirmation and negation be true together' (1975a, 265). These principles are summed up by Aquinas's observation that 'a substance is a thing to which it belongs to be not in a subject' (1975a, 128).

We will explore Aquinas's culture of error in the *Summa Contra Gentiles* now in two relations: first in God known by man, and second in God known by himself. We will see that the former works with the ambivalence or the culture of error, while the latter prioritizes the error of culture.

*God known by man*

Man's thought is in error in that he can know *that* God exists but cannot comprehend *what* He is. Man's finite power can never 'be on a par with the infinite object' (1975c, 187). They are never equal and therefore 'no created intellect may comprehend it' (1975c, 187). Philosophy is a finite power in that natural reason can prove the existence of God. But faith makes this more available to those who cannot devote their lives to study. That God is beyond reason serves to humble those arrogant enough to assume they know the true. Natural reason proves that the ordered universe needs a creator of order, and can provide certain of its attributes, that it is immutable, eternal, incorporeal, and simple. But these are essentially negative in showing how different God is from everything that is known in the finite mind.[14] He is neither body, nor accident, nor in time, nor potency, nor matter, nor composite. Faith is a higher form of knowledge, but the knowledge of Christ and the Apostles is higher still. Even visions of God only reflect the likeness of God for the mind can go no higher than 'that whereby a cause is known through its effect' (1975c, 161). As such, God is named and known 'from His effects' (1975a, 148). This means that neither through knowledge, nor demonstration, nor faith, is it possible 'for man's ultimate felicity to come in this life' (1975c, 162).

Man is also in error regarding self-knowledge. In God understanding is being – we will return to this point later – but in man 'being is not its act of understanding' (1975e, 82) and therefore is not perfect. Nothing besides God 'can be its own being' (Aquinas, 1975b, 153). Since man's understanding of himself is always mediated by and always 'pertains to some object' (1975c, 105), it is never a pure act of intellect as being.

But the soul is important for Aquinas for it carries ambivalence as the culture or re-formation of error. 'The end and ultimate perfection of the human soul lies in its transcending by knowledge and love the whole order of creatures, thus reaching up to the first principle, which is God' (1975b, 295). He sees the soul as the moving form of the body, and as containing both the active and the potential intellects. This view of the soul as the form of the moving body is at odds with Plato, Averroes, Alexander of Aphrodisias, Galen, and Empedocles, all of whom in various ways did not believe the soul could be the form of the body. Against all of them, Aquinas argues that the soul is the form of the body because it meets two criteria. First, it is the principle of the being of the body, and second it communicates this principle to the body in a unity of one act of being. Together the form of the intellectual substance is also the body's form, which is the human soul, and this, for Aquinas, is not counter to Aristotle who, for example, argued for soul and body in the constitution of the heavens. The soul and the body need no third party to unite them because to be the act of a body is the essence of form (although disposition does come between form and its reception in matter).

In discussing man's knowledge of God, Aquinas accuses Alexander of Aphrodisias and Averroes of making man's end in God and thus the education of the soul futile. They argued that if the active intellect was to be joined to a person this needed the person to know and understand all of the principles of the speculative sciences. Since for Aquinas no such likeness to God is ever knowable, man would never know God as his true end. For Aquinas the active intellect is 'united with man in substantial being' (1975c, 141) and is the soul, or part of the soul. Against much mediaeval Islamic philosophy Aquinas does not believe that man's knowledge of God is mediated by an active intellect that is separate from the understanding. Rather, for Aquinas, the soul is where the active intellect is already united with man, and wherein the likeness of God will appear. This leads Aquinas to reiterate the principle that although the soul can know *that* it is, and can know this through itself, this is very different from knowing *what* it is. Some have claimed the latter in ecstatic visions, but Aquinas prefers the view that it is in and as the first principles of understanding that the 'image of divine truth is reflected universally in the minds of all men' (1975c, 161) and that with Augustine, as with St Paul, man sees God through a glass darkly.[15]

The *Summa* also argues for the re-formation of error through grace and providence. In grace man achieves 'the likeness to God' (1975d, 234), while in miracles, revelation, law, Scripture, and the hierarchy of beings man knows God's providence over the world. In the latter, man learns of God's goodness in acting for the benefit of those who are of a lower order of being.

*God known to himself*

Here Aquinas holds the error of culture against the truth in God by employing Neoplatonic logic. Contradiction for God is impossible. If God moved himself then it would be like a teacher teaching himself the same knowledge he already has, and this would mean that 'the same thing would be possessed and not possessed by the same being – which is impossible' (1975a, 91). Alternatively, if God is moved by another type of motion this opens up an infinite regression, which is also impossible. Thus, says Aquinas, 'we must posit some first mover that is not moved by any exterior moving cause' (1975a, 92),[16] and that the first principle of God is that he is 'absolutely unmoved' (1975a, 97). In addition, since God is not dependent upon any other for his being, he must be eternal and the efficient first cause of everything else.

In God being and essence are the same. This means that he is absolutely simple and uncompounded in any way. He knows all things without being a part of them, and is present in them as cause. He is the pure understanding of all things, and knows this essence as his own being. This understanding belongs to God alone for it has no potential, nor does it involve change or coming to understand something for the first time. There is 'no before and after in the divine being; everything is together' (1975a, 194). God's knowledge does not have the form of succession in the way that human knowledge does. In the *Disputation on God's Power* Aquinas makes the argument that the question as to whether the world had a beginning is a question made possible by God in creating time along with the world. God created the universe and willed it so that it would appear with a beginning. Questions, therefore, about a beginning being contradictory to an eternal being are nugatory. And in the *Summa Theologica* (I. 46) Aquinas repeats his belief that creation is not change.[17] That the world exists after it has not existed does not mean that its not existing was in time. The world created from nothing is God's will, which human reason cannot comprehend. God is an 'ever-abiding simultaneous whole' (1975a, 218).

Since being and essence are the same in God, when he wills his own essence it is willed purely for its own sake, and this is the good. Unlike man, in God 'being and understanding are identical, the intention understood in Him is His very intellect. And because understanding in Him is the thing understood ... it follows that in God, because He understands Himself, the intellect, the thing understood, and the intention understood are all identical' (1975e, 82). This means that divine generation is an 'intellectual emanation' (1975e, 83). In this unity or oneness the intention of this self-creating intellect is the word of God, or is God understood as and by himself. The word, therefore, is his absolute being. The love of God for himself, for goodness, shows that his pure will desires only the good. This internal impulse of God to himself is the holy spirit. It is this love of his own goodness that is the reason for creation, that is, for willing that there be other things. 'The only thing that moves God to produce creatures is His own goodness, which He wished to communicate to other things by likening them to Himself' (1975b, 141). Thus it is through the holy spirit that man is brought to 'the beatitude of divine enjoyment' (1975e, 124) in preparation for his likeness to God in perfect operation.

### Summa Theologica

Written between 1265–74 and never completed, the *Summa Theologica* reasserts the Neoplatonic principles of the error of the culture of finite thought, and of the culture of this error, that were established in the earlier *Summa Contra Gentiles*.

### God known to man

In the error of the culture of finite thought man knows God logically in natural Neoplatonic reason, which is the way that God communicates himself in the universe to man. Natural reason means God is known only negatively, as what he is not. But, and beyond the senses and the imagination, man's intellect is a gift from God so that in the culture of error, he might still be known to man. But faith in revelation will also be needed because of the limitations of the finite intellect.

As in the *Summa Contra Gentiles* the soul is seen as the means of this divine education. It is able to take in pure intellectual concepts but will never be able to know immaterial substance perfectly because the embodied soul has to work with its representation in material objects.

All positive names attributed to God 'fall short of a full representation of Him' (I.13.2). Man also learns of God from law and divine ordinance. There is in man an intrinsic principle of the good which knows that it must act in pursuit of itself. The principle and the end come from God, but the voluntary pursuit of it belongs to man. Virtue is in the well-ordered soul that knows to act justly. Divine law is present in man as the law of nature that is inclined to its own proper act and end. As such, 'every act of reasoning is based on principles that are known naturally' (II.I.91.2) because God has 'bestowed on each thing the form whereby it is inclined to the end appointed to it by Him' (II.II.23.2). Human law should seek the common good, peace and justice. When a human law is contrary to God's commandments it should not be obeyed. Indeed, in the struggle between the spiritual and the material worlds, man will move nearer to eternal happiness the more he abandons the material world, although it need not be abandoned altogether, since he can use 'the things of this world [to] attain to eternal happiness, provided he does not place his end in them' (II.I.108.4).

Finally, in the third part of the *Summa Theologica*, Aquinas looks at the way in which God is known by man as incarnate. It is God's nature to communicate himself as goodness, and the highest mode possible for communicating this was to be united in flesh with creatures. Christ lived as the person of the word, and existed in 'the mystery of the union of the two natures in Christ' (III.2.6).

## God known to himself

Here Aquinas prioritizes the error of the culture of finite thought in relation to the perfection of God. God has his essence and his existence as a pure act without any potentiality. He is pure form and, untouched by matter, he is infinite. In Part I, the 14th question notes that God has no division within himself, knows himself perfectly as substance and existence, is the first cause of all things, knows everything including the future without change to himself, and is spontaneous, immediate, and whole. For man, truth is defined by conformity of intellect and thing, but in God truth and being are the same thing. Therefore, in the divine intellect, truth is the very act of understanding and being 'simply and immediately' (I.16.4). God, the divine intellect, 'is truth itself' (I.16.5) and is immutable. It is also the case that the will of God is one with his intellect in that what he understands he also wills. It is his will to spread his goodness to others, thus 'it befits the divine goodness that other things should be partakers therein' (I.19.2). God's love is also a pure act and is thus a love without passion.

### Ambivalence

The culture of error in Aquinas is grounded in the same principles that characterize mediaeval Christian philosophy. Foremost here are the laws of non-contradiction, of cause and effect, and of the absurdity of infinite regression. Thus, God is the first efficient cause because infinite regression opposes itself and cannot therefore be true. God is not subjective substance because finite thought is contrary and opposed to eternal truth. Reason based on sense perception, analogy, and likeness is dependent upon an object and is not therefore both being and essence. Each of these principles posits the impossibility of truth containing contraries existing together and at the same time. Everything that is part must be restored to the whole; everything that is compound must be reduced to the simple; everything that is effect must find its cause; and everything thought is error and must be returned to its perfection in that for whom being and will and intellect are the one essence. Thus the conception of God, in Aquinas as in other mediaeval Christian cultures of error, is the positing of thought as error in relation to the true.

Yet as we saw there is ambivalence in Aquinas's treatment of the contradictions realized in the law of non-contradiction. God needs to be undivided *and* to be part of each particular. He needs to enjoy undivided knowledge yet to have knowledge of all particular things he has created. He needs to will his own goodness in such a way that in the multitude of created things this truth can fail to be known in itself by that which it has created specifically for this purpose. Aquinas has to deny that God creates out of any heteronomous necessity, yet His goodness seemingly needs creatures for it to be itself, that is, to be good. God makes things only so that they may serve his end, but is he also dependent upon creatures for the fulfilment of his own essence? If God created man with free will, in likeness to himself, then creation contains the same ambivalence that we find in finite reason. It can oppose itself.

Equally Aquinas mediates the ambivalence of creation by arguing that it is 'relation by essence' (1975b, 56). God can create that which will oppose him without this being in any way an opposition within the creator. He also recognizes that there is the threat of contradiction between free will and God's providence. For example, he recognizes that God has providence over all things, but also that the natural hierarchy of the superior over the inferior means that providence is enacted by intermediaries. This extends to the question of predestination. Predestination is certain, but can be helped by the secondary actions of intellectual creatures. Who is saved depends on God's will, but it is enacted by the choices of the creature.[18]

A second example of ambiguity in free will is that a good act, freely chosen, must conform to the divine will. The problem arises in knowing how a particular act serves God as the universal end. The creature does not know what God wills in particular cases for it is only in heaven that the truth of the particulars will be clearly seen in the universal. Aquinas seeks to resolve this rational ambiguity between universal and particular by employing grace as a middle between them. If law is God's external help in guiding man, grace is his internal intervention. When God gives the gift of grace he implants 'an eternal good, which is Himself' (II.I. 110.1), and one that allows man to choose freely those things that are demanded by grace, or by God in man. It is, therefore, the law of perfect liberty, or freedom, prompting man inwardly to choose to do the right thing. In this way man's free interior movements 'are ordered' (II.I.108.3). Equally, because free will is always based on a prior reflection and, as cause and effect, cannot extend *ad infinitum*, God is the first principle of man's free will. Human nature can be raised 'by the help of grace to a higher end' (II.I.109.5), a help that man must be willing to receive as God's gift and to be inspired by it and inwardly moved toward God. Reason knows this in the contradiction that 'free will can only be turned to God, when God turns it' (II.I.109.6). This negation of free will will become self-negation when, in modernity, reason finds itself in and as the work of the aporia as a whole.

Thus the culture of error here is *error* in its being grounded according to the law of non-contradiction, of cause and effect, and of the impossibility of infinite regression, but it is also *culture* or re-formation in all of the ways in which Aquinas mediates oppositions with formative middles, not least of which are grace and the soul.

## Duns Scotus

Duns Scotus also exhibits ambivalence in his approach to the logic of thought within the culture of error. It is an ambivalence that has provoked debate in particular about his relation to Thomist thought. Of significance here are his ideas of being and univocity.

In his *Oxford Commentary on the Sentences of Peter Lombard* he makes the case for being as the most fundamental transcendental element and having both material and immaterial existence. Being is the condition of the possibility of there being anything at all, including the distinction between the infinite and the finite. Since man is moved to know substance through the senses and not directly from substance itself, it must follow that an accident is 'none other than the concept of being'

(1987, 6). This ambiguity of being as of God and man remains grounded in Neoplatonic logic. Since the less perfect presupposes the more perfect, as the finite presupposes the infinite, so the creature presupposes the creator. Scotus even clarifies Ockham's razor by ensuring that the principle of non-contradiction is inserted within it as its logical premise.[19] 'Among beings which can produce an effect one is simply first' (1987, 39)[20] or else cause becomes impossible, lost to infinite regression, and 'a circle in causes', he states, 'is inadmissable' (1987, 39). 'Of necessity, some first being able to cause exists' (1987, 45) and since 'nothing can come from nothing, it follows that some nature is capable of causing effectively' (1987, 41) and as its own ultimate end.

The ambivalence here is that God's being, like that of everything else, is known only *a posteriori* and never by a true knowledge of God. However, here Scotus does not leave the gate open for nihilism of an indemonstrable God. Rather, it is because being is common to God and man that he can be known. How he can be known is 'univocity', something that substance and accident share. Univocity is the concept or the logical idea in which God is defined not just *by* the principle of non-contradiction, but *as* that principle. It is the condition of the possibility of God and man *being*. 'I designate that concept univocal', he says, 'which possesses sufficient unity in itself, so that to affirm and deny it of one and the same thing would be contradiction' (1987, 20), adding that contradictions 'do not form a unity' (1987, 73), and that true propositions cannot admit of contraries existing simultaneously. Further, his proofs of univocity are grounded in cause and effect and the fear of infinite regression. Without univocity man's certainty about God, or any object, becomes infinitely uncertain. Analogies of God in the finite intellect, presuppose univocity or they are nugatory. Faith too has meaning only because there is univocity. Finally, the intellect must possess the formal concept of God – its univocity – in order for metaphysics to be possible. Every enquiry into God by way of metaphysics is only possible because the formal notion of God has univocity with its imperfect knowing in creatures. To this extent, culture or re-formation *a posteriori* in Scotus lies in the *a priori* structure of the condition of the possibility of the *a priori* and the *a posteriori*, and this condition of possibility is the univocity of being or, the same, the being of non-contradiction *per se*. This is a radical attempt to think the truth of the culture of error, one that points towards the Kantian revolution described below in Part III.

Scotus adheres to the ambivalence of the culture of error, then, by way of univocity. It is, as it were, the very power or capacity of being to will itself. It is a middle between God and man for it is the pathway by which the latter might know himself in the former. But it has no possibility within it of another middle term between its being and its attribute. In this latter, then, it also carries the error of the culture of finite thought. In univocity it remains the case that the created intellect cannot know the essence of God. Univocity here does not compromise the unknowability of God to the creature, but it does serve to reduce the separation between them. It is the condition of the possibility of metaphysics, of God being known at all, but it does not compromise the absolute independence of God. It is 'impossible for our intellect to possess a natural and intuitive knowledge of God' (1987, 31). That is for God alone to have. When the finite mind thinks infinity, it does so by considering one thing after another in time, whereas the infinite intellect can know all things at once. All creaturely contemplation of God is beneath that of God who thinks himself as the singular essence. This confirms the error of the culture of thought. Unlike the finite intellect, 'the intellect of the First Being knows everything else that can be known with a knowledge that is eternal, is distinct, is actual, is necessary, and is prior by nature to the existence of these things in themselves' (1987, 60–1).[21] In comparison the finite intellect has only 'defective truth' (1987, 130).

## Towards reason

The aporia of mediaeval Christian philosophy is its unhappy consciousness. God is posited as everything that consciousness is not. He is not body, accident, in time, potential, matter, or composite. God is his own cause and effect, he is pure act, and he is immediate self-mover. As such, he is posited as unknowable in finite thought. Subjectivity is antithetical to God, and the further the divine is pushed out of human consciousness, where thought is taken as error, the more unhappy the subjective consciousness becomes. Thought here is both the solution to the problem of this alienation and unhappiness, and it is the problem of the solution in that it undermines its own work. This is why mediaeval history of philosophy is both the culture of error and the error of culture. The solution it posits – perfection – is the grave of its own life, negating itself and producing only further unhappiness and a greater desire for resolution. What lies ahead for the history of Western philosophy is for thought and subjectivity to learn and recollect that the unknowability of God is in fact reason's misrecognition of itself. This negative education will be explored later in Part III.

# 4
# Mediaeval Islamic and Judaic Philosophy

## Introduction

Our interest in this chapter will be in the engagement of mediaeval Islamic thinkers – al-Farabi (c. 870–950), Avicenna (980–1037), al-Ghazali (1058–1111) and Averroes (1126–98) – and the Jewish thinker Maimonides (1135–1204) – with Neoplatonic logic and philosophical principles. Here too we will see how the error of the culture of finite thought coexists with the culture or education carried in such errors.

## Al-Farabi

### The one and emanation

Al-Farabi works with a culture of error in distinguishing the perfect being of the one from the finite thought that knows him. Grounded in the principles that 'contrariety is itself a deficiency of existence' (al-Farabi, 1998, 133), and that compound existence is 'defective' (al-Farabi, 2001a, 53), al-Farabi is clear that the one is the first cause of all that exists, and imparts motion without itself being moved. He holds to the Aristotelian view that what cannot be different is substance, and what can be different is merely contingent and accident. As Aristotle holds the unmoved mover to be actual intellect, or thought thinking itself,[1] so al-Farabi sees in God this same self-relation where 'the essence which is thought is the essence which thinks' (1998, 71).[2] The finite mind can only know this as a tautology, or in error, for 'the One whose identity is intellect is intelligible by the One whose identity is intellect' (1998, 71).

Al-Farabi employs the concept of emanation to explain how the unmoved mover creates the universe without change or opposition in himself. Henry Corbin argues here that al-Farabi's notion of emanation is triadic in having three acts of contemplation. Al-Farabi says,

> From the First emanates the existence of the Second. This Second is, again, an utterly incorporeal substance, and is not in matter. It thinks of (intelligizes) its own essence and thinks the First. What it thinks of its own essence is no more than its essence. As a result of its thinking of the First, a third existent follows necessarily from it; and as a result of its substantification in its specific essence, the existence of the First Heaven follows necessarily.
>
> (1998, 101)

This is repeated for the remaining levels of creation or intellectual spheres. The first heaven, the existence of the third, is not in matter, and as such it too thinks its own essence and therein is the soul that thinks (its relation to) the first. Again an existence follows necessarily from this as the actual essence and existence of this soul (the first heaven) which is contemplating its essence in the first intellect. The new existence, this new 'third' to intellect and its soul, is the sphere of the fixed stars. There are a further eight intellectual spheres that are created in this way, each being a sphere of a particular planet.[3] Here al-Farabi states that

> [e]ach of the ten (intelligizes) its own essence and thinks the First. But none of them is sufficient in itself to attain excellent existence by thinking its own essence only, but it acquires perfect excellence only by thinking together with its own essence the essence of the First Cause.
>
> (1998, 117)

In each case, the existent sphere is the thought of the first intellect but at an ever-increasing distance from its source. This distancing increases the need for the intellect to become attached to matter and this is the significance of the 11th sphere or the active intellect. Al-Farabi has to hold to the spheres being independent of matter if they are truly to be the mind of God, and he resolves the contradiction of the planets being form and matter by arguing that each of the spheres of the intellect after the first intellect, have substrata which are not wholly intellect but imply no opposition or change to the divine intellect for whom emanation is substantial knowing and being of self.[4]

## Human divine education

Al-Farabi explains the nature of the relation of the finite intellect to God by way of education within the culture of error. The emanation of one sphere to the next is a gradual corruption of the pure intellect until, after the lunar sphere, the intellect is only potential and requires its actuality in material objects. The path from man back to the intellect is the path of philosophy; for in philosophy man learns to think without physical objects, to think intellectually. Man comes nearer to God 'only by becoming actual [or "actually"] intellect' (1998, 83) and it is only when man's thought is completely separated from matter that his knowledge of God 'will be at its most perfect' (1998, 83). Man and God are related by the active intellect (*nus poietikos*) which mediates between the simple and the composite. It is the 11th level of emanation and is therefore furthest from its source but closest to material. In this ambivalence it gives form to matter and returns matter to form.[5]

Al-Farabi is clear on the political implications of this model of emanation in the mind. The man whose 'soul is united as it were with the Active Intellect' (1998, 245) is the man whose rational faculties are open to divine revelation. Such a man is the Imam, and as a ruler he will know that wisdom and virtue require cognition of the one through philosophy. Such a man is educated by both the material and the immaterial and his learning is a midpoint between God and existence. This culture of error learns 'from both directions' (2001a, 62) at the same time.

This education for man's highest wisdom can be attained in three ways: through demonstration in and by philosophy; through trust expressed for the teacher by the pupil; and, for those unable to grasp such demonstrations, through symbol and by imitation. Of these, al-Farabi notes that 'the knowledge of the philosophers is undoubtedly more excellent' (1998, 279). He adds that nations may have different religions but 'all have as their goal one and same felicity and the very same aims' (1998, 281). Nevertheless, while philosophers will agree on the truth, different symbolic representations in different religions may lead to disagreement. In line with Plato's *Republic*, al-Farabi argues that the most potentially virtuous characters should receive an education that will prepare them to take their places as the leaders of cities or nations. Again with Plato, he sees that the philosopher-ruler will not only comprehend theoretical matters – metaphysic and logic – but will also have the skill needed to teach such matters and to do so 'for the benefit of all others' (al-Farabi, 2001b, 43).

There is an added sophistication to the education that al-Farabi identifies in the error of finite thought. In *The Attainment of Happiness* he argues for a logic of philosophical education. He reasons that a principle (B) that is the cause of beings (A1, A2) both precedes A1 and A2 yet is also dependent upon them for the principle (B) being actually known. This contradiction where each is the possibility of the other is seen as the necessity of the primary principle (C). The principle (C) here is triadic for it is the condition of the possibility of the experience of a principle and the condition of the possibility of the experience of the effects of these principles. It is, as it were, the relation of their relation. This leads al-Farabi to remark that in investigating the true one should seek not just its principles, but also 'the principle of its principle and [ ] the principle of the principles of its principles' (2001b, 21). This shares the significance of univocity in Duns Scotus and looks towards synthetic *a priori* judgements in Kant.

Al-Farabi's culture of error, then, has education at its centre. Man's potential intellect can be re-formed by the God that makes itself known in and as the education of the active intellect. But this mediaeval culture of error, like its counterparts, does not yield the substance of triadic experience in loss and negation and as such, it does not commend recognition of the notion of Western subjectivity. As such, Corbin is perhaps right to point out that al-Farabi's philosophy is less Platonic and more Prophetic. His case is that the active intellect, identified as the angel Gabriel, is not to be rationalized but is to maintain its divine mystical character. Here Corbin asks whether the relationship between Islam and philosophy is 'possibly one of irreconcilable opposition?' (Corbin, 2006, 164).[6] Al-Farabi himself, however, is convinced that divine truths are 'true philosophy and the true philosopher' (2001b, 47), and that philosophy is essential for the Imam and the legislator. But even at this early stage in our chapter on Western Islamic and Judaic philosophy we can note that the triadic structure here, of emanation and of the trinity in mediaeval Christian philosophy both commend a culture of error, but neither comprehends the rationality of error as subjectivity.

## Avicenna

### Being

Avicenna is perhaps best known for working with the priority of being. This remains grounded in the logic of noncontradiction, cause and effect, and the absurdity of infinite regression. The logic of the necessity of being in Avicenna shares with Aristotle the priority of the actual over the potential. Everything that exists is contingent upon the fact that it is. What *is* has being as its own cause and effect. As for Aristotle, 'act is prior to potency' (Avicenna, 2005, 143) because possibility depends upon actuality for its being possible. Everything, including metaphysical questions about origin and God, is dependent upon the priority of being. This priority of being is grounded in the law of noncontradiction such that what is possible cannot oppose itself by being impossible, and what is actual cannot be otherwise. The priority of being is a principle of first cause. Since there are existents there must be a principle of necessary being. The fact of existents makes a necessity of being irrefutable. This necessity is the first cause and is without cause. Equally, the threat of 'infinite regress' (2005, 23) is also proof that there must be a cause of all causes and a principle of all principles. The priority of being is necessarily the first cause because it is the cause of itself and is where infinite regression stops.

## Characteristics of God

Avicenna's culture of error shares the Neoplatonic view that God is the simple existent and that only his principle is 'knowledge of truth absolutely' (2005, 215). Only that which is simple and necessary is 'permanently true in itself' (2005, 38) while what is compound, dependent, mutable, or understood only in relation to or in terms of something else, is false. Human consciousness, tied as it is to objects for its knowledge via a soul that is dependent upon the body, is error in comparison to the simple, the eternal, and the unchangeable.

God knows himself as the necessity that is being. His nature is intellectual and is free of matter. 'Because it is in itself an intellect, being also intellectually apprehended by itself, it [itself] is the intelligible [belonging] to itself' (2005, 285). He is the 'intellectual apprehender' (2005, 285)[7] and is 'the order of the good in existence' (2005, 327). As such, he is eternal and is a self-cause, and the proof of this is the multiplicity of existents that cannot cause themselves. He is related to the multiplicity of existents through his essence and is not therein corrupted by such a relation. In this culture of thought as error, Avicenna takes to describing the characteristics of God via the negative method of saying what God is not. He has 'no genus, no quiddity, no quality, no quantity, no "where," no "when," no equal, no partner, and no contrary.... He has no definition and [there is] no demonstration for Him. Rather, He is the demonstration of all things' (2005, 282–3). Indeed, after the fact of his individual existence there remains only the means of 'negating all similarities of Him and affirming to Him all relations' (2005, 283). He is 'above perfection' (2005, 283), having not only an existence belonging to him, but also being the source by emanation of every other existence.

## Creation and emanation

Creation is the act of divine thought thinking itself. This necessity has no potentiality, nor is it known by God as an intention to create. It is not, as Corbin puts it, a *'coup d'état* in pre-eternity' (2006, 171) for there is no time when the necessary existent was not necessarily existing. Avicenna has to try to explain how it is that the intellect can create or think itself in such a way as to avoid a relation, since all 'relation is finite' (2005, 274).

He offers a triadic model of God's mind. There is apprehension; apprehension of itself as necessity; and apprehension as the principle that knows its own necessary being. It would be wrong to think of this chronologically, for that would risk the first apprehension being potential.

> The plurality it has is not [acquired] from the First. For the possibility of its existence is something that belongs to it in itself, not by reason of the First. Rather, from the First it has the necessity of its existence. Then the plurality, in its intellectually apprehending the First and intellectually apprehending itself, is a necessary consequence of its necessary existence from the First.
>
> (2005, 330)

As such, for Avicenna, nothing can escape being known by God. 'Not [even] the weight of an atom in the heavens and the earth escapes Him' (2005, 288).[8]

Intellectual apprehension in the one also brings into existence the order of the good. There is one mover that is the object of love but 'each sphere has a particular mover and a particular object of love' (2005, 325). This means, in turn, that each sphere has a soul that is 'a universal, intellectual exemplar of the species of its act' (2005, 325), a soul that imparts motion to the sphere which is the intellectual apprehension of the good. Corbin says here that the souls are pure imagination and that 'their aspiring desire for the Intelligence from which they proceed communicates to each heaven its own motion' (2006, 171). God is, as it were, life itself, where there is no distinction between knowing and will. It is emanation and it is 'munificence' (Avicenna, 2005, 295), as it is absolute and pure 'enjoyment' (2005, 297).

There is also a triadic structure, or, for Corbin, a 'phenomenology' (2006, 171), to Avicenna's notion of emanation. Emanation is intellect when it apprehends its source; it is soul in apprehending itself as intellect; and it is body in existing as the sphere. This is repeated

from one intellectual sphere to another through the hierarchy of the
ten spheres of intellect, and their motion of soul and transcendental
body. Avicenna confirms that this is the state of affairs in each sphere
'until it terminates with the active intellect that governs ourselves'
(2005, 331).[9] The first existence to come from the one is the rank 'of
the spiritual angels called "souls" – namely, the active angels – then the
ranks of the celestial bodies ... until the last [of these] is reached' (2005,
358). Thereafter begins the existence of matter that is receptive to the
forms of the elements. 'The best [in this descending terrestrial order of
existence] is the human, then below the human the animals, then the
plants' (2005, 358).

### The divine in man

The culture of error for Avicenna sees the active intellect emanating
knowledge and ideas into human souls whose contemplative intellect
has learned how to turn itself towards this active angel. A rational soul
seeking the happiness of the intellectual can know the teleology of
universal motion, the structure of the cosmos, the order of the first principle in its emanation down to its lowest existent, providence, and the
unchangeableness of God, although none of these will be learned unless
the soul frees itself from the errors of this world and attends only to the
celestial world. The highest of the rational souls will be prophets, for
they can hear the speech of God and see the angels and thus are those
to whom revelation is given. The soul in Avicenna is 'a single substance'
(Avicenna, 1952, 33). In *Avicenna's Psychology* he notes that divine intuition is the highest form of rational knowledge. Intuition learns from
within and requires little or no instruction in order to make contact
with the active intellect. In such souls the middle term of the syllogism –
that by which all intelligible truths are obtained – can be carried as a
form of immediacy such that divine truths are known intuitively. Such
a man is imbued with divine spirit which is, says Avicenna, 'a kind of
prophetic inspiration ... [and] the highest human faculty' (1952, 37).

   This prophet has the role of lawgiver to the people, and he will be differentiated by his performing miracles. He will teach the people of God
of the need to obey God, of the afterlife of bliss that awaits the obedient, and the misery that awaits the disobedient. But he will not teach
them the harder transcendental truths of God that are known to the
prophet, for 'it is not for everyone that [the acquisition] of divine wisdom is facilitated' (2005, 366). It is in large part the attachment of the
human soul to the human body that prevents the people from enjoying
perfection. The finite mind is limited to the error of an imitation of the

good. However, it can be reeducated by the overflowing of light from the necessary existent, a motion that is present as love and desire for the good, but which cannot be completed in finite substance. Thus, what is left to ordinary human souls is to imitate the good 'by enduring in the [state of] the most perfect perfection' (2005, 314). In *Remarks and Admonitions* Avicenna states that it is his own intention in this work to protect divine truth from 'the ignorant [and] the vulgar' (1984, 3) and from those incapable of the thoughts required to comprehend it. It must suffice for a teacher to employ symbols and parables when teaching of the nature of God. But since a prophet appears only rarely, the people must be taught how to draw nearer to God in their own lives, through fasting, pilgrimage, and other acts of worship, the highest of which is prayer with its demands for purification and cleanliness.[10]

Avicenna's culture of error, then, is Neoplatonic in that it is grounded in principles that define the culture of finite thought as error in relation to the true. He holds to the definitions of true and false that are determined in the logic of noncontradiction, cause and effect, and infinite regression. But he is very concerned to establish the means for an educational relationship between God and man, although the man who conjoins with the first principle will be rare and extraordinary. It is also a characteristic of Avicenna's philosophy that the hierarchy of the universe be reflected in the hierarchy of the educated man over the majority who remain ignorant. The mediaeval culture of error holds this to be necessary and restricts culture to those who are led by their awareness of error, through philosophy and reason, to pursue elusive truths.

## Al-Ghazali

### Scepticism

The singular importance of the culture of error in the work of al-Ghazali is that he knows and explores the Western culture of philosophical thought as error. He learns this first from a deep scepticism regarding Western philosophical reason. In 1095 he left both his family and his job as a Professor at Baghdad University to pursue a solitary pilgrimage through the Muslim world on a quest for inner truth. His uncertainties regained a sense of equilibrium in Sufism. Here he found a unity of theory and practice where truth is known in states that are experienced rather than in words that merely describe them. These states required a rejection of earthly passions and delusions, and as a result he lived out a six month period of vacillation during which time he could not eat or teach, and fell ill. In the contradictory pull of earthly desires and heavenly salvation, he was left powerless and unable to choose between them. Yet only in this aporetic state of paralysis did it become possible for him, finally, to turn to God.

Inspired, now, by 'the light of prophecy' (al-Ghazali, 1980, 81) al-Ghazali records what he has learned that is beyond error. Alone among the theologians, philosophers, and Batamites, only the Sufis' total absorption in God was free from error. In the light of prophecy, beyond intellect, he held that true knowledge is disclosed to the spirit 'in such a manner that no doubt can exist with regard to it, and no error can tarnish it' (Corbin, 2006, 181). This disclosure, says al-Ghazali, is 'the direct seizure by the thinking soul of the essential reality of things' (Corbin, 2006, 182). This thinking soul receives intelligible forms from the universal soul which contains all knowledge as potential. On returning from his pilgrimage to his family and work, he is able to state the humility that underpins the power of what has been revealed to him, and of the kind of teaching it demands from him.

> I believe with a faith as certain as direct vision that there is no might for me and no power save in God, the Sublime, the Mighty; and that it was not I who moved, but He moved me; and that I did not act, but He acted through me. I ask Him, then, to reform me first, then to use me as an instrument of reform; to guide me, then to use me as an instrument of guidance; to show me the true as true, and to grant me the grace to follow it; and to show me the false as false, and to grant me the grace to eschew it.
>
> (1980, 92–3)

This gnosis becomes the basis for his expression of the culture of error in his major work, *The Revival of the Religious Sciences*.

## Contra philosophy

It is in philosophy and its practitioners that al-Ghazali finds a source of error for Islamic theology. His own culture of error is an education against the error of such culture. Critical of Socrates, Plato, Aristotle, al-Farabi, and Avicenna, he demonstrates why the truths of logic, mathematics, and the physical sciences are not relevant to religion, and that metaphysics contains the three most important errors; that men will not have their bodies after death, that God does not know particulars, and that the world is eternal and uncreated. He concludes that not only is philosophy inadequate in providing true meaning, but also that reason alone is 'incapable of fully grasping all problems or of getting to the heart of all difficulties' (1980, 71).

His most famous book in the West, *The Incoherence of the Philosophers*, takes up this attack on the errors of the philosophers, and in particular of Avicenna's view that the earth has existed eternally and God knows only universals. What al-Ghazali mounts here is a defence of the robustness of God and his prowess and autonomy as an infinite and unknowable power, and an attack upon the effect that philosophy is having on Islamic theology. He notes that under the sway of al-Farabi and Avicenna, intelligent men are turning their backs on Islamic duties by imitating so-called truths of the Ancients. Bluntly, he argues that the ignorant are better off than these learned men, for it is better to be blind to truth than to comprehend it falsely. *The Incoherence* also claims that religion and philosophy may share the same truths, but they are not arrived at through the same means. Proof of God is not in reason but in revealed religious law and the intuitions of the prophets.

The method of *The Incoherence* is essentially negative. Al-Ghazali aims to reveal the incoherence or error of the philosophers by reveal-ing contradictions in their doctrines. He does not offer any affirmative doctrine of his own.[11] He is sceptical about the idea of rational necessity that the philosophers presume for themselves. Metaphysics, he says, has never been able to prove the logic of the syllogism, and its reason has no greater claims to validity than others who use reason differently. Indeed, the title *The Incoherence of the Philosophers* aims to show how the presumption of rational necessity in philosophy can be turned against itself. One bare assertion of the truth of reason is worth just as much as another. Corbin notes that the word *Tahafut* in the title means not just incoherence but also breakdown, collapse, and destruction, and he emphasizes its carrying a negative reciprocity between different parts of a whole. Thus he suggests that a better translation of the title is *The Autodestruction of the Philosophers* in order to highlight how the means by which they assert their truths is the same as that which negates and undermines their arguments. Their incoherence or autodestruction is where reason opposes its own necessity. As such, Al-Ghazali's target here is the error of their culture.

*The Incoherence* acts as a critique of what al-Ghazali sees as the pagan logic of noncontradiction, cause and effect, and the absurdity of infinite regression. For example, the idea that an eternal God cannot have cre-ated the universe is grounded in human but not divine logic. It makes the assumption that something is impossible for God, and this assump-tion puts man's knowledge of God above God himself. Al-Ghazali argues that it is perfectly possible for God to exist both before and after the creation of the world. The 'and' between God who was without the world 'and' who was with the world, is for al-Ghazali a neutral term carrying no reflective or rational necessity other than that God was alone and then God willed the world. Since nothing is impossible for God he must be able to will a second essence. Moreover, and against the culture of error in mediaeval philosophy, there is no necessity to assume a third thing in order to resolve two things which seem to contradict each other.

Al-Ghazali here finds the very idea of philosophical logic to be autodestructive or aporetic. Judgements of necessity are grounded in a perceived (logical) need to explain (logical) contradictions in God's essence, but such judgements employ the same logic that needs explaining. This in turn assumes that logic tells man what is and is not possible for God, which is to doubt his omnipotence. Rational necessity in the syllogism is a third term between propositions that seem impossible to us, but cannot be impossible for an all-powerful God. For al-Ghazali, then, the 'must' of the syllogism should be replaced by a neutral 'and' that does not restrict God's power. The third element is 'a relation necessary with respect to us [only]' (al-Ghazali, 2000, 32), that is, to the finite mind. Because this finite philosophical mind cannot 'comprehend an existence that has a beginning except by supposing a "before" for it' (2000, 32), it is always adding categories of time and space to a truth that needs no further supplement. As such, the philosophers are always trying to prove the necessity of a pre-eternity, missing the fact that it is a necessity only according to the limited scope of human reason. It is revelation that lifts man beyond this limited reason to a comprehension of the full power and truth of God.

Al-Ghazali makes a very significant philosophical point here. He reveals how philosophical logic and rational necessity ground their truth in a merely finite standpoint, and that therefore all their judgements of God are complicit with this error. In a more modern guise, this dependence of truth upon the mind that thinks it constitutes the Kantian revolution (which we look at later in Part III), though this is not the implication that al-Ghazali finds here, preferring revelation and intuition to the synthetic *a priori* judgement.

It is not that al-Ghazali is trying to show the inconsistency of any one view of the philosophers but of all of them, because they are all grounded in the positing of rational necessity as needed to resolve God's apparent contradictions. The arguments of the philosophers autodestruct because philosophy is grounded in a notion of reason that excludes the truth of God, an exclusion which makes him merely finite and self-contradictory. This leads the philosophers to believe that God needs saving from contradictions that, in truth, He is not affected by. The philosophers only achieve a decrease in God's power. There is nothing, says al-Ghazali, in theoretical reflection or rational necessity, that should prevent one from asserting that 'the First Principle is knowing, powerful, willing; that He enacts as He wishes, governs what He wills, creates things that are varied and things that are homogenous as He wills and in the way He wills' (2000, 76).

## The relation of emanation

In *The Incoherence* al-Ghazali believes he is thinking in ways that philosophical reason deems impossible. Emanation provides a further example here.

When al-Ghazali summarizes the cosmologies of al-Farabi and Avicenna, he draws attention to the efforts of the philosophers both to protect God's unitary substance and essence, and yet to explain how the manifold emanates from him in such a way as not to compromise this essence. Yet in their argument that the first intellect is one *and* that it has body, soul, and mind in ten spheres that emanate from it, their cosmology is autodestructive according to its own logic. In keeping God's essence free from plurality they are forced to argue that knowing himself as a principle is different from knowing himself as himself. The former is essence, while the latter is only an effect of a cause. Thus they are forced to posit a strict separation between essence and its effect. Al-Ghazali's criticism here is that this logic rules out the possibility of God in relation to or with himself as two essences. It is only the concept of rational necessity that leads the philosophers to posit the need for a third thing that can explain away such an impossible relation. For al-Ghazali, revelation has no problem in accepting the impossible as 'a relation' (2000, 102) within the omnipotence of God.[12] Such relation, for al-Ghazali, can realize plurality in a way that does not autodestruct the essence of God, for relation achieves essences where philosophical logic achieves only multiplicity in an essence. We can note here that this debate has similarities to that of a more modern philosophical debate. Post-foundational philosophy has given priority to multiplicity over the logic of the principle of noncontradiction and the principle of the one and of identity that accompany it. In some ways, al-Ghazali's critique of the presuppositions carried in philosophical logic resembles that of Derrida who has sought to show *différance* suppressed in and by the logic and hegemony of difference-opposition, and of Deleuze

who argues for a neutral 'and' of relations without the logic of cause
and effect.

## Culture and error

It has been observed that al-Ghazali employs the same logic in his work
that he is criticizing. It is true that the proof of autodestruction is itself
grounded in a logic of what is and what is not, for autodestruction posits logic contradicting itself, and contradiction here is posited as error.
But there is a case for arguing that perhaps al-Ghazali is not claiming
that his own thought is free from aporia. This would credit al-Ghazali
with a culture of the error of culture. In his *Letter to a Disciple* he can
be seen working autodestruction into his advice on how to live according to what is true and to discard that which is false. For example, he
argues against the philosophers that no one who contemplates rational
knowledge at the expense of good deeds in the world, will be saved. 'If
a man studied a hundred thousand intellectual issues and understood
them, but did not act on the strength of them, they would not be of
use to him except by taking action' (2005, 8). However, he shows too
that deeds in themselves are not sufficient to gain paradise, for salvation also requires divine grace. In expressing this antinomy he does
not seek to avoid for himself the truth of autodestruction or aporia. He
quotes from Ali ibn Abi Talib saying, 'whoso believes that he will attain
his goal without effort is a wishful thinker. And whoso believes he will
reach his goal by the expending of effort is presumptuous' (2005, 12).
In the kind of chiasmus that will be found in Kant some 700 years later
al-Ghazali notes that 'knowledge without action is madness and action
without knowledge is void' (2005, 16). Depending on how one chooses
to look at this, this is either inconsistency in al-Ghazali or precisely
the truth of his claims regarding the universality of autodestruction
repeated, now, in his own work. Perhaps we can say that for Western
philosophy al-Ghazali raises the aporia of philosophical reason to an
unavoidable totality, one in which error is educational, while education
remains error.

## Averroes

Averroes mounts a critique of al-Ghazali and his attack on philosophy.
But the terms of this critique are not straightforward. Averroes believes
that al-Farabi and Avicenna, who are the main targets of al-Ghazali's
*The Incoherence*, have themselves misinterpreted fundamental tenets of
Aristotelian philosophy. This means that al-Ghazali's comments may

be apt in relation to al-Farabi and Avicenna, but not to Aristotle. It is to retrieve an accurate and faithful account of the latter against al-Ghazali, al-Farabi, and Avicenna that Averroes sets as his task. As is well known, his work led to Latin Averroism in the West, although Corbin claims Averroes himself for the East. We will return to this later.

Averroes's most famous book, called *The Incoherence of the Incoherence*, is a direct response to al-Ghazali, and he argues in it that al-Ghazali's book should in fact have been called just *Incoherence* without the qualification of *The Philosophers*, since it is he and not them who is incoherent. However, in his *Decisive Treatise* Averroes mediates this view somewhat, arguing that al-Ghazali 'intended only good' (Averroes, 2001, 22) in wishing to increase human understanding, and that the Book of God clearly instructs man to use his intellect to reflect on God's creation, and therefore commands man to practise philosophy and syllogism, even if these tools were handed down by the Ancients who were not Muslim. God can be known through a comprehension of his works, and this can be uncovered by philosophy because 'truth does not oppose truth' (2001, 9).

### The first principle and the active intellect

Averroes criticizes the role of the active intellect as a mediator between God and man in Avicenna's cosmology. Where Avicenna argued for emanation in the spheres of the intellect, Averroes holds to the more Aristotelian view not of an act of creation but of an eternal and continuous act of God knowing himself. As such, Averroes sees no need for the angel-souls found in Avicenna's cosmology, through and by which the imagination received prophetic and mystical symbols independent of the senses. But Averroes goes further. He argues that the active intellect lies in the soul and is the active power of the soul to move potential or material intellect to actual intellect. His criticism here is that a separate active intellect makes the human intellect too passive and merely receptive. Indeed, if the active intellect is not in the soul, but separate from it, then intellectual activity is merely an accident of the soul and not its principle, an error which threatens the truth of God's universe.

At stake then, between the two cosmologies is the identity of the first principle and particularly how it can know itself. When the first principle contemplates itself it has a triadic structure of angelic self-awareness in the emanation of intellect, soul, and body which constitutes the ten spheres of al-Farabi's and Avicenna's cosmos. However, Averroes argues for a very different understanding of how the first principle knows himself. He argues that since God knows himself as the cause of the universe, he knows his creations also as their cause. This means that God's knowledge cannot be understood in the error of its finite representation of universal and particular. God's knowledge of particulars is knowledge of being their cause. Thus he knows all particulars but without change implied in doing so. Emanation and progression are replaced here by continuous self-knowing as and of itself as the first cause. Thus, God knows particulars 'in their noblest mode of existence' (Averroes, 1987, 135), that is, by knowing them as caused by its thinking them. The terms universal and particular are only effects of this knowing and thus are merely human categories open to change. As proof Averroes argues that the inherent pluralism in the model of emanation where self-knowing as essence has two forms does not conform to Aristotle's notion of the monad in Book XII of the *Metaphysics*. For Averroes this thought which moves itself, desires itself, and this good is the ultimate good because it is the purest necessity, uninfluenced by anything external. There need be no differentiation here for the simple monad is simply itself, and is a love that is the moving principle of all life. As such, Averroes has no problem arguing that God can be both simple and plural, substance and the living manifold, unchangeable and infinite in actual form. Unity is the cause of plurality. Al-Farabi and Avicenna are in error when they treat the simple merely as a number, from which only one can come.

Averroes is concerned to restore an active agency to the soul and to criticize the Ash'arite theologians who sacrificed all agency to God's absolute omnipotence, and to argue that the role of the active intellect is much more materialist than what the theologians allow. With Aristotle, Averroes emphasizes that universals exist in actuality, in particular things. God is cause, but cause is actual. He does not therefore cede to Plato the independent and transcendental existence of universals beyond their existing. In giving priority to the actuality of the soul in the person, Averroes is weakening the hold in Avicennism that spiritual individuality requires an active intellect that remains separate from matter. Nevertheless, even though Averroes was trying to argue for God in the soul, it was his assertion that the active intellect is one for all men that led Aquinas and others to see him repeating the errors of those he claimed to be correcting.

## Cause and effect

To understand what Averroes means when he says that God knows himself in particulars as cause and not as number, we need to explore his idea of 'cause'. He criticizes al-Ghazali for his attack on the philosophers and his seeing their idea of the universal existing eternally as doing away with the need for God altogether. Al-Ghazali argues that God can intervene in ways not conforming to cause and effect whenever he chooses, and as such the law of cause and effect is an insufficient principle on which to explain the origin of the universe. Averroes is prepared to hold to the principle of cause and effect, arguing that all facts and knowledge are inescapably the result of a cause.

> Intelligence is nothing but the perception of things with their causes, and in this it distinguishes itself from all the other faculties of apprehension, and he who denies causes must deny the intellect.[13] ... Denial of cause implies the denial of knowledge, and denial of knowledge implies that nothing in this world can be really known.
>
> (1987, 319)[14]

From this, Averroes takes the Aristotelian line that if there are causes and effects, there must be a first cause. This avoids a *reductio ad absurdum* of a never-ending chain of cause and effect. The Ancients, says Averroes, introduced the idea of the eternal and unchanging being precisely because cause and effect must have their truth in the being that is their cause and because movement in time requires a mover. God, therefore, is 'the mover who is the condition of man's existence' (1987, 34) as he is of heaven and earth and all that lies between them.

While reinforcing the Aristotelian principle of cause and effect, he also argues that neither al-Ghazali nor the philosophers have understood how God is cause but not effect. He does not accept that God works in the same way as man does, acting either by necessity or desire. God cannot be impelled by anything outside himself to act in any way at all, nor can God act from need or desire since this suggests a lack on his part. Thus, Averroes sees God's will and knowledge as both different from that of man and as unknowable by man. This is the basis for Averroes's own interpretation of creation. The universe is eternal because something cannot come into being from nothing. But it is also created in the sense that God continuously knows himself as the cause of all compounds of form and matter. Human existence is eternal and created, for in God's thinking of himself there is a unity of cause and effect unknown in the finite universe.[15] This argument that sees the movement of the prime mover as 'partly eternal, partly temporal' (1987, 237), that is, eternal as a whole but temporal in its effects as experienced by those effects, has become known as *creatio ab aeterno*, or continuous

creation.[16] Similarly he argues that God can know and not know something at the same time. Thus, for Averroes divine and human knowledge cannot be compared. Anyone who argues that human and divine
knowledge are commensurable 'makes God an eternal man and man a
mortal God' (1987, 285).

## Double truths

We note that Averroes uses Neoplatonic logic here to reveal the culture
of thought as error in relation to God, but that God is not restricted by
this same logic. This ambivalence in logic has led to the interpretation
of Averroes as holding to double truths. These are, for example, that
God as cause is both eternal and temporal, that the active intellect is
both transcendental and in the soul, that the intellect is potential and
actual, that the monad is one and many, and that the words of the
*Koran* are eternal and interpreted.

There is ambivalence too in the ways these double truths of the culture of error are to be taught. He does not defend the teaching of such
equivocation to the masses. Instead he defends the need for interpretation (*ta'wil*) in dealing with the different innate abilities of the devoted.
He defines the role of interpretation as 'drawing out the figurative significance of an utterance from its true significance without violating the custom of the Arabic language with respect to figurative speech in doing so'
(Averroes, 2001, 9), that is, revealing the interpretative significance from
utterances taken at face value. In other words, interpretation requires the
learned to find the figurative in the true so that the laws and pronounce-
ments will be revealed according to 'people's innate dispositions' (2001,
10). Verse 3:7 of the Koran is taken here to be the justification, where God
says that only those well-grounded in knowledge will understand the
reasons for ambiguities in the text, they themselves being necessary due
to the different capacities of people for comprehension. Teaching must
differentiate between demonstrative (philosophical), dialectical (theological), and rhetorical (non-interpretative) methods, the latter being the
only one safe for the education of the masses. Heresy and chaos would
result if the masses were taught of differences within interpretation.

It might also be said that there is a double truth in Averroes's doctrine
of double truth. Corbin notes that Averroes's work gave rise to a Latin and
political Averroism in the West that could not and did not take hold in
future Islamic philosophy. He claims Averroes for Islam in the tradition
of *ta'wil* and cedes Averroism to the West. The reason, he says, is that the
idea of the philosopher-theologian was always different in each tradition. Averroes never believed himself to be working with a double truth

or with two contradictory truths. Even in noting that chaos threatened unless one distinguished between the exoteric meaning of the text and its more esoteric significations, Averroes nevertheless knew that 'it was always the same truth that was present at different levels of interpretation and comprehension' (Corbin, 2006, 245). The contradiction of the double form in fact belongs to Latin Averroism. It has its actuality in the separation of God and man such that, in Aquinas, the active intellect is seen as present in each soul. This, Corbin interprets in terms of a socializing of Islamic mysticism where personal communication with God through the active intellect becomes personal separation from God, with the church assuming a mediating role. Corbin's argument here implies that what Luther reclaimed from the church through opposition to its dogmas was already present differently in the mediation of esoteric Islamic religion. Where the separation of God and man became the opposition of church and State in the West, Islam never ceded the intermediary to the finite, as such. Corbin argues that the freedom from church dogma that Averroism offered the West must be seen in contrast to the freedom from 'an oppressive orthodoxy, from a legalistic literalism of a *shari'ah*' (2006, 250) which could be obtained 'by means of the *ta'wil*' (2006, 250).

Averroes's culture of error conforms to the positing of thought as error in relation to the true. Aristotelian logic reveals the proof and the necessity of God. But God himself is relieved of having to conform to the logic that proves his existence. This retrieves for the West a *culture* of error that over the next centuries inspires a renaissance of interest in the activity of the human agent. But this renewed rationalism will carry with it the ambivalence that grounds it. It will enact an agitation in the culture of error and its logic of noncontradiction. At its core, this agitation is the experience of knowing *that* God is but not, by the same proof, *what* God is. Averroes's culture of error is a skillful attempt to unite rival camps in Western thought within ambivalence. But the history of Western philosophy is beginning here to face up to the strength – even the universality – of the thought of the error of culture known in and by itself. From 1270 onwards Aristotelian Averroism in the West began to be condemned as heretical for giving priority to reason over faith. But this is also the culture of error continuing to determine itself as the rationality of subjectivity.

## Maimonides

We turn now to the Jewish culture of error found in Maimonides's *Guide of the Perplexed*. Its design is itself perplexing, and so we begin by examining this perplexity as an education regarding the ambivalence of error.

## Open concealment

Maimonides aims to explain the significance of ambivalence in Scripture to someone whose philosophical doubts threaten the solidity of his religion. A subsidiary aim is to relieve this perplexity by revealing the secret inner meanings of certain parables in Scripture whose external meanings perpetuate confusion. However, he does not intend to resolve this perplexity, only to guide the perplexed individual 'in his perplexity until he becomes perfect and he finds rest' (Maimonides, 1963a, 17). This guidance will be presented by way of contradiction and obscurity.[17] Maimonides warns the reader to seek little more from him than chapter headings (as the Babylonian Talmud also advises its readers) and even these are not arranged coherently, this because it is his purpose 'that the truths be glimpsed and then again be concealed' (1963a, 6–7). In the Introduction to Volume III, he states openly that he will speak of the truth by a method of open concealment, withholding divine truths from the uneducated general populace. The *Guide* is not aimed at those who live in complete darkness. Indeed, it is made clear by the sages that 'the reward of him who conceals *the mysteries of the Torah*, which are clear and manifest to men of speculation, is very great' (Maimonides, 1963b, 415).

Maimonides begins with the equivocation of religious language and image. The terms that make God appear corporeal, having human features, affections, place, and movement have a double truth that can satisfy the unlearned multitude and the scholar. God is represented in error as having a body because 'the multitude cannot at first conceive of any existence save that of a body alone; thus that which is neither a body nor existent in a body does not exist in their opinion' (1963a, 56). Attributes like seeing, hearing, and speaking are assigned to God habitually so that the multitude can know him. The *Torah* speaks in the language of man, thus addressing itself to the imagination of the multitude and to the fantasies of God that 'come to them from the age of infancy' (1963a, 57). They are yet to see that the corporeal qualities attributed to God will change their meaning if they should come to comprehend him intellectually. Equivocal terms, therefore, both give a picture of God to the unlearned and have the possibility of reforming the corporeal into the intellectual. An education in tradition is necessary for the multitude while education in mystery is appropriate for the few. However, the truths of divine science are revealed only in rare flashes of lightening and no one must think that 'these great *secrets* are fully and completely known to anyone among us' (1963a, 7). They certainly cannot be communicated directly.

## Man knowing God

The error of the culture of finite thought in Maimonides means that God 'cannot be apprehended by the intellects, and that none but He Himself can apprehend what He is' (1963a, 139). He holds to the view that multiplicity or composition in God is an error that stems from restricting oneself only to the external meanings of the prophets. God's essence should not be comprehended according to the external meaning of the relation of the created to the creator but within the truth of the logic of noncontradiction. His essence is 'one and simple' (1963a, 122) even if this lies beyond the comprehension of man. As such, God can have nothing in potentiality because that would mean that God lacks something of himself. He cannot be potentially perfect, only actually perfect.

Maimonides also notes that error is contained in human language when speaking of God. When man speaks of God he does so as if he were speaking of attributes. Terms like 'one' and 'eternal' are used as predicates of God. This 'looseness of expression' (1963a, 133) is unavoidable, for man can speak only through 'the instrumentality of the customary words, which are greatest among the causes leading unto error' (1963a, 132).[18] When using the *'language of the sons of man'* (1963a, 133) in this way, one should again look for the deeper meanings of such terms in the Scriptures.

The culture of error means for Maimonides that God can only be known in thought negatively. If God is described affirmatively then such assertions inevitably take the form of predicate which immediately implies a deficiency in his oneness. Against this, 'the attributes of negation do not give us any knowledge in any respect whatever of the essence of the knowledge of which is sought' (1963a, 135). Negation, itself an error, protects against the furtherance of error. Primary among these negations is that God is not multiple or compound. When we say that God is powerful we mean that he is not powerless; that God is knowledgeable means that he is not ignorant; and that he is living means that he cannot be not living. Thus, in the culture of error

> when the intellects contemplate His essence, their apprehension turns into incapacity; and when they contemplate the proceeding of His actions from His Will, their knowledge turns into ignorance; and when tongues aspire to magnify Him by means of attributive qualifications, all eloquence turns into weariness and incapacity.
>
> (1963a, 137)

Maimonides sees quantification here in that the more attributes one negates, the nearer one gets to God. As such, knowledge of God can be cumulative, with those coming later benefitting from earlier work. The man who remains with a God of positive attributes 'has abolished his belief in the evidence of the deity without being aware of it' (1963a, 145). The prophets only ever assign attributes to God in order 'to direct the mind toward nothing but His perfection' (1963a, 147).

## Creation

Against Aristotle, Maimonides holds that God created the world in time but he does not wish to assert this dogmatically. He reasons that those who see God as a creator posit a time before creation, which reduces creation to potential and imperfection. Against this, Maimonides employs the Aristotelian priority of actuality arguing that even potentiality – the time before creation – is actual and that God, as actual, is always already eternal in his existing as his essence. As such, God as maker and first cause mean the same thing; creation is eternally actual, and actuality is always creation.

But equivocation is again Maimonides's method of man's divine education. He does not choose between rival doctrines of eternity and creation, since they are not antithetical to each other. He criticizes both Christian and Islamic theology and philosophy for beginning with doctrines they hold to be true, and then making up systems of thought that fit these doctrines. Thus Maimonides defends Aristotle's premises that God is a unity, eternal, and non-corporeal, but argues in addition that it makes no difference to the necessity of the prime mover whether the world was created in time out of nothing or not. The case for the existence of God as the mover is the same for both sides of the debate. He is binding them together around the proof that, whether eternal or created, the logical contradiction of a *reductio ad absurdum* proves that God must exist. Maimonides's case here for eternity and creation is that eternity is a divine construction rather than a divine essence. The appearance of the eternal nature of generation and corruption is itself part of the creation of finite time. Circular motion has no beginning because it has been created this way. The eternal, therefore, is only an effect of creation *ex nihilo*. The logic of this argument, says Maimonides, is 'a great wall that I have built around the Law' (1963b, 298) to protect it from those who attack it.

## The active intellect

In considering the active intellect, Maimonides is again concerned to see in Aristotle what is and what is not compatible with Judaism. He describes in detail the Aristotelian view of emanation as eternal motion, noting that the relation of the active intellect to the elements is similar to the relation of the intellect and its sphere, and that both relations mirror that between potentiality and actuality. He sums up Aristotelian cosmology as follows:

> All spheres are living bodies, endowed with a soul and an intellect, having a mental representation and apprehension of the deity and also a mental representation of their own first principles. In that which exists, there are separate intellects that are in no way a body. All of them overflow from God, may He be exalted, and they are the intermediaries between God and all these bodies.
>
> (1963b, 259)

Again, Maimonides points to the agreements between Judaism and Aristotle on relations within the cosmos, while acknowledging also that Judaism holds that God created its governing forces and Aristotle holds that they are eternal. However, it is not contrary to Judaism that God should overflow his goodness to the intellects and the spheres up to and including the active intellect, which then moves matter into actual formal existence. Emanation or overflow is a fitting and appropriate way to think about the actions of a God who is not a body. Emanation realizes *separate* intellects and movement within them without being compromised by composition in doing so. This emanation continues to the active intellect which is the principle and cause of movement, actuality, and intellect in the human world of existents. This overflowing is life itself and it is what makes the finite intellect able to apprehend its own truth. Thus there is nothing Aristotle says on emanation 'that is not in agreement with the Law' (1963b, 265).

## Culture of error

Maimonides holds to the Aristotelian principle that in God 'the essence that apprehends is undoubtedly the same as the essence that is apprehended' (1963a, 122). For God to will and to create is not differentiated in his essence, for God is he who creates everything that is created and knows it to be himself. This is captured for Maimonides in the name of God given to Moses, 'I am that I am' (Ex. 3.14).[19] God, then, is not a compound of attributes but is 'the necessarily existent' (1963a, 155). Again, Maimonides is concerned to separate the error of finite judgement from the essence of God who is 'one and simple' (1963a, 122), noting again that man can speak only through 'the instrumentality of customary words, which are the greatest among the causes leading unto error' (1963a, 132), which is why God's truth can only ever be stated negatively.

Maimonides is also at one with the core of mediaeval philosophy in holding earthly matters as a force for corruption by compound and multiplicity. He associates it with the basest human qualities, most particularly eating and copulation. Form, by contrast, he knows to exist without matter and to be pure. All the commandments and the prohibitions of the Law are 'only intended to quell all the impulses of matter' (1963b, 433) and he advances the case for the ascetic lifestyle of those who prefer 'to be a human being in truth' (1963b, 433) and who wish to see through the 'strong veil' (1963b, 436) of matter that carries error. However, where God is 'constantly an intellect in actu' (1963a, 166), man has potential which makes such constant actuality logically impossible. Thus man achieves a unity with such actuality extremely rarely as it is reserved for the prophet who can, at times, know God in his unity rather than through the human mind. In God himself there is no potentiality whatsoever because he is not sometimes apprehending and sometimes not. He is always actual because actuality is his essence and existence.

But Maimonides's view of the error of culture in respect of the human related to God is also a culture of error in and through the ambivalence carried by error as divine education. For example, to the assertion that, if God creates or acts at one time but not at another this suggests that the unchangeable God is changed in moving from potentiality to actuality, Maimonides counters by saying that the term 'action' here is equivocal. As with the active intellect, so also, the non-corporeal acts without matter and therefore without change. Also, to the belief that if God wills to create the world then his choice of when is affected by external constraints, Maimonides again argues that there is equivoca-tion. A corporeal body has the purpose of its will in something external to its essence and may well be affected by something external to it, but God's will 'does not exist in any respect for the sake of some other thing [and] is not subject to change' (1963b, 301). Finally, against the claim that the eternal God can only create that which is eternal, Maimonides says that this presumes to know of God's wisdom which is unknowable for man, and that God's purpose can change, and the world with it, without change in God, for his will is self-determining.

In Maimonides's culture of error, then, error is clearly distinguished from the true. No man can know how God works. It is the case that just as men cannot apprehend the true reality of God's essence, so neither can anyone know the true reality of God's knowledge. Thus Maimonides is clear on the following divine principles: that God knows at all times; that his knowledge is neither multiple nor finite; and that nothing is hidden from him. The terms knowledge, purpose, and providence are all equivocal when applied to God and to man. Truth arises in knowing how things are ascribed differently to God and to man. All the things that man knows 'follow upon His knowledge' (1963b, 485), which precedes that of man. We cannot know as God knows for 'our knowledge does not grasp the future or the infinite' (1963b, 485).[20]

However, as we have illustrated, the *Guide* also illustrates how the culture of error has within it the ambiguities necessary for a higher education. The parables and stories, and language and images in Scripture have the double significance of meeting the needs of the educated and the uneducated. This equivocation evinces a perplexity in which God is known and is known as unknown at the same time, although not by the same people. A man incapable of speculation must accept the authority of the speculative man, while at the same time the learned man keeps the divine secrets safe through formative ambiguity. This is Maimonides's own method of education about this education in the *Guide*. The Scriptures, the laws, and the *Guide* itself are no less than 'a gracious ruse' (1963b, 532) by which error maintains its educational significance.

## Conclusion

The Islamic and Jewish cultures of error explored above reveal the domination of Neoplatonic logic within them. Even al-Ghazali's critique of logic is a logical critique. But from the perspective of present recollection, much can be made of a period in which the Western Christian, Muslim, and Jew spoke of and to each other in a shared philosophical language, having common concerns, and being willing to engage with each other. When, in Chapter 7 below, we look at the present history of Western philosophy we will have to return to the issue of how Western voices can speak to each other, and to those who are 'other' than the West. A new, modern culture of error may well be discernible as the ground and groundlessness of this work. But this is mediated by the fact that the mediaeval culture of error has, in the modern mind, educated itself to the point where it can speak the identity of its ambivalence. This identity is modern Western subjectivity.

# 5
# Rationalist Philosophy

## Introduction

Between the mediaeval cultures of error and the modern aporetic philosophical mind are the rationalist philosophies of Descartes (1596–1650), Spinoza
(1632–77), Leibniz (1646–1716), and Locke (1632–1704). Our interest in
these thinkers concerns their employment of Neoplatonic principles in rationalist cultures of error. Their defining feature is that they eschew doubt and
ambivalence as significant or formative in revealing truth. However, these are
different kinds of cultures of error to those that preceded them. Previously
cultures of error held thought to be in error in relation to the true, but held
also to the idea that the ambivalence of thought – its culture – was educative. The new rationalist cultures of error now find truth in rational thought
and error in its ambivalence. The mediaeval cultures of error are reconfigured
now in the rational errors of culture. The advance this represents takes reason
beyond its status merely as error and opposed to truth in itself. But the cost
of this is that the means by which rationalism – the culture of reason – can
learn from its experiences of itself are cast aside. Reason extends itself here
into everything except itself. In the search for the clear, the distinct, and
the unambiguous, reason withdraws from its own conditions of possibility.
In particular, Descartes, so often seen as the beginning of modern western
philosophy, is only an abstraction – a very important one nonetheless – of
reason taking responsibility for itself from within its own groundlessness.

## Descartes

### Doubting doubt
The *Rules for the Direction of the Mind* (1628) and the *Discourse on Method*
(1637), both announce the standpoint of Descartes' philosophy against

doubt and dialectic. His experience of scholastic negation has, he says, left him with only an 'increasing recognition of my own ignorance' (Descartes, 1985, 113) from which he concludes that philosophy needs clear and reliable rules of deductive reasoning which will lead unambiguously to what is certain. It is mathematics and not philosophy that delights him 'because of the certainty and self-evidence of its reasonings' (1985, 114). For nine years Descartes endeavoured to rid himself of all faulty opinion and error, confessing here only his own ignorance.

Nevertheless, the logic that sustains the chain of deductive reasoning is the same logic that has underpinned previous cultures of error. Descartes accepts the logic that the simple precedes the compound, that some singularities lie beyond human powers of comprehension, that it is contradictory and therefore wrong that something can come from nothing, or that the less perfect can create the more perfect, and that God is not corporeal but intellectual. These are, in essence, the Neoplatonic principles of non-contradiction, cause and effect, and the absurdity of infinite regression. They underpin Descartes' philosophical method in that he sets out to doubt everything that can be doubted so that, by stripping them away, whatever is left must be the most simple and incontrovertibly true. In the first of the *Meditations* (1641) he concludes that there is not one of his former beliefs 'about which a doubt may not properly be raised' (Descartes, 1984, 14–15).

The most simple element that survives all doubt is the thinking I, the *cogito*. Descartes rehearses this in the *Discourse*, the *Meditations*, and the *Principles of Philosophy* (1647). The proof of the *cogito* lies in the logic of non-contradiction.

> It is a contradiction to suppose that what thinks does not, at the very time when it is thinking, exist. Accordingly, this piece of knowledge – *I am thinking, therefore I exist* – is the first and most certain of all to occur to anyone who philosophizes in an orderly way.
>
> (1985, 195)

The thinking I is always something rather than nothing.

The indubitable *cogito* also has within it the indubitable idea of God. In the Third Meditation he reasons that 'something cannot arise from nothing' (1984, 28) and that what is more perfect 'cannot arise from what is less perfect' (1984, 28).[1] In addition, he accepts that even though one idea might lead to another there 'cannot be an infinite regress here; eventually one must reach a primary idea' (1984, 29), an archetype containing all of the perfection that is in such ideas. He reasons, therefore, that if in his thought of God the perfection is so great that the mind cannot conceive of itself as the cause of the thought, then some other thing must exist which is the cause of such perfection. Finding nothing in the description of the infinity of God that could have originated in his own mind, Descartes states that 'it must be concluded that God necessarily exists' (1984, 31). The idea of God in man is the effect of God as the cause of the idea. 'The whole force of the argument lies in this: I recognize that it would be impossible for me to exist with the kind of nature I have – that is, having within me the idea of God – were it not the case that God really existed. By "God" I mean the very being the idea of whom is within me' (1984, 35). But he reasons that since God is perfect and has no potentiality, finite knowledge could never achieve this perfection in itself.

The Fourth Meditation looks into the mind of God to see if and why he allows his creatures to think erroneously. In God Descartes finds no error, but he admits to error in the finite judgements that man is able to make. The source of error is where the will extends itself to make judgements which are beyond the finite comprehension of the intellect. The will is free to make such judgements and is in this sense in the image and likeness of God. The error lies not in the gift of free will but in the use it is put to by his creatures. Comprehension in the intellect should always precede assent or denial by the will. Thus suspension of judgement on everything except that which is clear, distinct, and certain will avoid error in rational thought. This is what Descartes believes himself to be doing in the *Meditations*.

Nevertheless, as with the mediaeval cultures of error, Descartes does identify pedagogical significance in finite error. For example, to the question as to why God made man's judgement open to error and to imperfection, Descartes makes several responses. If errors occur with God's concurrence then one must admit to being more perfect for having free will than not having it. If God has intended that the mind make errors, then it must be the case that, in his perfection, it is better to be able to make mistakes than not to be able to. In any case, for Descartes God is working in ways beyond the grasp of mere human knowledge. One needs to look at finite error within the bigger picture of its function in the universe overall. Descartes says he can have no complaint 'on the grounds that the power of understanding or the natural light which God gave me is no greater than it is; for it is in the nature of a finite intellect to lack understanding of many things' (1984, 42). He sees error as proof of God's ordinance, that there may indeed 'be more perfection in the universe as a whole because some of its parts are not

immune from error, while others are immune, than there would be if all
the parts were exactly alike' (1984, 42–3).

Descartes here is entering the mind of God to find divine ordinance
in the existence of error and falsity. At the very least, error is an education into the limits of the creature and his gifts from God. God cannot
deceive and therefore there must be a higher *telos* to the limitations of
man's finite comprehension. Those things that can be understood, and
those that cannot, must have their author in God and must be part of
His providence, because He who is so supremely perfect 'cannot be a
deceiver on pain of contradiction' (1984, 43).

Descartes' philosophy then looks backwards and forwards at the same
time. In looking backwards the pain of Neoplatonic contradiction is
the logic of God's universe making itself known. It is contradictory to
assume that the *cogito* can be doubted, that God does not exist, that
God deceives us, that he is not perfect, and that what he wants us to
understand is not clearly able to be understood. Contradiction, here,
is assumed to be the method by which God communicates himself.
Descartes employs Neoplatonic logic as a culture of error and as the
error of culture in finding truth in that which eschews contradiction
*and* in knowing that God must logically exist but not knowing what
God is. God gave man as much intellect as he deemed necessary and
no more. Thus, error is in the finite intellect even though the intellect
is the home of the proof of God. The soul's dependence upon the body
is one of the main sources of such error. These errors are privations and
negations, but they are human errors, not divine. The mind has the idea
of God within it as an 'utterly necessary and eternal existence' (1985,
197) but in man the will is needed to assent to judgements made in
the intellect, and the will often extends beyond that which is clearly
perceived.

But his philosophy looks forwards in that he believes he has produced
an absolutely rational proof of God's existence from the chain of deductive reasoning based on things as they really are in the universe. He
believes this to be a victory of clarity and certainty over the dialectical
obfuscations that cloud scholastic philosophy. Descartes believes that
he has overcome the doubt that characterized mediaeval proofs of God.
This begins an education for reason wherein it learns of its independence in a self-justifying logic that cannot be gainsaid. In the *Principles*
Descartes criticizes Aristotle and his followers for grounding principles
in less than perfect knowledge, the proof of which, he says, is that
Aristotle's principles 'have not enabled any progress to be made in all
the many centuries in which they have been followed' (1985, 189). But

Descartes believes he has removed the uncertainty from these principles and given them an unequivocally rational and irrefutable basis. At one and the same time, Descartes here gives reason its absolute clarity by overcoming its ambivalence, yet, and ambivalently, makes it impossible for this clearer reason then to learn of itself from itself. Thus he reveals the error of dialectical culture by establishing reason as the overcoming of such error. Making reason admit to the fact that its errors were only its own lack of clarity about itself is Descartes' essentially modern philosophical significance in the history of Western philosophy. But having therein cast culture as error, reason's victory is Pyrrhic for it wins totality but loses the conditions of the possibility of this totality. This must await the modern Kantian and Hegelian philosophical revolution.

## Spinoza

In Spinoza's rationalism necessity is the education that teaches of finite freedom as error and of nature as the universality of that necessity. What this rationalist culture of error reveals here is reason made its own truth without ambivalence or sophistical dialectic. What it loses, however, in the rationalist positing of the error of culture is any possibility of its own culture or re-formation, which in turn suppresses the possibility of modern Western freedom and subjectivity.

### Simple understanding

It is Spinoza's view that there are three types of knowing. From the senses comes chaotic knowing, from reason comes the clear and distinct truth of ideas adequate to their objects, and from intuition comes the adequate ideas of the essence and eternity of God, from which it proceeds to adequate knowledge of the essence of things. This latter knows God as what is existing or as nature. Thus, in Spinoza the 'more we understand particular things, the more we understand God' (Spinoza, 1992, 214).

His *Treatise on the Emendation of the Intellect* (c. 1662) reveals the Neoplatonic *telos* of his philosophical project. He seeks for 'a new guiding principle' (1992, 235) that will bring eternal and supreme joy. He recognizes that this means giving up any pursuit of riches, honours, or sensual pleasure, and that 'love towards a thing eternal and infinite feeds the mind with joy alone' (1992, 235). It is a weakness of the human mind that it cannot comprehend this truth, although man can seek this supreme good in 'the knowledge of the union which the mind has with the whole of Nature' (1992, 235). His goal, then, is to acquire this union and to emend or purify the intellect so that 'it may succeed in understanding things without error' (1992, 236) and achieve 'the highest human perfection' (1992, 236). The only mode of perception that can work without error is where a thing is perceived from its essence as self-caused, or from a proximate cause where knowledge of such an effect, he says, 'is nothing other than to acquire a more perfect knowledge of the cause' (1992, 257). What remains, then, is to find the best method for arriving at such perception.

Also of interest in the *Treatise* is his distinction between the idea of an object (its *essentia objectiva*), the actual existence of this object (its *essentia formalis*), and the implications of this distinction for infinite regression. Since an idea is something different from its object, one idea can be the object of another idea, and so on *ad infinitum*. But whereas the argument for the first cause is based in the logical impossibility of infinite regression, Spinoza argues that the idea of an idea adds nothing to the first idea. Infinite regression is stopped at source because 'in order to know, I need not know that I know' (1992, 241). In fact, its logic is reversed by Spinoza, for 'in order to know that I know, it is necessary that I must first know' (1992, 241). The 'given true idea' (1992, 242) is therefore proof of 'the given idea of the most perfect Being' (1992, 242) and involves no equivocation or ambiguity. The first knowing is the whole knowing. For Spinoza, this is a circle of sound reasoning involving nothing vicious or absurd. No method for seeking the truth is needed beyond this proof. But, in losing infinite regression, Spinoza here suppresses the dialectic and negation that ground infinite regression. Do not be put off, he says, by paradoxes in reasoning for they are already contingent upon a greater truth, that 'there must first of all exist in us a true idea as an innate tool' (1992, 242).

This is not the chain of deductive reasoning found in Descartes, but they both arrive at an irrefutable point of certainty in the rational intellect. This point of certainty is again grounded in Neoplatonic logic. Spinoza argues that something is impossible if it would be contradictory to itself to exist; necessary if it would be contradictory to itself not to exist; and possible if its existence or non-existence were not contradictory and where necessity or impossibility were dependent upon unknown causes. Thus, 'if the nature of the known thing implies necessary existence, we cannot possibly be deceived regarding the existence of that thing' (1992, 250). As with Aristotle, where understanding *simpliciter* knows the explanation of an object to be that it cannot be otherwise, so for Spinoza it is the real that corresponds to ideas by which the true may be distinguished from the false. As such, a true thought is intrinsic to itself 'without reference to other thoughts' (1992, 251) and without reference to a cause beyond the intellect. When we possess 'such knowledge of God as we have of a triangle, all doubt is removed' (1992, 254).

## Knowing God

In his *Theologico-Politico Treatise* (1670) Spinoza takes this same approach to religion and to the Bible. Since God is the cause of all things, the more man knows of nature the more he gains knowledge of the essence of God. This 'natural divine law' (Spinoza, 1889, 61) is innate and common to all men at all times and is its own reward. Thus everything that is truly described in Scripture must have happened 'according to natural laws' (1889, 92) for what is contrary to nature, and therefore to reason, is absurd and 'to be rejected' (1889, 92). It is indisputable that 'nature preserves a fixed and unchangeable order, and that God in all ages, known and unknown, has been the same; further, that the laws of nature are so perfect, that nothing can be added thereto nor taken therefrom' (1889, 96). Even miracles are 'natural occurrences' (1889, 97).

Spinoza's emphasis on knowing the clear and distinct extends the knowledge of God to all men endowed with natural reason. Spinoza criticizes Maimonides's belief that the truth of Scripture cannot be made plain to the ordinary man and must therefore not be sought, arguing instead that it must be available to the natural faculties of mankind. This marks a new stage in the principles that underpin the history of Western philosophy. The mediaeval cultures of error reserved their ambivalence for the few. When rationalism eschews ambivalence for natural reason it democratizes truth by assigning it to a universal natural reason regarding the clear and distinct truths that exist in the world. 'Scriptural doctrine contains no lofty speculations nor philosophic reasoning, but only very simple matters such as could be understood by the slowest intelligence' (1889, 175). What doctrines the Bible does contain for philosophy are very few and very simple. The aim of the Bible is not to make man learned (of Plato and Aristotle) but to make men obedient, that is, to know God in love of one's neighbour. The universality of natural reason leads Spinoza to argue for democracy as the form of government most fitted to individual liberty.

The *Ethics* (1677) displays most clearly the relationship between Neoplatonic principles and Spinoza's rationalism in knowing God. Substance is self-caused existence, since it would be 'contradictory' (1992, 33–4) for substance to depend on anything else. Because the human mind is determined first by one cause, then another *ad infinitum*, it can be neither absolute nor the free cause of itself. Thus men are in error when they 'think they are free' (1992, 95).

The same logic applies to the existence of God. First, existence presupposes an entity whose essence is existing as existence. This is grounded in the logic that it would be a contradiction if existing were not the truth of its own nature, of itself. Second, this contradiction means there must be an order of 'universal corporeal Nature' (1992, 37), since nothing existing can annul its necessity (and something not existing is of no import). Thus, 'neither in God nor external to God is there any cause or reason which would annul his existence. Therefore God necessarily exists' (1992, 37). Third, existing is a greater power than not existing, but it would be absurd to suggest that finite existing entities are more powerful than an absolutely infinite entity. Since we exist, so too must that whose essence is existing. Perfection in this sense presupposes our existence, and is the necessity of God's existence. Spinoza concludes 'there is nothing of which we can be more certain than the existence of an absolutely infinite or perfect Entity' (1992, 38). A little further on he observes that 'God is substance which necessarily exists; that is, a thing to whose nature it pertains to exist, or – and this is the same thing – a thing from whose definition existence follows' (1992, 46). As such, in God existence and essence 'are one and the same' (1992, 46).

Each of these proofs is grounded in the Neoplatonic logic of non-contradiction, cause and effect, and the absurdity of infinite regression. They also lead Spinoza to conclude that absolute substance is indivisible, that there is only one God, that he is not corporeal, that he is the 'efficient cause of all things' (1992, 43) that exist, and that he acts only from necessity. Spinoza is critical of those who get embroiled in disputes about creation and eternity, or God knowing universals or particulars, seeing such disputes positing God's intellect or nature in human and therefore contradictory terms. Since God's intellect is the divine essence prior to all things, it must be different from man's intellect.

### Contingency and freedom

Because all things are modes of God's existence there can be 'no contingency' (1992, 51) for 'whatever is, is in God' (1992, 51). This safeguards against contingency or infinite regression in thought, for 'every idea which is in us is absolute' (1992, 86). As such, truth is God's nature and its own standard. There is no need here for a potential intellect, since intellect is always in the act of itself, always an attribute of God's natural, infinite, and eternal self-causing. Reason here understands things as necessary rather than contingent, and knows this necessity as 'God's eternal nature' (1992, 93).

Freedom then becomes a matter of ignorance regarding God's necessity. Nature does not act for man's benefit, as he often supposes, but only as God's absolute essence. To the modern mind this looks like a suppression of freedom by an over-determining God. The source of this suppression lies in Spinoza holding culture as error in relation to the rational understanding *simpliciter*. In this way, Spinoza's thought is more strictly Aristotelian than Neoplatonic. His lack of interest in the phenomenology of relation in the thought of God and in his being known, removes significance from philosophical experience altogether. When this relation *is* acknowledged by Spinoza, he sees it only as a contradiction and dismisses it as unsustainable. In so doing, the thought of God and of freedom are refused substance by the logic of non-contradiction which deems it the error of dialectical culture. The universality granted to God eschews the free knowing of universality.

### Error of culture

Here, then, we see in Spinoza how the culture of error is grounded in positing the error of culture. Spinoza eschews as equivocal, culture and its dialectical sophistries by uniting God and reason in and as the necessary truth of all that is clear and distinct. Reason is freed from error by being placed within the eternal necessity of God's nature. As such, God and reason are the one universality with no requirement for pedagogies of opposition. But in this view of error as the culture of finite thought, the mind is refused its own self-learning, and refused the means by which to carry out Western philosophy's central maxim: 'Know Thyself'. Natural reason, based on clear and distinct truths of what actually exists, teaches necessity over contingency. But the cost here is of culture *per se*. Spinoza's rationalism is only ever the abstraction of rational substance, never its own self-determining re-formation of itself.[2] Nevertheless, the gains of overcoming error are clear for Spinoza. To know God's will in our ideas, as in our volitions, is to learn to act for God's will, which will produce the greatest happiness is us, and a 'complete tranquillity of mind' (1992, 100) resulting from a stoicism regarding God's necessity. This will be 'to do freely what is best' (1992, 100), and in social relations this means living without hate or envy, and always being ready to help others. The highest good that a man can attain is the knowledge of God, for that, he believes, is truly to know himself. In sum, the highest happiness for man lies in the 'self-contentment that arises from the intuitive knowledge of God' (1992, 196).[3]

## Leibniz

Leibniz argues that each individual substance in the world is 'like a mirror of God' (Leibniz, 1998, 61). His early text, *Discourse on Metaphysics*[4] reveals the Neoplatonic logic that grounds this view. An effect 'always expresses cause, and God is the true cause of substances' (1998, 68). A substance includes all its predicates, which can therefore be deduced from it. By contrast, an accident cannot claim accidents as its own. Equally a substance is unique and their number cannot be increased or decreased. They are as God in that they carry an imprint of his infinite wisdom and omnipotence. As such, 'God is in all [and] is intimately united to all created things' (1998, 84).

Here he distinguishes between the necessity and possibility of a substance. Necessity is that which must happen to an individual substance because its contrary is not possible without contradiction. So, the character of a circle is absolutely necessary, for it already contains all that will and can happen to it. If a contrary is possible without contradiction, this is an appearance of contingency where choices look possible. But they are not possible because even if the less perfect does not contradict the perfect, it is nevertheless true that God will make happen what is perfect and necessary. Leibniz holds here to the principle of God as non-contradiction, as perfect, simple, and first cause, while yielding the appearance of contingency to the finite misunderstanding of the nature of substance.

The soul 'expresses God and the universe' (1998, 78) because God puts ideas in the soul as an expression of his essence. Because of this the mind is able to know and to understand what the senses see. The soul expresses God 'as an effect expresses its cause' (1998, 80) but it is independent in that it must think its own thoughts. It is in this independence and spontaneity, paradoxically, that the soul corresponds most closely to what happens – what must happen – in the universe. Man can choose, but he is determined to choose that which is most perfect. In the later *Monadology* (1714) Leibniz argues that monads with bodies are living things, and with souls are animals. Every organic body is therefore a kind of 'divine machine' (1998, 277).

Leibniz also accepts the Neoplatonic idea of God as mind. 'Minds certainly are the most perfect of beings, and express the Divinity best' (1998, 87) because God is a mind, and it is 'only minds that are made in his image [or are] children of his house, for only they can serve him freely, and act with knowledge in imitation of the divine nature' (1998, 88). Thus, 'a single mind is worth a whole world' (1998, 88), although while non-spiritual substances express the world rather than God, spiritual substances express God rather than the world. God therefore derives 'infinitely more glory from minds than from all other beings' (1998, 88). Happiness is where God flourishes, and to make men 'perfectly happy, all that God asks is that they should love him' (1998, 89).

Regarding infinite regression, Leibniz argues in the *New System*[5] (1695) that material objects are always divisible *ad infinitum* into those parts which constitute them. One contingency cannot explain another. The problem then is to explain how God as a unity of form is present in this infinite reduction. Here Leibniz turns to substantial forms as 'atoms of substance' (1998, 145) arguing that only these can be 'the absolute first principles of the compositions of things' (1998, 149). These atoms of substance, then, 'by means of the soul or form' (1998, 148), correspond to what is called the I. This distinguishes rational souls from mere natural machines. The atoms are 'metaphysical points' (1998, 149) and are both 'indivisible and real, and without them there would be nothing real, since without true unities there would be no multiplicity' (1998, 149).

On the question of the relationship between the soul and the body, Leibniz admits the difficulty posed by the independence of each substance. His solution is to argue that God created the soul so that its own spontaneous action also conforms to things outside it. The effect of each substance reflecting the whole universe in its own particular way is a 'perfect agreement between all these substances' (1998, 150) as if they communicated with one another. It is in this way that from the unity of a substance there arises multiplicity without changing the substance. Such a theory of agreements 'gives a wonderful sense of the harmony of the universe and the perfection of the works of God' (1998, 151), as well as offering a 'surprisingly clear proof of the existence of God' (1998, 152), since such agreement could only have come 'from their common cause' (1998, 152). Every mind expresses the universe, and thus 'each mind should always play its part in the way most fitted to contribute to the perfection of the society of all minds which constitute their moral union in the City of God' (1998, 151).

In his *Principles of Nature and Grace, based on Reason* (1714) Leibniz argues for these atoms of substance as monads, from the Greek *monus* meaning unity or one.[6] The whole of nature is full of the life of these substances. Monads have no parts, no shape, no beginning or end. They cannot be made or unmade, cannot be destroyed and will last as long as the universe. But they can change. Thus, one is distinguished from another 'by its internal qualities and actions' (1998, 259). The perception of a monad is its representation of external things in the simple, and its appetitions are the movement from one perception to another. Thus, simple substance can exist together with multiplicity, for change is only the variety of its relations to external things, and life consists of just such changes. All monads are linked because every monad represents the universe, albeit in accordance with its own point of view. The harmony of the universe is in the accordance between perception and motion, as it is therefore in the union of soul and body.

Monads also address the issue of infinite regression. Matter provides no sufficient reason from within itself to explain motion in the universe. 'Therefore the sufficient reason, which has no need of any further reason, must lie outside that series of contingent things, and must be found in a substance which is the cause of the series [and] carries the reason for its existence within itself' (1998, 262). God is the name of this 'final reason for things' (1998, 262). God is proved *a priori* because something that contains no contradictions must necessarily exist, and proved *a posteriori* because contingent things exist.

In the *Monadology* Leibniz further explains that all created monads are limited to the perfection which they individually possess. They can be moved and changed by each other because God obliges one perfection to adapt to the perfection of another. A monad is deemed active if it is the explanation of what is changed, and passive if it is what is being explained. It is 'this *interconnection*, or this adapting of all created things to each one, and of each one to all the others, [which] means that each simple substance has relationships which express all the others, and that it is therefore a perpetual living mirror of the universe' (1998, 275). It means that there is 'universal harmony [where] every substance exactly expresses every other through the relationships it has with them' (1998, 276), even though each monad is limited and differentiated by its distinct level of perfection. In addition, all rational minds are part of the city of God, in which there is harmony between nature and grace. Since God is perfect, love will have its most perfect expression in the love of God and will provide 'genuine tranquillity of mind' (1998, 265) in the certainty of a happy future. But since God can never be known completely, this tranquillity will strive for new pleasures and new perfections.

Leibniz is able to conclude then that in his system of interconnection there is a perfect harmony not only between efficient causes and final causes (contingency and necessity) but also between nature and grace (God as designer of nature and monarch of minds). The paths of nature lead to grace. It is man's task to be devoted to God the designer, and the efficient cause of what is, but also devoted to God the master, the final cause of all that is. To love this is to be content with whatever God brings about, knowing that we can never fully understand God's will, but knowing also that it is perfect. The rational mind has the advantage in that it can know and understand the system and science of the universe of created things. Because the mind is the image 'of the divinity itself' (1998, 280), it can not only imitate God in its activity, but also 'enter into a kind of community with God' (1998, 280) to make up the city of God, a 'moral world within the natural world' (1998, 280).

### Overcoming ambivalence

Leibniz adheres to Neoplatonic logic in justifying how the mind can arrive at knowledge of the self, of substances, of the immaterial, and of God. The principle of non-contradiction enables the mind to judge as false that which involves contradiction 'and as true whatever is opposed or contradictory to what is false' (1998, 272). The principle of sufficient reason holds that 'no fact could ever be true or existent, nor statement correct, unless there were a sufficient reason why it was thus and not otherwise – even though those reasons will usually not be knowable by us' (1998, 272). Both of these principles are grounded in the positing of actual thought – aware of itself as aware of itself – as error. The contradiction of the principle of contradiction is therein suppressed, and the principle of sufficient reason is abstracted from its own logic and culture of autodestruction.

   This rationalist suppression of error as culture grounds itself still in the Neoplatonic principles of non-contradiction, first cause, and the absurdity of infinite regression. Reason is brought to universality by overcoming errors associated with dialectical scholasticism, arriving at the clear and unequivocal evidence of God in the created universe. Perhaps even more than Spinoza, Leibniz fathoms a harmony in the universe in which all things are connected as God's ordinance. Yet at the same time he displays how reason, by its own work, is becoming increasingly powerful in recognizing that it, and it alone, is clearly and distinctly the house of God. But in casting culture merely as error, here again, reason is denied the possibility of its own philosophical education. In Leibniz there is an experience of reason, but one that in prioritizing rational harmony over rational equivocation suppresses therein the oppositions in which reason can be its own free self-determination.

## Locke

John Locke offers a gateway to the modern Western philosophical mind, even though Locke himself does not pass through it. His stance is that of the rationalist against the dialectical obfuscations of the scholastics.

He sees the philosopher as the under-labourer who must remove the mediaeval rubbish 'that lies in the way to knowledge' (Locke, 2004, 11). In scholastic disputation, truth is decided only upon rhetorical flourish and not on rational demonstration. These scholastics, says Locke, are 'bookish men' (1996, 189) who learn little from their studies, except how to 'talk copiously' (1996, 189) on either side of a dispute, the superficiality of which only serves their own vanity. The art of rhetoric serves only to 'insinuate wrong ideas, move the passions, and thereby mislead the judgement' (2004, 452). The popularity of rhetoric is commensurate with the inaccuracy of meanings carried by words. The result is that the sciences have been 'over-charged with obscure and equivocal terms' (2004, 454) employed by so-called learned men who become 'more *conceited* in their ignorance, and *obstinate* in their errors' (2004, 454). The under-labourer by contrast will 'use no word, till he views in his mind the precise *determined* idea' (2004, 14) of the object that the word represents. He does not need Aristotle, says Locke, in order to be rational.

## Demonstration

Against equivocation and inaccuracy in thinking, Locke advocates a rational demonstrative method for philosophy, one aware of the limits of the understanding that must be employed as the tool of rational enquiry. The correct conduct of the understanding should be to conform itself to truth by endeavouring 'to know and think of things as they are in themselves' (1996, 188), and words should be restricted to describing things that are clear and distinct, and without ambiguity or equivocation. The certainty of knowledge can only come from direct experience of objects, 'things in themselves, as they exist' (2004, 569). Knowledge cannot be extended beyond direct experience. Man's reason therefore can only work on the ideas of particulars that he has in his own mind. 'The immediate object of all our reasoning and knowledge, is nothing but particulars' (2004, 601). This leads Locke to conclude that we can have no knowledge of substance in general.

In the *Essay Concerning Human Understanding* (1706) Locke distinguishes between simple and complex ideas. Simple ideas accurately portray real things. Complex ideas are only archetypes and are not intended as copies of anything in the real world. Ideas themselves are generated only by sensation from external objects and by reflection on the internal workings of the mind. The key to the activity of the under-labourer is the demonstrative method. Demonstration in philosophical reasoning shows 'the agreement, or disagreement of two ideas, by the intervention of one or more proofs, which have a constant, immutable, and visible connexion with one another' (2004, 577). When this concerns the ideas of real objects, there we arrive at 'certain real knowledge' (2004, 508) and when, as in mathematics, we find agreement between archetypes, 'there is certain knowledge' (2004, 508).

The criteria for judging agreement and disagreement between ideas are found in the 'natural power' (2004, 468) of the mind. They are identity, difference, relation, fixedness, and actual existence without the mind – God being an example of the latter. Intuitive knowledge sees agreement or disagreement immediately, needing no intervening ideas.[7] Demonstrative knowledge, on the other hand, is not immediately knowable and requires intervening ideas to mediate, by reasoning and proofs, in order to arrive at certainty. It is in the intervening ideas, which confirm agreement or disagreement between the ideas, that new knowledge is developed. Such intuition is the work of reason, which Locke calls 'natural revelation' (2004, 616). Thus, this learning and education lie not in application of universal principles but in an intuitive self-certainty that is clear and unambiguous. The true light is the truth of propositions and the validity of its proofs. Reason 'must be our last judge and guide in everything' (2004, 621). However, the longer the chain of proofs required in demonstrative knowledge, the further from its original clarity it travels. Indeed, the possibility of demonstrative knowledge proceeding *ad infinitum* is avoided only by the intuitive certainty between the intermediate ideas that locate agreement and disagreement between simple or complex ideas. Intuition is the condition of the possibility of demonstrative proof. It is the proof of proof.[8]

### Error as limit

But Locke is also clear that human knowledge has limits. He notes that the mind has no knowledge beyond that of which it has ideas, and that there is no possible knowledge beyond intuitive or rational agreement and disagreement. He notes that even with the greatest effort 'our knowledge would never reach to all we might desire to know concerning those ideas we have; nor be able to surmount all the difficulties, and resolve all the questions [that] might arise concerning any of them' (2004, 480). This limit should not prejudice the mind against what God is able to do. Where we meet these limitations we can 'content ourselves with faith and probability' (2004, 481), including in regard to the afterlife.

Locke here sides with uncertainty against transgressing the limits of knowledge. So, for example, in regard to the question of the soul's materiality, Locke notes that each side of the debate will be driven to its contrary. Dogmatically siding with one view or the other will not deliver peace or truth. In the face of such oppositions, there is nothing to be gained by fleeing to the opposite opinion for that too will be 'clogged with equal difficulties' (2004, 482). There is no safety in avoiding one set of 'seeming absurdities' (2004, 482) by taking refuge in the contrary 'which is built on something altogether as inexplicable' (2004, 482) to our comprehension. It seems here that Locke's advice is to learn from such antinomies of the limits of finite knowledge, and to accept that these will not be overcome, particularly with regard to knowing the truth of essences. It is past controversy, he says, that we have something in us that thinks – our doubts about it confirm this – but every substance that exists has something in it 'which manifestly baffles our understandings' (2004, 482). Our ignorance is 'infinitely larger than our knowledge' (2004, 490).

It is beyond the mind to know 'the nature and hidden causes of those ideas' (2004, 282). God is made up 'of the simple ideas we receive from *reflection*' (2004, 284) put together to make up the complex idea of God. God is therefore 'the best idea of him our minds are capable of' (2004, 285), formed by adding infinity to the simple ideas we receive in reflection. Thus the idea of God arises from our ideas, but his essence, as simple and uncompounded, is unknowable to us. This positing of essence as uncompounded, places Locke within the ancient and mediaeval paradigm of Neoplatonic logic, for even though we represent God to ourselves in the best way we are capable of, this is still error compared to his true and unknowable essence. His warning is that the idea of God is only a complex one made up of simple ideas that arise in sensation and reflection. Therefore we can have no ideas beyond these simple ideas, and we must not mistake the power of combination for substance in itself. We do not know things by their real essences. 'Our faculties carry us no further towards the knowledge and distinction of substances, than a collection of those sensible ideas, which we observe in them' (2004, 397). As such, it is obvious that 'the internal constitution, whereon their properties depend, is unknown to us' (2004, 397). Falling within the paradigm of the unknowability of the infinite in the finite, he confirms that 'the workmanship of the all-wise, and powerful God, in the great fabric of the universe, and every part thereof, further exceeds the capacity and comprehension of the most inquisitive and intelligent man' (2004, 397).

### Innate principles

The *Essay* begins by arguing that there are no innate or originary principles stamped on the soul in its very beginning. The two principles in speculative science that have the greatest claim to being innate are (1) that what is, is and (2) that one thing cannot be and not be at the same time. These principles, even though they need no other proof, cannot be innate because they do not command universal assent; they are not already within each new-born child and they are not known by all people. In addition, if moral principles are innate and accepted on their own authority and without examination, then how can 'anyone's principles [ ] be questioned?' (2004, 90).

The logic of Locke's argument here is Neoplatonic. If such principles were imprinted on the mind of the child at birth, then the mind would have to know and perceive them. But it would offend the law of non-contradiction for something to be in the mind but not perceived, or in the understanding but not understood, because this would require it to be and not to be at the same time. It would be a further contradiction to argue that a man needs reason to discover the innate principles that he already knows, for here a man would know and not know them at the same time. As we will see later, it is Locke's positing of thought as an instrument, combined with his Neoplatonic principles of non-contradiction that rules out the possibility of the innate being known negatively in and as its own form and content, or as recollection. In the absence of the innate and of recollection, and as is well-known from Locke, the mind is established as a *tabula rasa*, 'white paper, void of all characters, without any ideas' (2004, 109), and furnished by way of direct experience of objects in sensation and reflection. Locke's task then becomes that of discerning the correct conduct of the understanding in the absence of innate principles.

Correct conduct here is essentially demonstrative method. Too many men, he notes, are satisfied with their own limited knowledge, embracing 'error for certainty' (1996, 175) and eschewing the habit of rational deductive understanding. The task for the understanding is to 'establish the truth beyond doubt' (1996, 180) in the ways described earlier. This requires that man lay his own prejudices open to argument and rigorously examine himself. Evidence must overcome prejudice and true opinion will be loved for no other reason than that it is true. This true endeavour can easily be corrupted when men 'espouse opinions that best comport with their power, profit, or credit, and then seek arguments to support them' (1996, 189). Too often, he bemoans, the mind 'is amused with uncertainties' (1996, 190) when it should be securing truth by demonstration. The rational creature must pursue truth freely and for himself, and not trust anything on the authority of others. Even though human nature – being human – cannot 'be perfectly kept from error' (1996, 211), says Locke, 'I never saw any reason yet why truth might not be trusted on its own evidence' (1996, 212). This is man's defence against error. In reason God has ensured that 'the candle, that is set up in us, shines brightly enough for all our purposes' (2004, 57). Indeed, '*viresque acquirit eundo*' (1996, 215) – it acquires force as it goes.[9]

In addition, although the idea of God is not innate, God has given man what he needs in order to discover God's work and purpose. If children were to be placed on a deserted island having no notion of God, they would still conclude his existence from the constitution and causes of things around them, which, once arrived at, would 'propagate and continue amongst them' (2004, 96).

## Thought as instrument

A case can be made for Locke being a gateway to the modern Western philosophical mind, even though it is not necessarily a gateway he would have approved of. We saw earlier how he returns to Neoplatonic logic for his own work, and how even though existence and non-contradiction are not innate principles, they are intuitive certainties. However, these Neoplatonic certainties in Locke carry their own culture of error – not in the mediaeval form of aporia and ambivalence, but in the new rationalist spirit where reason knows itself to be all reality, and wherein nothing is known without it. In fact, Locke posits reason as *separate* from a culture in which it can be experienced as re-forming itself. Thus, it acts as the standard of truth for everything except the conditions of the possibility of its being known by itself within the contradictions that ensue.

This becomes apparent in the beginning of the *Essay* when Locke discusses thought as an instrument. His aim is to make the understanding its own object in thought, its own idea, so that in employing it as the instrument for seeking true knowledge, the mind will restrict itself only to what the understanding is capable of. This is a task with phenomenological significance which, however, Locke pursues without phenomenology. In line with the principles of non-contradiction, cause and effect, and the absurdity of infinite regression, he separates the instrument from the truth it seeks, for it is deemed an error for thought to be seen as truth. Pure substance is retained by Locke as unknowable because it is mediated by reason. His rationalism grants direct experience of objects only at the cost of truth itself. Thinking thought as an instrument, separate from truth, posits thought according to Neoplatonic logic. Indeed, an enquiry into the correct conduct of human understanding carries this positing with it. It presumes that truth and thought are contradictory to each other, because thought involves the error of the infinite regression of cause and effect that only the truth – uncorrupted by such thought – can ultimately prevent. Or, again, the instrument is separated from the content which it thinks, in such a way as to rule out the very possibility that Locke seeks, namely, that the understanding becomes its own object.

Locke's rationalism, then, is of reason as a method abstracted from its experiences of being so posited. The very culture that is unavoidable for reason here is suppressed so that it can be employed as an instrument that conforms to its own limits regarding its objects. But these limits are not proved. They are already posited in the nature of the task that has been set. Locke's rationalism therefore faces backwards in refusing contradiction as substance, and in holding that the understanding must conform to its object. As such, he rules out metaphysics and a science of the logic of reason. But he points towards the modern mind in holding reason as universal human understanding. For Locke, this universality must rid itself of the scholastic baggage of equivocation, ambiguity, and confusion which is grounded in a lack of rationality, in order for reason to assert its sovereignty. But *without such equivocation*, reason loses its actuality. This will be recovered in Kant and Hegel, who will retrieve culture now within the universality of reason and retrieve therein education and re-formation, this time for a reason that is sovereign, but not yet (in Locke and Rationalist philosophy) vulnerable to or in this sovereignty. Reason, in the rationalist philosophy of Descartes, Spinoza, Leibniz, and Locke has become the principle of all life. What now awaits it, once again, is to retrieve death from within this life.

# Part III  Modern Philosophical Education

# 6
## The Modern Mind

### Introduction

The modern mind gives voice to the re-formations of thought that have occurred in the history of Western philosophy. It is the mind that is now able to speak of itself as determined within the cultures of error, and as the actuality of the learning of this (self-) determination. As such, the modern mind is a present recollection of itself. This recollection can be stated in a number of ways. It is the retrieval of death in life, of the slave in the master, of truth in error, and of Hegel in Kant. It also retrieves the social relation in the metaphysical relation. Essentially, it is the groundlessness of modern thought whose ground or truth lies in this, its self-negation. In this chapter we will describe some of the shapes of this groundlessness from Kant and Hegel to Derrida. In the final chapter below we will think this groundlessness as the standpoint of the West in relation to God, to the other, and to death.

We have seen above how the history of Western philosophy has struggled to reconcile thought with truth because it has posited the aporetic thinking of truth, or culture, as error compared to truth in itself. But the ubiquity of culture becomes the universality of modern reason. It is where reason knows universality not in the object, but in the work of knowing the object. The modern mind is grounded in the equivocation of its mediation of all things. Its search for truth now returns to itself, specifically to try to comprehend how it is the condition of the possibility of the experience of objects. It looks to these conditions, now, as the truth of all knowing. This modern mind is Kant (1724–1804) and Hegel (1770–1831), and some of the shapes that their relation has taken are explored later as Marx (1818–83), Adorno (1903–69) and Habermas

115

(1929–), Kierkegaard (1813–55), Nietzsche (1844–1900), Heidegger (1889–1976) and Derrida (1930–2004).

## Kant

Kant's *Critique of Pure Reason* (1791/87) sets out to discover the conditions of the possibility of our experiencing of objects. He argues first that experience requires objects in time and space that can be intuited by the senses. This *a priori* sensibility is the transcendental aesthetic. Second, there must also exist the conditions by which intuitions become known in ideas. These ideas can be *a posteriori* if they are grounded in empirical objects and *a priori* if they deal solely with ideas. In the latter Kant makes possible a metaphysics – one where thought can be its own logical form and content – where before him the cultures of error posited only the unknowable. This metaphysical form and content is transcendental logic. It would be wrong to see the transcendental aesthetic and the transcendental logic as independent of each other. Kant famously observes that since the understanding can intuit nothing, and the senses can think nothing, so 'only through their union can knowledge arise' (Kant, 1968, 93). 'Without sensibility no object would be given to us, without understanding no object would be thought. Thoughts without content are empty, intuitions without concepts are blind' (1968, 93).

The advance here in the history of Western philosophy is that reason accepts its being the unavoidable mediation of all objects of knowledge. Its task now is to know itself *as* this mediation. Here emerges the Janus face of Kant's philosophy. Culture is no longer eschewed as error, but neither, as we will see, is it comprehended as its own truth.

Kant divides the transcendental logic into analytic and dialectic. The analytic explores the concepts that ground the understanding and the principles by which concepts express sensible reality. This is the question of truth for it concerns the criteria for judging 'the agreement of knowledge with its object' (1968, 97). But such criteria need to find a correspondence between the knowledge of all objects and one object. Kant acknowledges that it would be 'absurd' (1968, 97) to unite universal and particular in the latter. Since the matter of the object is precisely what defines it as not general, a criterion of agreement based on the particular 'would by its very nature be self-contradictory' (1968, 98). According to the law of non-contradiction, then, truth must rest in the transcendental logic of forms that are uncorrupted and uncompounded by particular matter. This logic, 'in so far as it expounds the universal and necessary rules of the understanding, must in these rules furnish criteria of truth' (1968, 98).

Kant here is mediaeval in holding form, matter, universal, and particular apart according to the law of non-contradiction, but modern in exploring the conditions of the possibility of non-contradiction as logic in their own right. This ambivalence in Kant is found in the possibility for logic to be non-contradictory but also to be in contradiction with its object. The logic of pure reason is 'the negative condition of all truth. But further than this logic cannot go. It has no touchstone for the discovery of such error as concerns not the form but the content' (1968, 98). The logic of thought is always correct, and error is restricted to the thinking of objects. On this basis Kant distinguishes himself from the Ancients, for whom logic was dialectical, and who treated logic not as a canon of judgement but as an organon of objective knowledge. Logic, with them, says Kant, was 'never anything else than a *logic of illusion*' (1968, 99), a 'sophistical art of giving to ignorance ... the appearance of truth' (1968, 99). They held that the transcendental logic of the form of understanding was transferable to the knowledge of the content of particular objects. In a distinction, then, that both champions and suppresses the education of the modern mind, Kant states that 'logic teaches us nothing whatsoever regarding the content of knowledge, but lays down only the formal conditions of agreement with the understanding' (1968, 99). This distinction becomes the transcendental analytic and the transcendental dialectic. The former is 'a logic of truth' (1968, 100) dealing with the 'elements of the pure knowledge yielded by understanding, and the principles without which no object can be thought' (1968, 100). But there can be no *a priori* knowledge of things, and in the transcendental dialectic Kant guards against the extension of transcendental logic beyond its own sphere of validity, against, that is, 'sophistical illusion' (1968, 101).

Here Kant claims to overturn the cultures of error in the history of Western philosophy. His Copernican revolution reverses the presupposition that knowledge must conform to objects, arguing now that objects must conform to knowledge. He asserts here the priority of metaphysics. The understanding has rules *a priori* that both precede and are independent of the objects they perceive. It is these *a priori* rules, and their concepts and principles, to which the object must conform. These rules are not given in or by experience; they are what make experience comprehensible. Thus, and famously, Kant says, 'the conditions of the *possibility of experience* in general are likewise conditions of the *possibility of the objects of experience*, and for this reason they have objective validity in a synthetic *a priori* judgement' (1968, 194). With this, Kant seeks to overturn the cultures of error which posited contradiction as other than truth, and, in finding contradiction in thought, therein judged thought as error. He tries to separate the logic and truth of thought from its illegitimate extension to the knowledge of objects. Against centuries of philosophy which held thought unable to know the true, now Kant finds truth in thought itself. He offers 'the secure path of a science ... [which] enables us to explain how there can be knowledge *a priori*' (1968, 23). It is absolutely revolutionary in the history of Western philosophy for Kant here to find truth in reason, and to claim that 'we can know *a priori* of things only what we ourselves put into them' (1968, 23). It is this radical aspect of the Kantian revolution that defines the modern mind, and which is referred to below when describing the Kantian shape of this modern mind.

However, the Kantian revolution that promotes reason as universal also backs away from the infinite reduction threatened by having truth as the effect of thought. Here Kant holds to one further culture of error. He argues that 'we can never transcend the limits of possible experience' (1968, 24) and that as such the knowledge gained is always conditioned. Positing truth in Neoplatonic fashion here as unconditioned, he concludes that *a priori* knowledge 'has to do only with appearances' (1968, 24) and, therefore, – and 'therefore' here is a mediaeval logic – 'must leave the thing in itself as indeed real *per se*, but not as known by us' (1968, 24). This culture of error opposes the full implications of the Kantian metaphysical revolution. Thought cannot think the unconditional without contradiction because a representation of the unconditional in thought is posited as an oxymoron. On the other hand, when it is supposed that representation does not conform to objects as they are in themselves, 'but that these objects, as appearances, conform to our mode of representation, *the contradiction vanishes*' (1968, 24). Logic, for Kant here, is 'the negative condition of all truth' (1968, 98) and, conforming to the Neoplatonic positing of truth that having negation as its other, as negative it cannot also be true. Thus, *a priori* synthetic judgements have their objectivity in the correspondence of two conditions: the possibility of experience and the possibility of objects of experience. But together they do not arrive at knowledge of truth in itself. In this way, Kant's transcendental logic is mediaeval and modern. It is the modern philosophical version of the metaphysics that knows that God exists but not what God is. It is of greater philosophical significance than mediaeval metaphysics because it extends this insight from God to the whole of what is understood and (not) known. Metaphysics comes of age here because the conditions of its own possibility are now its own groundless foundation. It is not just God that can be known as not known, it is everything, including metaphysics itself. What makes Kantian metaphysics so universally destructive of assertion and illusion, is also what robs that metaphysics of any ground beyond its being the negative condition of all truth. Thus, Kant's view is mediaeval in being only negative in relation to truth, but is ground-breaking and essentially modern in extending negativity to the mediaeval view. Essentially Kant articulates the ground of metaphysics as the negation of the negative relation to God in the history of Western philosophy to date. Kant universalizes the presupposition that thought is error in comparison to what is true in itself, and in doing so points modernity forward to the metaphysics of the totality of contingency. But at the same time he continues to lean on the presupposition that this unavoidable totality is still error when compared to truth. Kant's metaphysics here is truly the crossroads where the mediaeval and modern meet, but while he yields to modernity the conditions of its possibility, Kant himself does not yield fully to these conditions.

Kant's Neoplatonism is evident in the culture of error that he retains. He holds cause and effect as pure *a priori* concepts or categories, relieving them therein of any actuality as recollection in the conditions of the possibility of experience. Equally, the positing of the conditioned as error remains justified in a Neoplatonic view of the absurdity of infinite regression, for 'what necessarily forces us to transcend the limits of experience and of all appearances is the *unconditioned*, which reason, by necessity and right, demands in things themselves, as required to complete the series of conditions' (1968, 24).

Kant sought the unconditioned in the will in his *Critique of Practical Reason* and in the imagination and the principles of pleasure and dependence in his *Critique of Judgement*. That he was forced to do so is witness to the dialectic between thought and object that metaphysics repeats but does not overcome. Subsumptive judgements are not pure. Rather they bear witness to a power struggle that pure reason cannot avoid. The hope that the unconditioned might be found in pure practical reason is also dashed when duty appears within a dialectic of power over both nature and the imagination. The third *Critique*, finally, is itself in dialectical struggle with the other two *Critiques*, something recognized in Kant's attempt therein to ground principles in the conditional or the particular. Whichever way Kant shakes the dice he cannot avoid throwing a dialectic between the pure and its corruption by its others. This whole problem stems from and is grounded in the mediaeval remnants in Kant of the positing of thought as error. Thought, as error, will always be constituted by a dialectic of power with its others, precisely because it has eschewed a notion of otherness as part of the truth of itself. Until it sees the truth of error, thought will work in the illusions of thought that does not know itself.

## Hegel

Hegel completes Kant's metaphysical revolution, but in such a way as to change our understanding of what 'completes' means here.

As with Locke, Kant seeks to examine the faculty of cognition prior to its enquiry into truth in order to ascertain its suitability for such work. Hegel's criticism of this is twofold. First, it posits truth separate from thought, and second it therein already employs truth – that is supposedly the object of the enquiry – prior to the enquiry. Even though Kant agrees 'we can never transcend the limits of possible experience' (1968, 24), his positing of truth as unconditional is nevertheless the condition of the possibility of separating truth from thought. For Hegel here, 'to examine this so-called instrument is the same thing as to know it' (Hegel, 1975, 14). Indeed, to hold to the possibility of examining thought before using it 'is as absurd as the wise resolution of Scholasticus, not to venture into the water until he had learned to swim' (1975, 14).[1] In short, the conditions of the possibility of experience being likewise the conditions of the possibility of objects of experience, applies just the same to the method of the critical philosophy. Thought is already the instrument and the object of the enquiry. Truth, here, asks to be understood within this negation of its unconditional ground.

This request is met by Hegel in the *Science of Logic* in such a way as to complete the metaphysical revolution begun by Kant, by re-forming the Neoplatonic principles that have guided the history of Western philosophy to this point. In the 'Introduction', Hegel argues that it has been a prejudice of the history of Western philosophy that form must be abstracted from content, containing nothing of its own, and that it only has content when it fills itself with something external to it. This is to assume that form cannot be its own content and cannot be known in and for itself. This is the presupposition that Kantian critical philosophy both exposes – in arguing that thought should no longer have to conform to its object – and also repeats – by arguing that truth cannot conform to its being known. In a way, says Hegel, ancient metaphysics did better than Kant for it understood that 'the knowledge of things obtained through thinking is alone what is really true in them'

(Hegel, 1969, 45). Anaxagoras laid 'the foundation for an intellectual view of the universe' (1969, 50) and Aristotle tried to turn metaphysics into logic by turning the conditions of the possibility of human experience in the universe into a collection of definitions and propositions. That the critical philosophy neither rejects this nor advances it, gives the appearance that the system of logic is complete. This should be evidence enough, says Hegel, that logic in fact is 'in need of a total reconstruction; for spirit, after its labours over two thousand years, must have attained to a higher consciousness about its thinking and about its own pure, essential nature' (1969, 51).[2]

The history of Western philosophy for Hegel, and as we have presented it earlier, has been dominated by *reflective* understanding. The reflective subject is life posited as identity, and death and loss posited as other. As such, a content that is negated in being thought, is a content other than its being thought. The *a posteriori* as a category is subjective logic, or the positing of experience as error against the objective logic of unconditional, unthinkable *a priori* truth. What is ruled out here is metaphysics *per se*, or that the experience of logic can be its own form and content. The *Phenomenology of Spirit* chronicles ways in which the Western mind's pursuit of truth repeats the incompatibility and incommensurability of objective logic of thought and the subjective experience of that logic. Logic, by its own Neoplatonic definition, rules out the possibility of its own form and content as metaphysics. As such, the history of Western philosophy is the history of the misrecognition of logic in reflective thinking because reflective thinking posits logic separated from itself. The contradictory experiences that result, further entrench the logic of reflection. Even the critical philosophy, which knows the groundless universality of experience, takes against contradiction, as life takes against death. Reflective reason, as such, has no life of its own. It fails to recognize that 'the contradiction is precisely the rising of reason above the limitations of the understanding and the resolving of them' (1969, 46). 'Resolving' here is *Auflösen*. In this context it means that reason sees itself learning about itself, just as in Plato the sun sees itself shining. What is 'resolved' here is the separation of reason as the condition of the possibility of experience from reason as an object of that experience. But experience is not somehow at an end here. It is continuing but with form and content known as education by education, rather than eschewed merely as error. In the Neoplatonic history of Western philosophy, thought and form were never considered 'on their own merits and according to their own peculiar content' (1969, 47).

Hegel then sets out to show how the Kantian revolution can be pushed further in order that the contradictory experience of logic becomes its own form and content in philosophical learning. Here Hegel is prepared to accept death or loss as part of the truth of the Kantian revolution. The critical philosophy has already 'turned metaphysics into logic' (1969, 51) by noting that the conditions of the possibility of experience were also the conditions of the possibility of objects of experience. Kant proved 'the objectivity of the illusion' (1969, 56; italics removed) that thought should conform to the object, and 'the necessity of the contradiction which belongs to the nature of thought determinations' (1969, 56; italics removed). But this logic was itself refused as an object of experience, and thus the conditions were kept apart from any subjective logic that might come to know its own truth. As such, the thing in itself remained 'a beyond' (1969, 51). Kant's chief aim was 'to vindicate the *categories* of self-consciousness as the *subjective ego*. By virtue of this determination the point of view remains confined within consciousness and its opposition' (1969, 62). As a result, 'it has something left over, a *thing-in-itself*, something alien and external to thought' (1969, 62).

## The notion

Hegel acknowledges that the Kantian synthetic judgement *a priori* is a profound development in the history of Western philosophy, recognizing as it does the groundlessness that inheres when the conditions of the possibility of experience are also the conditions of the possibility of objects of experience. Indeed, 'it contains the beginning of a true apprehension of the nature of the Notion' (1969, 589). But Kant does not let the synthesis speak for itself. Hegel notes that 'the very expression *synthesis* easily recalls the conception of an *external* unity and a *mere combination* of entities that are *intrinsically separate*,' (1969, 589) both encouraging and in itself reproducing the misrepresentation of spirit as essentially reflective. Thus, at the same time as prioritizing the subjective thinking-ego over objects, Kant retains the ancient prejudice that thought – and dialectical thought in particular – is error. He grants no possibility to thought having aporetic learning as its own form and content, and cannot therefore think the conditions of the possibility of categories in relation to each other as *thought as such*. When relieved of this prejudice thought will be seen to have 'within itself the capacity to *determine* itself, that is, to give itself a content ... in the form of a system of determinations of thought' (1969, 63). Seen positively, now, and as actual self-determination, contradiction posited as error in the Neoplatonic history of Western philosophy is 'nothing else but the inner negativity of the determinations as their self-moving soul, the principle of all natural and spiritual life' (1969, 56). There is, says Hegel, only stupidity in the presuppositions that 'infinity is different from finitude, that content is other than form [and] that the inner is other than the outer' (1969, 41).

This form that is content is the notion. First, it is the notion in the form of being, that is, as it is in itself. This is the shape of objective logic. Second, it is the notion existing for itself, free and self-determining. It is the subject, and as such is subjective logic. It is where substance becomes itself, freely and necessarily. This self-relation of form and content is a critique of traditional metaphysics which posited form devoid of content. This metaphysics intended to explain the world objectively, as we have seen earlier, by positing thought, with its dependence on content, as error, leaving pure form floating freely above the corruption of being known finitely. Now, in Hegel and in the notion, objective logic is substance known in itself, known, that is, as the positing that deems it unknowable; and subjective logic is this positing having the illusion of substance *as its own self-determination*. This self is subject. It is the individual who knows itself determined in the negation of its illusory objective standpoint.

> This infinite reflection-into-self, namely, that being is in and for itself only in so far as it is posited, is the *consummation of substance*. But this consummation is no longer *substance* itself but something higher, the *Notion*, the *subject*. The transition of the relation of substantiality takes place through its own immanent necessity and is nothing more than the manifestation of itself, that the Notion is the truth, and that freedom is the truth of necessity.
>
> (1969, 580)

We will explore in Chapter 7 what this freedom looks like in the modern world.

## Groundless philosophy

Hegel is well aware of the mess that this creates for philosophy and for the thinking of truth. Famously he says that the true is 'the Bacchanalian revel in which no member is not drunk' (Hegel, 1977, 27). He recognizes too how philosophy will seek an easier path for itself. Thus, in the *Shorter Logic* he defines philosophy not in terms of the critical method, but in terms of logical aporia. When thought becomes not just the condition of the possibility of experience, but also the condition of its own possibility as an object of experience, it therein 'comes to itself' (Hegel, 1975, 15). But in doing so 'thought entangles itself in contradictions, i.e. loses itself in the hard-and-fast non-identity of its thoughts' (1975, 15). Critical thought resists this as far as truth is concerned. But Hegel does not. He resists protecting thought from its own logical contradictions, and does so by refusing to presuppose that truth must be different from such contradictions, refusing, that is, to believe that truth is different from the way every other object of thought is known. 'To see that thought in its very nature is dialectical, and that, as understanding, it must fall into contradiction – the negative of itself – will form one of the main lessons of logic' (1975, 15).

What is at stake between Kant and Hegel is the nature of illusion. For Kant, dialectic is illusion when it tries to bring the transcendental analytic into the actual world of objective propositions, for it achieves only an appearance of truth, while in fact failing to comprehend truth *a priori* in the conditions of the possibility of understanding and judgement. For Hegel the *a priori* is illusion when it tries to protect itself from the dialectic of its being known, for it achieves only the appearance of truth while in fact avoiding what truth must learn of itself from being known. What Kant finds to be illusion and error, Hegel finds to be phenomenology and necessity. Rather than avoid contradiction in the thinking of truth, Hegel is able to embrace it as precisely what learning about truth looks like. In the *Phenomenology* he describes this as 'the pathway of *doubt*' (1977, 49) that thought cannot avoid if it is willing to learn from itself, about itself, when it makes itself its own object. The mind can view such difficulty as undesirable and seek to return to a more peaceful way of life where the thought of truth can be kept from its own dialectic. But if philosophy is being honest with regard to what its experiences are teaching it, it will know that thought cannot provide for itself such peace. Its integrity is at stake here. Consciousness suffers the violence of the unrest of the dialectic at its own hands. It disrupts any and every standpoint that thought might wish to insist upon.

> When consciousness feels this violence, its anxiety may well make it retreat from the truth, and strive to hold on to what it is in danger of losing. But it can find no peace. If thought wishes to remain in a state of unthinking inertia, then thought troubles its thoughtlessness, and its own unrest disturbs its inertia.
>
> (1977, 51)

## Neoplatonism against itself

Hegel's completion of the Kantian revolution finally yields the logic of Neoplatonic principles that has been suppressed in and by reflective understanding. This completion, however, does not mean a finality or an end to the history of Western philosophy. It means, rather, that thought finally undermines the last refuge of reflective thought. In the *Phenomenology* Hegel states that if it is the fear of thought falling into error that creates mistrust of thought, in comparison, say, to revelation or even to the synthetic *a priori* judgement, then 'it is hard to see why we should not turn round and mistrust this very mistrust' (1977, 47). In a question that finally demands that positing in philosophy be made its own immanent enquiry, he asks, 'should we not be concerned as to whether the fear of error is not just the error itself?' (1977, 47).

This is to ask that Neoplatonic principles in the history of Western philosophy finally be held to account for their positing of truth as other than thought, as unchangeable, as unconditional, and as simple, and for positing the absurdity of infinite regression and the necessity of a first cause. This positing of philosophical principles has been the condition of the possibility of Western philosophical work. They have been the essence of philosophy in that, as Duns Scotus remarked, 'we experience that we assent to propositions such as the first principles without a possibility of error or contradiction' (Duns Scotus, 1987, 142). But for Hegel, the idea that thought is error is an error of thought. It is the error that 'presupposes that the Absolute stands on one side and cognition on the other' (1977, 47), or that truth must be different from its being known or thought. Yet, as Hegel showed in regard to the critical philosophy, what is deemed incapable of knowing truth is the same instrument used to state such a truth. For Hegel this leads to an obvious and necessary truth of its own; that truth *is* known when it is not known. What other conclusion could thought arrive at than the one that stares it in the face, even though in doing so it disrupts the whole basis of the history of Western philosophy? Perhaps another conclusion might be that, with Kant, this conclusion itself posits a correspondence between the conditions of the possibility of experience and of objects of experience, which grants a sovereignty to thought that is illegitimate, or at worst, imperial. Hegel's reply to such criticism, in keeping with the critical philosophy, is that there is nothing that does not contain the immediacy and mediation – the experience – of its being cognized. In fact, it is an illegitimate presupposition of sovereignty that it *cannot* or *should not* be known in this way. The criticism that Kant and Hegel grant sovereignty to thought presumes for itself greater sovereignty in doing so than the Notion claims for itself. It is a much more common view of Hegel that he has established the idea of truth or the absolute over and against the groundlessness of the conditional nature of knowledge. In fact, the real picture here is precisely the opposite. Hegel has yielded truth to its own logic, and logic to its own truth, in comprehending that truth *is* the groundlessness of the conditional.

## Kantian and Hegelian modernity

Modernity is the Hegelian experience of Kantian experience. It is the self-consciousness of division, no longer as alienation but as a formative education. As we argued earlier, the Kantian revolution reveals the groundlessness of thought and of the object of thought. Hegel comprehends the re-formative import of the groundlessness of the Kantian revolution to be logic and metaphysics, or the notion. Kantian and Hegelian modernity, then, is the re-education of life regarding death, of the master regarding the slave, of truth regarding Neoplatonic conceptions of error, and of thought regarding negation.

But neither Kant nor Hegel alone is the experience of modernity. Kantian experience without Hegel is empty, for it does not have its own form and content in logic and metaphysics. Hegelian experience without Kant risks immunity from the actual negative experience of abstraction. True, Hegelian experience carries with it the groundlessness of mediation, and in this sense contains Kantian experience within it. But, as many interpretations of Hegel bear witness to, an abstract reading of Hegel finds only bare assertion of unity, missing the work of the Kantian experience that determines it. Such readings are found in supporters and critics of Hegel alike. Hegelians who argue that the ladder to the *Science of Logic*, that is, the *Phenomenology of Spirit*, can be kicked away, threaten to rob logic and metaphysics of their groundlessness in reason. This would leave the absolute in Hegel as an assertion abstracted from social and political experience, something that such commentators would then have in common with those who read Hegel as the anti-democratic, self-appointed sovereignty of Western reason and as the master discourse. What this misses, in effect, is the Kantian experience in the Hegelian experience. Just because the science of logic is its own form and content does not mean it is independent of the experiences that are formative of that form and content. Logic is not a replacement for experience, it is the philosophy of experience. Such a philosophy is recollection, and recollection, as the *Aufhebung*, retains what it negates.[3] This is why modernity is Hegelian and Kantian, and is, in passing, that in which the contradictions of modern bourgeois social relations persist, known but not overcome. Modernity is the age of the notion, but remains within the relation of master and slave, self and other, life and death, and God and man.[4] It is the age of aporetic philosophical education about itself. It is where culture as re-formation becomes itself as reason and as enlightenment, but also where culture returns against itself as the self-(re-)formation of this identity of reason.

Modernity is also Kantian and Hegelian in spirit. Spirit refers to the way that mind knows itself. It appears as different social and political shapes at different times in the history of Western philosophy. We have seen it appear as an abstract totality in the Ancient world, or as a template of spirit without the self-determination that exists as the question of freedom. In the mediaeval cultures of error, spirit was mind knowing itself as alienated from truth and blaming itself for the alienation. Now, in modernity, reason is mind knowing itself as the unavoidable totality of what is to blame. This is one of its most difficult and confusing shapes, because modern reason has its ground in the free individual. In the cultures of error it learned that the I, as the interminable source of the corruption of the true, was also unavoidable in relation to (the failure to know) the true. The I, at first blamed for corrupting the true, now has this unavoidable universality as its own ground, a ground known by itself as needing no other. Modern reason, therefore, is positive as the universality of the negation of (alienated) truth. It is where error becomes itself as the rational I, or as the groundlessness of its being the conditions of the possibility of experience and the conditions of the possibility of objects of experience. Error becomes reason in Kant, but this does not mean that Kant is wrong. When postmodern critics lambast reason for its self-appointed sovereignty, they fail to understand that spirit, here, builds its house on the universality of negation, not assertion. This becomes significant when reason investigates itself in philosophy, for it means that spirit is absolute only when it negates itself. This is hardly the strategy of something aiming at world domination.

Two observations remain here regarding the truth of reason as error having its actuality as the truth of the rational individual. These are, first, the complications that beset spirit in trying to recognize itself as modern reason, and second, the implications for philosophy, and for the *metaphysical* and *social* relations in particular, of this difficulty.

Spirit as modern reason is not clearly apparent to itself. It is the condition of its own possibility, but this, its actuality, appears as the natural consciousness of the reflective individual. Paradoxically, then, the modern shape that spirit takes as the condition of the possibility of its being known, is to appear as its opposite, as not conditioned at all. It is in this misrecognition of spirit by itself that modern reason is sovereign as the free Western individual. But spirit in modernity exists as an *actual* individual. When this actual individual seeks to comprehend its truth, it is faced with the problem of somehow speaking of the unity, the collective truth, of each sovereign individual. As we will see later, this defines the antinomy of modern social and political thought. What spirit means in and for modernity is that the search for the truth of the modern mind is autodestructive or autoimmune. It attacks and undermines itself. This is because what it seeks – spirit – has already taken the shape that makes the search necessary. The conditions that pre-determine the search are the same conditions that determine its failure. If this was a culture of error, spirit would interpret this failure as a weakness of the I, and try to re-form itself in likeness of that which is without error. But in modernity, spirit as reason can no longer sacrifice itself without returning to itself aware of the hypocrisy that this is still rational work. Spirit, here, has to learn something different about itself, and this is that its universality lies in the aporia of its experience of itself that is both Kantian and Hegelian.

The second implication of the aporetic shape of modern spirit concerns the fate of philosophy. When error becomes the universal negativity of reason, reason takes positive and concrete shape *without* error, that is, without the experiences that have been its re-formative self-determination. These errors are the truth of reason, and although they are out of sight now, they are not out of mind. Kant established modern reason as the universality of error by recognizing that the conditions of the possibility of experience were likewise the conditions of the possibility of objects of experience. Yet he also granted *a priori* pure reason immunity from this rational ground-lessness. This imports into modernity a division which will definitively characterize it, namely, the division of theory and practice such that any universality of the former and particularity of the latter are forever cast as incommensurable. Reason now has its actuality in an impossible totality: to unite that whose conditions of possibility are division. Reason pre-determines itself as the division of theory and practice, and all attempts at unification are already premised on the identity of division. This is the aporetic shape of modern reason, and in practical philosophy it is the division of legality and morality, necessity and freedom, and autonomy and heteronomy.

But, as we have seen, the aporia of modern reason has more to teach us. Thought as error is the dualism of theory and practice. This means that philosophy is the divide thinking itself, but can only appear as divided in doing so. This is its natural appearance. Philosophy reacts badly to its modern appearance when it abstracts itself from division, and works only formally. Such formal philosophizing is a *ressentiment* against spirit, against the social and political shape that mind takes in modernity in seeking to know itself. The philosophy of this modern appearance of truth has been pursued best and most faithfully by those for whom philosophy is social and political theory, or the aporia of theory and practice pursued by itself.

How and where, then, has modernity tried to make sense of its Kantian and Hegelian constitution? It is the loosely termed European or Continental style of philosophizing that has sought to work within the pre-determined conditions of the divide between theory and practice and tried to find ways of expressing the aporetic totality of doing so. It is to this Kantian and Hegelian tradition then that the history of Western philosophy must look if it is to find the truth of thought as error challenging itself to think itself in the social relations that are its modern appearance. We will look at seven representatives of this tradition now, who all share the concern to think the truth of modern social and political relations. In them, the social relation returns to a relation with the metaphysical relation such that the totality of spirit might again announce itself, even if only in the aporias that present it. In this sense our seven philosophers are all philosophers of spirit. They are united perhaps behind Adorno's claim that 'politics aimed at the formation of a reasonable and mature mankind remain under an evil spell, as long as they lack a theory that takes account of the totality that is false' (Adorno, 1991a, 28). But they are not all united by the conclusions they draw from such difficulty. If anything characterizes the Continental tradition, it has been a concern to protect the notion from any dogmatic or ideological totalizing. The cost has often been to miss the ways in which such protection is also ideological.[5]

## Marx

Marx's political philosophy is Kantian in the modern sense of working with the groundlessness of reason wherein the conditions of the possibility of experience are likewise the conditions of the possibility of objects of experience. This is expressed in his notion of ideology where the material conditions of experience are likewise the material conditions of the production of objects of experience. This is a powerful addition to Kant's revolution in metaphysics, arguing that the conditions of the possibility of experience are of a historically and socially specific type, those of modern capital and labour.

When Marx is writing against Hegel he prioritizes the material over the intellectual, asserting that 'it is not the consciousness of men that determines their existence, but their social existence that determines their consciousness' (Marx, 1975, 425). Equally, Marx rejects the Hegelian experience of groundlessness as spirit by positing a new and not yet present social relation. Communism is to be the truth or the resolution of the antinomy of theory and practice. This attempt to know Kantian modernity in a way different from Hegel in effect returns the experience of capital and labour as ideology to ideology. Communism is based not on the actuality of political experience, but on positing political experience as error in comparison to a truth that resolves the groundlessness in Marx's notion of self-determining species being. The return of this positing to the ideological conditions of its own possibility is the culture of Marx's social philosophy. But, lacking any recognition of such a culture, the ideological subject of modernity is denied its own truth. The result is that Marxist revolution is re-formed by its own conditions of possibility. Assertion against such re-forming is inevitably a terror over and against actuality or present consciousness. The assumption that knowing the ideological conditions of the possibility of experience and its objects is no longer ideological, is itself ideological, grounded in the positing of actual thought as error. Its tyranny consists in suppressing the metaphysics of appearance wherein ideology is itself known ideologically.

However, when less self-consciously trying to turn Hegel on his head, Marx approaches the totality of Kantian and Hegelian modernity in his theory of commodity fetishism. The relation between capital and labour is the condition of the possibility of social and political experience. It is likewise the condition of the possibility of its being an object of this experience. The object that contains these conditions of possibility, expressing them as natural rather than as produced within a specific mode of production, is the commodity. The commodity expresses the totality that is false, but by way of its illusion as a natural object. The social relation that men enter into in order to produce the goods needed for their survival appears as a metaphysical relation between objects. In this appearance the social relation appears as the natural law of individuals and their competition against each other for resources. The conditions of the possibility of this appearance appear completely separated from experience, and belong to the metaphysics of the commodity rather than the community.

In the appearance of the commodity, then, the social relation and the metaphysical relation – themselves the groundlessness of modern reason – hide their relation to each other; the social in the autonomy of the free wage labourer and the metaphysical in the natural appearance, that is, exchange value. Commodities usurp the social and metaphysical relation that in truth belongs to the modern mind, or spirit. properly speaking express the truth of modernity.

## Adorno and Habermas

The problem of the totality that ideology takes in the commodity as the condition of the possibility of experience and of objects of experience, is taken up by Hegelian Marxism around reification and objectification, in particular within the critical theory of the Frankfurt school. The aporia that accompanies reflection upon the form of modern reason that is groundless in the totality of ideology is expressed in the relation of the dialectic of enlightenment, which itself is expressed in the relation between Adorno and Habermas.

Adorno attempts to express social relations within the logic of the commodity. This logic is Kantian in that its totality is groundless and in that this totality is grounded in an ideological self-reproduction of the conditions of possibility determined by capital and labour. The ambition here is Hegelian in that it attempts to think this totality in full awareness of its being compromised by its complicity within these conditions. For Kant this vicious circle is dialectical illusion. For Marx it is self-determining *praxis*. But for Adorno it is a challenge to think the whole even though it is false. The dialectic of enlightenment thinks the whole of the conditions of the possibility of experience to be corrupted and negative in their expression as objects, and thus as myth, and thinks the whole of the conditions of the possibility of objects of experience to be groundless in their conformity to that myth. The latter is enlightenment regarding the myth of enlightenment. The dialectic of enlightenment, here, is the logic of culture or reform that becomes commodity or industry, wherein, as Adorno remarked, 'no theory today escapes the marketplace' (Adorno, 1973, 4).

Adorno's melancholy at the implications of the dialectic of modernity stems from his rigour in holding to the totality that is false. He is sanguine about the possibility for revolutionary change and is treated badly by his students towards the end of his life. He was made well aware that 'suffering caused by a negative condition – in this case by obstructed reality – turns into anger toward the person who expresses it' (Adorno, 1991b, 172–3), and, in turn, 'how easily the subordination of theory to praxis results in the support of renewed suppression' (1991b, 172). Yet his melancholy in the dialectic of enlightenment also reveals a modern version of the fear of reduction *ad infinitum*. Negative dialectics resists the reduction of consciousness to identity or totality. Critical thinking is held fast by knowing that objects do not go into their concepts without leaving a remainder, and this remainder for Adorno is a source of hope, and a ray of light into the prison cell. This reverses the mediaeval fear of infinite regression. There the fear was of a lack of identity for truth. Now, in Adorno, the fear is of identity as a standpoint. But this is grounded in a positing of thought as error, namely, the shape of thought that thinks its own conditions of possibility within the dialectic of enlightenment. Here it is Adorno's stance against his understanding of totality in Hegel that drives him to resist aporetic thought as its own truth, as self-re-for-mative, or as having meaning as its own condition of possibility.

As such, Adorno resists the dialectic of enlightenment as culture, that is, as thought's self-determination, for fear of it coming to rest in an ideological standpoint of Hegelian totality. He distinguishes his own philosophy from Hegel's because 'Hegel's philosophy contains a moment by which that philosophy, despite having made the principle of determinate negation its vital nerve, passes over into affirmation and therefore into ideology' (Adorno, 2000, 144). In fact, the posit-ing of affirmation as ideology is itself ideological, and passes into the aporetic logic of the dialectic of enlightenment. When Adorno says of Hegel that he does not 'carry the dialectics of non-identity to the end' (1973, 120), in fact it is Adorno and not Hegel who presupposes what does and does not conform to the absolute. This presupposition is not mediaeval in content, but it is Neoplatonic in intent, for it carries the same prejudgement of thought, this time as the dialectic of enlighten-ment, as error. Adorno's modernity is Kantian in its recognition of the totality that is false, but un-Hegelian in not yielding the truth of this false totality to itself. Ultimately in Adorno, ideology is still unknowable as its own truth.

Habermas commends Hegel and Adorno for revealing how modern subjective reasoning repeats a negative dialectic, and how this circular phenomenology is one which 'the Enlightenment cannot overcome by its own power' (Habermas, 1987, 20). Such a task requires infinite rather than finite powers. Since Kant revealed this for modernity, and Neoplatonism before that, it is an insight that 'should be trivial by now' (Dews, 1992, 199). Habermas seeks an antidote to the 'paradoxes of a self-negating philosophy' (Dews, 1992, 99) found in Hegel and Adorno, finding it in his theory of communicative action. Communicative action has the same function for Habermas against Hegel and Adorno that the transcendental method had for Kant against the illusions of dialectic. In this case, it acts as a foil to the groundlessness of the dialectic of enlightenment by offering a communicative and intersubjective lifeworld that grounds the negativity of subjective consciousness. The Habermasian project, then, is Kantian in comprehending the groundlessness of the subjective conditions of possibility of experience and its objects, but is not Hegelian in that it seeks to resolve this dilemma intersubjectively.

However, it is together that Adorno and Habermas might be said to constitute the experience of Kantian and Hegelian modernity. Both share the view of reason as negative and self-defeating. For Habermas this points the dialectic of enlightenment back to its rational ground in intersubjective communication. Here myth (or groundlessness) becomes enlightenment. But the basis of doing so is the positing of thought and its aporias of reflection as error. Habermas eschews the totality of consciousness that is false in favour of a prior condition that is the ground, then, of its aporetic subjective appearance. This is to say again that in Habermas myth becomes enlightenment because thought is also posited by Habermas as non-contradictory and within the impossibility of negative reduction *ad infinitum*.

On the other hand, Adorno is more faithful to the totality that is false. He knows that enlightenment inevitably and unavoidably returns to myth. But he also posits thought as error in holding that the totality, which is false, is not its own truth. Here, enlightenment's unending return to myth, its negative universality, is also posited by Adorno as error. Even where thought knows its groundlessness within the conditions of the possibility of experience that are also the conditions of the possibility of objects of experience, Adorno rejects groundlessness as true, particularly, he believes, as it becomes distorted in Hegel's notion. It is Adorno's positing of totality as non-contradictory and ultimately as grounded in something other than its own groundlessness that avoids the difficulties that constitute the notion. When Adorno states 'the principle of absolute identity is self-contradictory' (1973, 318) as a criticism of the absolute, he remains wedded to the tradition of Neoplatonism in the history of Western philosophy, and does not yield to the truth of the modern mind.

However, while neither Adorno nor Habermas individually holds to the totality of Kantian and Hegelian modernity, together they can be said to do so. If in Habermas myth becomes enlightenment and in Adorno enlightenment returns to myth, then as a totality of revel and repose, of dialectic and enlightenment, they do constitute the substance of the Hegelian experience of Kantian experience. Their contradictory relation is the subject and substance of the notion. Together, in their opposition to each other, they commend the philosophical experience of the dialectic of enlightenment in which reason knows the truth of its groundlessness.

## Kierkegaard

Kierkegaard is willing to work with Kantian and Hegelian modernity and with the truth of error that constitutes this modernity. His use of pseudonyms is an example of this. The pseudonyms are not Kierkegaard. But since Kierkegaard is not himself, they are his truth. They are his being the truth of himself as error. His Kantian modernity knows the groundlessness of the relation of thought and object. The ambiguity of his authorship is the universality of this groundlessness. He knows that he and his pseudonyms are the same condition of possibility. They *are* only relative to each other. They share the lack of ground, or contingency, wherein each lies in the other.

His Hegelian modernity is expressed in each of the shapes of the experience of groundlessness taken by the pseudonyms. They are Kantian in their acknowledging of the non-author, and they are Hegelian in being experiences of that experience. The pseudonyms are Kantian. The difficulty of writing as non-author is Hegelian.

It is instructive to look briefly at some of the pseudonyms. In *Stages on Life's Way*, Johannes the Seducer claims that he is never trapped by identity. He lives true to his groundlessness by practising the deceit of seduction. As soon as a woman is ready to resolve the intrigue of the aesthetic of the chase, Johannes ensures her negation by ending the relationship. His escape is always ensured in advance. He enjoys the aesthetic of the chase for its own sake. Resolution of this intrigue is for him a lie. Judge William, also in *Stages*, makes the opposite response to the experience of groundlessness. He opposes an uncertainty signed in the heavens with one that needs living in real life. To live the negative requires the ethical, which, in turn, means that faith and religion are needed in order to hold the negative in temporality. He sees the Seducer as serving only an infinite possibility that is never realized, for that would destroy it. Marriage can live the truth of the negation that the Seducer never commits to. Kierkegaard is the Seducer, for he never married Regine, and he is the Judge, for his authorship is an actual marriage of infinite negative possibility and finite, actual, ethical negation.

Johannes de Silentio in *Fear and Trembling* reads truth as error into the story of Abraham on Mount Moriah. Abraham is required to make a groundless act, an act of faith in the truth that is also a temporal error. In his anxiety he has the leap of faith that what is error will be true. He could have abandoned the ethical by choosing faith, or abandoned faith by choosing the ethical. But he chooses the paradox and anxiety of faith in the world, and is rewarded by being spared the sacrifice. But Johannes is silent. He cannot make the leap of faith and cannot find truth in error. Not finding truth in error is the truth of error, however, and this is Johannes's own truth. Kierkegaard's Hegelian experience here is that of failing the test of groundlessness, and thus speaking its truth.

Vigilius Haufniensis in *The Concept of Dread* finds a logic in this anxiety, and is more closely still an Hegelian experience of Kantian experience. He reasons that sin came into the world by sin and thus posits itself. This contradiction of origin is not the Neoplatonic logic of first cause. It is the Hegelian logic and metaphysic of the notion in which infinitely reductive aporia is the truth of Kantian rational groundlessness. Haufniensis is Hegelian in working through the logic of positing.

Johannes Climacus is Kierkegaard's most philosophical pseudonym. He embraces the dialectic and searches for its true expression. His Kantian groundlessness is the thesis *de omnibus dubitandum*, everything must be doubted. In *Philosophical Fragments*, this becomes a logic of paradox moved by the passion or self-moving soul of thought. This paradoxical logic is the *Aufhebung*, or the philosophical and educational experience of the Neoplatonic logic of non-contradiction. Doubt is able to ground itself in its own groundlessness for, the relation between the conditions of the possibility of experience and of objects of experience are not dichotomous, but 'trichotomous' (Kierkegaard, 1985, 169) or triadic. It experiences itself as the relation between experience and objects of experience. This is the logic and metaphysics of the Kantian experience. 'Everything it says about the paradox [of truth in error] it has learned from the paradox' (1985, 53). In these philosophical fragments Kierkegaard can speak the truth of the paradox of Hegelian experience while still holding himself in opposition to Hegel.

As such, Kierkegaard retains his Kantian modernity in his pseudonyms, and retrieves Hegelian modernity in their mediation of his relation to the truth of error. His modern logic and metaphysics is the triadic notion of the experience of subjectivity that experiences itself as groundless. This, for Kierkegaard, is 'subjectivity's subjectivity' (1989, 242).

## Nietzsche

Nietzsche's Kantian and Hegelian modernity is in the eternal return of will to power. Will to power is the groundlessness of that whose condition of possibility undermines itself. The logic of this Kantian experience is not Neoplatonic but Hegelian, for will to power has its logic and metaphysic in its eternal return and is not posited as the error of infinite regression that requires a Neoplatonic solution. As such, the eternal return of will to power expresses the groundless totality of Kantian and Hegelian modernity.

This interpretation can be opposed by saying that Nietzsche is not working with the paradigm of subjectivity or consciousness that defines the philosophy of Kant and Hegel. But such an interpretation posits Kant and Hegel within Neoplatonic logic, which between them they are transforming by teaching of its own groundlessness. Kant's revolution overturns Neoplatonic unhappy consciousness by committing modern consciousness to a total collapse of any ground for its identity.[6] Hegel's revolution refuses to pre-judge this collapse as error against a truth posited free from such collapse. Nietzsche is opposed to the Neoplatonic paradigm of consciousness, seeing it as the history of an error in which consciousness comes to hate both mind and body. We have followed this same error in our presentation earlier, of the history of Western philosophy. What Nietzsche despises is the idea that truth decays when its logic of non-contradiction is corrupted. Will to power here is Nietzsche's revolution in the comprehension of subjectivity. It maps the same groundlessness of subjectivity as the dialectic of enlightenment. It is only the *ressentiment* of Neoplatonic subjectivity that causes subjectivity to avoid this revolution. This *ressentiment* in the higher man is the last vestige of the belief that thought is error.

Zarathustra is the new principle that comprehends this error as its own being and becoming. But Zarathustra is the truth of this new principle only in the errors of his teaching which Nietzsche describes in *Thus Spake Zarathustra*. In Kantian and Hegelian modernity, and now in Nietzschean modernity, it is the loss of subjectivity to the logic and metaphysics of its groundlessness that defines this modernity. The Hegelian notion is the experience of groundlessness as is the eternal return of will to power. The form of subjectivity that is essentially modern is aporetic, groundless, and total. It is the working out of this consciousness that is not itself, which is both Kantian and Hegelian modernity and Nietzschean modernity.

Nietzsche exhibits the logic and metaphysics of modern groundless-ness in the first of Zarathustra's speeches. This tells of the metamor-phosis of the spirit. The first change is of the spirit into a camel. It is strong and can bear the weight of much that is difficult including the oppositions of pride and humility and wisdom and folly. The camel carries these human difficulties into the desert where the second meta-morphosis occurs. Here the spirit of the camel becomes a lion. This lion is no longer prepared to be slave to Neoplatonic *ressentiment*, and seeks to become its own master and commander of its own freedom. There is, therefore, one last master to seek out, and it is the categorical impera-tive. That which says 'Thou shalt' must be overcome by 'I will'. If this is to succeed then 'values, thousands of years old' (Nietzsche, 1982, 139) will have to be defeated. The lion is the spirit that will create new values, speaking a 'no' to duty and a 'yes' to freedom for oneself. But, if these new values are to be created they must be free of the shape of spirit which, as a camel, sacrificed its strength to serve the Neoplatonic values of weakness, asceticism, and piety. The lion cannot return to this error or else he will only re-create old values. But the lion cannot forget his own history or his determination within the old values. New values require a third metamorphosis, where the lion becomes a child. The child here is a new beginning, an innocence, and a forgetting. These are the condi-tions now of the possibility of the spirit who wills his own will.

Left here, the story of the three metamorphoses opens itself to uto-pian fantasies ranging from the wild and imaginative to the deeply dangerous and fascistic. But this child of the third metamorphosis fails to appear in Nietzsche as a forgetting or innocence. Rather, what appears in Nietzsche is the aporia of the conditions of the possibility of experience, which are likewise the conditions of the possibility of the becoming of the child. This aporia is given its own form and content as the failure of Zarathustra, the failure of the man of the future to escape his conditions of possibility. He fails to find disciples, he fails to teach the death of God, he fails to teach the overman, he fails to stay on his mountain, and he fails to stay away from his mountain. As the teacher of the child and then as the teacher of the impossibility of the child, Zarathustra is the Hegelian notion that has its own form and content in the self-determining truth of the error.

The eternal return of will to power, then, is a revolution of the two-thousand-year-old view of Neoplatonic philosophy. But it is not a revo-lution that resists being re-formed by its own conditions of possibility. It is a critique of the most powerful – because they are the most obvious – standpoints of Neoplatonic logic. The will to power corrupts the idea of thought as error and of truth as the logic of noncontradiction by speaking of its aporetic totality as its truth. Nietzsche corrupts the principle of cause and effect by the logic of the eternal return, and in doing so reclaims for itself the logic and truth of infinite regression in and for itself. The eternal return of will to power demands a 'conscience of method' (Nietzsche, 1968, 238)[7] that does not reinstate cause and effect or the logic of non-contradiction. The failure of Zarathustra to become the child demands this same conscience of method, so that a new history of error as philosophy is not condoned. Such a new history may well have had a beginning, however, in the modernity of Heidegger.

## Heidegger

Heidegger's critique of Kantian and Hegelian modernity is Kantian to the extent that it is a study of the groundlessness of subjectivity. But Heidegger's response to the Kantian experience of groundlessness in consciousness is to give priority over this experience to *being*. Being is the prior condition even of the conditions of the possibility of experience and of objects of experience. In *Being and Time*, Heidegger argues that being has its own groundless constitution in *Dasein*, which is the being of being. It is the condition of its own possibility as the question of being, and has its own logic, one that trumps the logic and metaphysics of Kant and Hegel.

For some commentators, Heidegger's monumental achievement is to expose the modernity of Kant and Hegel as grounded in the suppression of being, which is originary and beyond thought. He offers an alternative to the Kantian and Hegelian modern mind, one that does not privilege consciousness, subjectivity, and negation. Its appeal is that it undermines the sovereignty that the intellect has assumed for itself in the history of Western philosophy and draws on a philosophical tradition that precedes even Socrates and Plato. For others, notably Adorno, Heideggerian philosophy is merely a tautological jargon of authentic being, where such authenticity replaces the instability of the dialectic carried in and by the modern mind.

Heidegger's case is that *Dasein* is both being and time. As being, *Dasein* is being-in-the-world as its own act of understanding. When being takes the appearance of the world at face value as an entity, then it works within the tradition of subject and object and the 'metaphysics of knowledge' (Heidegger, 1992, 86). But the true relation of being-in-the-world is *Dasein*. This encounter is not of subject and object but of being with itself. This extends to the character of care that is central to *Dasein*. Being-in-the-world includes within it the relational totality of being and otherness. 'Others' are given by being to itself in such a way that in otherness *Dasein* is at home with itself. Only when this is misunderstood does otherness appear in the form of a relation between individual subjects. Humanism for Heidegger therefore expresses only homelessness.

It is care that is the defining characteristic of *Dasein*. Enquiry and care are two of *Dasein's* most fundamental conditions which, in falling away from *Dasein*, describe the truth of its condition not *of* the possibility of existence, but *as* the possibility of existence *per se*.

It is in Part II of *Being and Time* that Heidegger turns to the enquiry of *Dasein* as temporality. When *Dasein* faces death it faces its most fundamental issue, that is, the possibility of a non-issue. Here is both anxiety and anticipation. It is the latter that is the condition of the possibility of possibility. In holding resolutely to this anxiety and anticipation, *Dasein* is truth in its authenticity and can experience for itself 'an unshakeable joy' (1992, 358). In this resolute anticipation *Dasein* is also the condition of the possibility of time. Being is always ahead of itself and behind itself in anticipation, for it is already fallen away from itself but always yet to come, and the constancy of anticipation is temporality, or the condition of the possibility of the being of time. The present of constancy is found in the moment of vision (the *Augenblick*) and is an ecstatic unity of past, present, and future. This ecstasy in constancy is in being as time and in time as being and it belongs not to the individual but to the community of the *Volk*.

However, the groundlessness of *Dasein* eschews the groundlessness of the modern mind. Whatever Heidegger's motives here, and whatever his motives in being a member of the Nazi Party from 1933–45, *Dasein* avoids the crisis of Kant's totality of conditionality by asserting its own form of authenticity. It grants itself immunity from Kantian and Hegelian modernity by removing itself to the priority of being. In effect, this establishes a ground against modern rational groundlessness. Such a ground was no doubt desired by those living in the Germany of the 1920s and '30s, and it was singularly powerful that *Dasein* should offer this ground in the authentic community that is the truth of its own being and its own time. But unavoidably, this authenticity is at home with itself against those who are judged inauthentic. When this opposition between the *Volk* and its historical and social other is comprehended within the authenticity of *Dasein*, it believes it has somehow avoided modern bourgeois social relations. *Being and Time* serves as an apology for rejecting political actuality. This is, in essence, a *ressentiment* against the totality of the Kantian experience, the dialectic of enlightenment, and the eternal return of will to power.

Indeed, *Dasein* is will to power without the conscience of method, where the latter knows of its determination in and complicity with error. This is what makes Heidegger's modern mind such a dangerous misconception of groundlessness. It finds will to power in the being of being but not in its eternal return in the totality of Kantian conditionality, or therefore, in the Hegelian notion. Heidegger's will to power asserts authenticity to itself by refusing the ambivalence of its eternal return in actual social and political relations.

Where Heidegger finds a crisis of the Western spirit, as Husserl had done before him, and tries to solve this crisis by a notion of authenticity, the Kant/Hegel tradition knows the continuing domination of modern social relations and knows too that this dominance leads to an ambivalence in all thoughts of overcoming such domination. This tradition holds to the truth that while it is a critique of the social relations that are its conditions of possibility, it is also, contradictorily, a defense of such experience against those who would step outside of this totality. Modern freedom opposes itself and defends this opposition. This is the ambivalence of the modern mind because it is the ambivalence of modern conditions of possibility. *Being and Time* opposes this freedom, but does not also defend it. As such, it warns the modern history of Western philosophy about what can happen when the conditions of possibility are eschewed in favour of a new philosophical reality that rides contemptuously over the conditions of possibility. *Being and Time* is a remarkable new reality, not least in the logical rigour of its own enquiry into the conditions of possibility. But new realities are terroristic if they are not both a critique and a defence of their conditions of possibility. *Dasein's* authenticity is seductive against Kantian and Hegelian ambivalence. But this should serve as a warning to the present history of Western philosophy that terror and fascism always accompany ambivalence, as impatience and frustration overcome by myth parading as enlightenment, including the myth that the dialectic of enlightenment is itself redundant. It is in this sense, the most dangerous sense of all, that Heidegger is able to confirm the end of philosophy on the altar of ingenuity and philosophical imagination.

## Derrida

Derrida has mounted the most serious recent investigation into the conditions of possibility within the modernity of Kant and Hegel. His philosophy has worked with the iterability of the conditions of the possibility of experience being likewise the conditions of the possibility of objects of experience. But he has done so in distinctive ways.

Derrida is Kantian in not avoiding the totality of experience. He is Hegelian in recognizing that this totality has a form and content of its own – difference-opposition – that is its *logos*. But it is the points on which Derrida distances himself from Kant and Hegel wherein his challenge to modernity is to be found. In *Glas* he enquires into the conditions of both experience and the experience of objects. A natural diversity is the condition of the possibility of experience, but as yet only an 'indifferent difference, an external difference, without opposition' (Derrida, 1986, 168). This condition of possibility can only be experienced as pressure and opposition. Thus, natural diversity is both the condition of the possibility of indifferent experience and the impossibility of this indifferent experience. The impossibility belongs to what Derrida calls *différance*. Desire, consciousness, and the will are all the result of this impossibility and express it as difference-opposition. Derrida resists the idea that *différance* can be a transcendental analytic precisely because there is no instance where *différance* is not already difference-opposition. It is also the case that any transcendental dialectic of difference-opposition is made impossible by its own autoimmune or aporetic relation to its own possibility. *Différance* at one and the same time shows the totality of modern reason *and* why this totality – which *does* exist – is also impossible. There is nothing that is not already difference-opposition, and there is nothing that is only difference-opposition. The modern mind is therefore at once 'the manifestation of difference ... *and* the process of its effacement or its reappropriation' (1986, 235–6).

*Différance*, then, is known in its impossibility. This has resonance with the Hegelian notion for, as we saw, the notion too expresses the form and content of dialectical or oppositional aporia. Here Derrida at times is very close to Hegel, and at other times impossibly different to him. Derrida, in accepting the totality of difference-opposition as the condition of the possibility of experience and of objects of experience, accepts too the totality of *Geist*, at least in so far as *Geist* is the totality known as misrecognition by that same misrecognition. *Glas* brilliantly executes this totality, not just in the way that it illustrates the appetite of *Geist* for all that is different – even the crumbs are hoovered up – but also in the way that *différance* can only appear within the totality of *Geist*. *Glas* begins by noting that it has already and unavoidably begun in the totality of the *Aufhebung*. If *Glas* begins by thinking that it is outside of the modern mind, then this can only be because it has not yet read Hegel. When it has done so it will realize that even though it was unaware of it, nevertheless it had already begun 'entrained in the circle of the Hegelian beginning' (1986, 4). One can also read the end of *Glas* as an inevitable return to this beginning, and that as such, *Glas* itself is one with this total circle of *Aufhebung*.

Derrida also employs the ambivalence of *différance* as social and political critique, notably in the strategy of *doubling*. Doubling registers the aporetic relation of possibility in its impossibility, and therein marks the totality of difference-opposition *and* the complicity within it of any form of opposition. But, even if Kantian and Hegelian modernity is irreducible, nevertheless the shapes that its aporias take are not all equivalent. As such, philosophical critique should undertake to explore which 'is the least grave of these forms of complicity' (Derrida, 1987, 40). The key terms in Derrida take their meaning from within the experience of this strategy. Deconstruction reveals the conditions of the possibility of meaning as determined within the text of difference-opposition. Iterability is the experience of the possibility and impossibility of *différance*. Autoimmunity reveals *différance*, but always as possible only in its own impossibility. Undecidability is the effect of deconstruction, iterability, and autoimmunity.

However much the Hegelian notion and *différance* might appear to share by way of aporia, Derrida never sanctions the notion being identified with *différance*. This is because Derrida sees absolute spirit as the total victory of difference-opposition, leaving nothing remaining that can register the impossibility of such a totality. Derrida here sees the absolute in Hegel as unable to preserve *différance*. As such, the *Aufhebung* is not the register or mark of the impossibility of totality, but only of its completion. But, in seeking to protect spirit from the notion that is, from its own form and content as logic and metaphysics, in fact, Derrida falls back on to the ancient and mediaeval tradition in positing the truth of thought thinking itself as error. Derrida does not go so far here as to posit an unchangeable God that is immune from corruption by finite thought. In fact *différance* is the opposite. It is infinitely changeable within the tradition that is its possibility and impossibility. If *différance* were able to speak its truth in ambivalence, and in the modernity of Kant and Hegel that is its trace, then its true form and content would be as it is thought. But Derrida disallows this. As such, he is caught between a mediaeval tradition that would relieve *différance* of its actuality in thought, and a modern tradition that would know *différance* to have its truth in the actuality of its being known. Derrida avoids the former because it is not Kantian enough, and he avoids the latter because it is too Hegelian. Towards the end of his life he spoke of the truth that is possible only in impossibility as a vulnerable non-sovereignty found in the impossibility or autoimmunity of sovereignty. This, he says, might be 'the name of God [that] would allow us to think something else, for example a vulnerable nonsovereignty, one that suffers and is divisible, one that is mortal even, capable of contradicting itself or of repenting' (Derrida, 2005, 157). The point is, however, that when thought is not posited as error, this is precisely the form and content, the logic and metaphysics of the notion.

# 7
# Present History of Western Philosophy

## Introduction

We have presented the history of Western philosophy as the story of ways in which reason has misrecognized its role in thinking truth. In Ancient Greece Plato and Aristotle exhibited the dialectical logic of this misrecognition. In the cultures of error that followed, Neoplatonism worked with this logic as the separation between thought and truth. In this separation subject and substance opposed each other, with subjectivity holding itself to be in error compared to the perfection of substance. In relation to this unknowable God, freedom became the work of human reason in and for itself. Freedom and God here have their determination in these same cultures of error.

The modern mind – and this is so often not comprehended in accounts of modernity – is where reason discovers that it is the cause and the effect of the separation between itself and truth. It is, therefore, where freedom and God are thought together, for it is where the metaphysical and social relations are thought of as one logic and content. This is where the condition of the possibility of reason's education about its own truth is likewise the condition of the possibility of its education about truth *per se*. This truth does not establish a new separation, as is inferred by those who still hold out against the Kantian experience of groundlessness.[1] Nor does it overcome or put an end to existing separations. Reason here is that which knows itself to be the condition of the possibility of experience and of objects of experience. Its only ground is itself, and this only negatively. The modern Kantian mind has this ground in its own aporetic nature, that is, in the experience of the separation of thought and object, theory and practice, or of God and freedom. As such, its ground is groundless. Kantian modernity remains without ground.

But the modern mind faces *itself* when it faces the aporia of being its own condition of possibility. What marks European speculative philosophy out as the modern mind is that it works within this aporia. In this work reason is being shown by its own contradictory truth that the idea of what truth is needs to be re-learned. When reason knows Neoplatonic principles of non-contradiction, cause and effect, and the absurdity of infinite regression to be based only in reason's misunderstanding of the role it plays in the logic of such principles, then it is opened to a new education about this as the truth of the modern mind. The question of how open it is to this, its self-re-formation, by being its own cause and effect is the question of how the Kantian experience of groundlessness relates to its Hegelian experience of itself.

The Hegelian experience of the modern aporetic Kantian experience is reason's self-re-formation in learning of itself in its groundlessness. Stripped of its Kantian aporetic conditions of possibility, Hegelian experience is interpreted as the assertion of overcoming oppositions. But the Hegelian experience has no logic and content without the experience of Kantian groundlessness. The *Aufhebung* in Hegel is what is learned about groundlessness from and in groundlessness. Only learning can hold such self-re-formation as its own activity and result. The modern Hegelian experience is therefore the idea of education as an activity in its own right and as its own end. It is this notion of education that marks out the development of the modern mind over Neoplatonic cultures of error. Most forms of Western philosophizing, however, remain wedded to Neoplatonic logic and continue to interpret Kantian groundlessness according to non-contradiction. Nevertheless, the modern mind holds within it the ability of reason to be re-formed by the experience of its role in such cultures, and holds, too, examples of this education that can be called on.

The previous chapter made this case for modernity as the Hegelian experience of Kantian groundlessness, and explored some of the ways in which philosophers have expressed this modernity. Now, in our final chapter, we will explore ways in which the Hegelian experience of Kantian groundlessness changes Western conceptions about itself and the world. If the Hegelian experience of the Kantian revolution re-formed the old order of Neoplatonic principles, we must ask now what the new logic actually look like in the modern world?

We will address this modern philosophical education by looking at three ways in which aporetic logic and learning changes fundamental conceptions, ways that can then cascade into other areas of thought that represent these conceptions. These three self-determinations of aporetic logic are in the relations of self and other, God and man, and life and death. All share the fundamental expression of this educative logic as the formative ambiguity in which negation is not itself. As self and other this is where 'I am already other and the other is not me'. As God and man this is where 'God is already other and God is not man'. As life and death this is where 'life is already other and death is not life'. Together they are the aporetic logic of the modern mind in which what is, is negative and educative.

## The time of recollection

However, before exploring these three aporetic determinations of modernity, we must acknowledge the method of this aporetic education in and as recollection. That it is a method is unavoidable. Hegelian education consists in the thinking of thinking. Having itself as its own object means that it falls within the groundlessness of the Kantian experience. But it also means that it posits the shape of the present conditions of the possibility of experience. It experiences such conditions as their cause and effect. In the modern mind cause is the autonomous and freethinking master, and effect is his other, the object. This is both the achievement of the history of Western philosophy to date, and another self-misrecognition. Some of the shapes of thought taken in recognizing this misrecognition – Marx, Adorno, Habermas, Kierkegaard, Nietzsche, Heidegger, and Derrida – were the content of the previous chapter. It is the failure to recognize this recognition as method, or as the standpoint of the master, which sees such recognition repeat itself as method without conscience, and without truth. The conscience of method speaks as the false totality in and as recollection. Here the standpoint of the master recollects himself posited as method. His truth is as method, and this truth is recollective of the truth of that method. Recollection here is groundless – because method repeats itself – and re-formative because in repetition there is learning. This structure of recollection will be drawn upon now in exploring the significance for and of actuality in Hegelian experience.

But there are other interesting features of recollection that merit mention here. Recollection is the method of present history of Western philosophy. As a list of chronologically arranged content, the history of Western philosophy is merely the *collection* of past events and ideas. It is only when it knows this content as itself that the collection and the past with it is recollected. Present history of Western philosophy recollects its own development in and as the past history of Western philosophy.

But expressed as mere collection, it can assert its past as an *identity*. Thus, for example, reason finds in the history of Western philosophy the path of its own development to its maturity wherein it realizes itself as the universality of what is known. This identity is the imperialism of modern reason over past (and present) cultures.

However, the modern mind also knows that the conditions of the possibility of its identity are likewise the conditions of the possibility of identity as an object to itself. The standpoint of imperialism – collection – undermines itself. This is the added educative significance of recollection carrying here both the Kantian experience of its groundlessness and the Hegelian experience of its re-formative truth in and as such learning. As such, present history of Western philosophy is both the possibility and the impossibility of its imperialism. Recollection un-grounds itself, and has its own truth in this circle.

But there is also a futural aspect to recollection. The circle wherein recollection recollects itself – its groundless Kantian experience – is as much recollection of the future as it is of the past. The past, here, is its own future recollected in the present. In this aporetic logic of recollection where the child is father to the man, so, the past is its future in the present. This does not mean that present recollection empirically knows what events will appear in the future. It knows that it is already what has become the future, and will become the future again. This displays one of the most important characteristics of recollection. It is open to the recollection of itself as the ambiguity of the totality that is false. It is open to itself as the false totality of its self-determination in time as it is to itself as the false totality of its groundlessness. Recollection has this openness to itself as its own truth in education and learning. The future is the name of this openness to itself.

As we will see later this concept of openness is not that of the master who, for example, says he is open to other cultures or to the views of his students – though he should be open to these anyway. Rather, the notion of recollective openness commends such a master to be open and vulnerable even to the mastery inherent in pluralism or critical pedagogy. Recollective openness is open to the autodestruction of these types of openness. It is this deeper and more radical notion of recollective openness that is discussed now in what follows.

Lastly, recollection is also the educative structure in which the metaphysical relation and the social relation return to each other in the history of Western philosophy. In recollection, logic is also content. This means that its metaphysics is also its actuality in experience. The metaphysical and the social share logic and content in the educative structure of recollective thinking. This is the same as to say that metaphysics and the social are the one logic and content of the *Aufhebung*, for it is where they know themselves in each other in the philosophical experience of their opposition. It is to the *Aufhebung*, then, as actual logic and content, and in the experience of the other, of God, and of death, that we now turn in order to explore the present history of Western philosophy after the revolution in which cultures of Neoplatonic error were made to face the truth of their own totality.

## Self and other

The first recollection we will explore is that of the relation of self and other, which has its truth in the aporetic logic and content of the modern mind. We will also extend this to look at the relation between the West and its others.

In Ancient Greece the metaphysical relation and the social relation were held together in the immediacy of the ethical order. Truth and the social order were transparent in and as life and death. The master was true as the immediacy of what is, and the slave was error as the immediacy of what is not, or as death, the other to life. But with Socrates this transparency recognized its own condition of possibility in thought. From this point, transparency became the site of the struggle between and within the metaphysical relation and the social relation. Transparency, appearing transparent to itself, misses the fact of its being known. This misrecognition, so often present in the assertions of what is obviously true or obviously absurd, has been followed earlier as the history of Neoplatonic principles in Western philosophy.

In Neoplatonic philosophy the relation of self and other was expressed in the unhappy consciousness wherein subjectivity was in error in relation to substance. What was transparent here was that substance must be true, and perfect, and other than the contradictions that thought produced in self-consciousness. The Kantian revolution in metaphysics finds universality in this transparent error, and therein returns the truth of substance to the conditions of the possibility of its being known. Transparency here is the obviousness that reason is the ground of all knowledge. Masked by this transparency, however, is the way that reason is also the groundlessness of that ground.

### Abolition of slavery

The abolition of slavery is a part of the history of Western philosophy. Reason that knows itself as the ground of all knowledge wages war against the irrational, that is, against that which does not yield to the freedom, independence, and autonomy of the thinking self. For a while, enlightenment reason was able to withstand the ambiguity in slavery that slaves are men who are not men, but in time reason prevailed over the irrationality involved in defending slavery. Negatively, reason's universality in the self-conscious minds of men undermined any and all irrational and arbitrary claims for the freedom of some minds but not others. This is the negative basis for the universality of modern rational freedom, where 'rational' here means the independent self-consciousness that thinks of and for itself. But, and as Nietzsche noted in *Twilight of the Idols*, the negation of non-freedom in pursuit of freedom is different from the freedom gained in victory.[2] The negation of the irrationality of slavery took on positive and merely abstract identity as the bourgeois master in modern social relations.

As the ground of knowing, then, reason is life that is certain of itself. This certainty is the independent and free mind of the bourgeois master. What is not *this* life is other than life, is not independent, and is not its own master. This other has the status only of an object. But the transparency of modern bourgeois equality and freedom hides something of immense significance. In the obviousness that slavery has been overcome, slavery is no longer visible. In addition, in being overcome, it is no longer a source of education for reason. It is no longer part of how the master defines himself. The logic and content of freedom that remains hidden in this transparency is the recollection of self and other in and for the modern mind. This we now pursue in the education of the modern master regarding the groundlessness of his ground.

In the transparency of modern bourgeois social relations there is an illusion. The illusion is of the free, autonomous, and independent person. This illusion becomes known first in the Kantian experience that the condition of the possibility of bourgeois freedom – the negation of all that is not mediated by reason – is likewise the condition of the impossibility of bourgeois freedom – negated by the same reason that grounded it. The identity of the master falls to the experience that its ground is groundless. This is an education regarding its being only an illusion. Having undermined the claims to universality of everything else, reason now finds its own universality – truth in the free self-consciousness – to be autoimmune or self-destructive in and as its dialectic of enlightenment. Myth is overcome by reason, but reason returns to myth by exactly the same standards that judge the incompleteness of everything else.

This means that the ground of the modern independent master collapses under the weight of its own truth.[3] This is the beginning of his modern re-education, first in the Kantian experience of the groundless-ness of his ground, and then in the Hegelian experience of this experi-ence in which he can find the logic and content of the master in the now hidden relation of master *and* slave. We will describe later some of the more obvious ways in which the master learns of his dependence in looking at the relation of the West and its others. Before that we will look at the Hegelian experience of the dialectic of enlightenment that lies at the heart of the modern conception of self and other, where we see the re-emergence of the slave in and for modernity.

### Modern master and slave

For Neoplatonic logic the contradiction of the identity and truth of the master means that the master is only error. Such a logic would again send us into a culture of error where truth is other than thought. But the Kantian revolution means that such cultures of error must find truth within the conditions of their own possibility. It is the Hegelian experi-ence, now, of this aporetic totality that can find truth in the error or con-tradiction of the master, and find it moreover in the mind of the slave.

When in the history of Western philosophy the master, as the cer-tainty of life, defines otherness as what is not life, or as death and nega-tion, the slave is included as this other. In fact, the slave here has his identity in two negations. First, he is a living death. He is nothing, and there is nothing about him that does not melt away and vanish. He is the impossibility that has existed in human relations as the effect of life taking itself as all possibility. Second, because the slave is essentially negative, when he experiences his negation at the hands of the master, then, because negativity is experiencing negativity, the slave achieves a mind of his own.[4] This mind of his own challenges Neoplatonic philo-sophical principles, for it is where error thinks itself as its own truth. In Hegelian terms it is the negation of the negation. In modern terms it is the Hegelian experience of the Kantian experience. In terms of social relations it is where the I learns of the truth of its contradictory identity from that which it has until then seen as its absolute antithesis.

The truth of the slave in the master here is in the logic and content of the Hegelian notion. It is the aporia of the freedom of the free man and has its own substance as the metaphysical and social relation. This relation is the truth of the negative that is not itself. It is determinate in the logic and content where 'I am already other and the other is not me'. This expresses both the groundlessness of the rational I in relation to himself, *and* the ground that this groundlessness has in not being the same as its other. It is in this relation of negation to negation that the modern mind achieves a mind of its own, and as such is the mind that is educated or re-formed in the experience. This education is recollection, for it is where the positing of the I and its other is recollected by itself as positing. Recollection is the only self-consciousness that positing can have. This is the fundamental openness of philosophical education, that is, that recollection is open to itself as positing. It is this openness to itself as aporetic that is its substance in and as learning, and not just once, but continuously in the repetition of the false totality that is always already posited.

Put another way, the logic and content where 'I am already other and the other is not me' is the triadic significance of the modern dialectical relation of self and other. 'I am already other' means that I have negated my independence by the same means by which I achieved it. Reason undermines reason. Thus, the independent mind is negated by the means of its independence. To be negated is to be brought into relation with everything that it defined against itself – insecurity, vulnerability, not-being, and death. When the slave returns to the master in the experience of his loss of sovereignty, he brings with him all these characteristics. The slave re-educates the master about how the master is also already the slave. 'I am already other' involves, then, the Kantian experience of the groundlessness of the master, for it is where the conditions of the possibility of sovereignty are likewise the condition of the possibility of the loss of sovereignty.

The second part of this aporetic social relation – 'the other is not me' – carries both the Kantian experience and the Hegelian experience of the Kantian experience. It is Kantian in recording how the self is other to itself. But it is Hegelian in that this groundlessness carries a dual significance. 'The other is not me' refers both to the truth of a negated I *and* to the truth of that which is also other to this negated I. It observes that 'I am not me, and neither are you', and states therein how the self and the other are experienced and 'self'-determined in modern recollection or philosophical experience. It states the truth of a relation between opposites that does not eradicate the opposition, but does allow the opposition to re-form itself in being known by itself. Learning, in its openness to itself, holds the truth of this relation as education, which is the third partner here in the notion of self and other. Wishful thinking that its difficulty is overcome in being recollected can only result in a new and perhaps more intriguing and disingenuous mode of suppressing its ground in groundlessness.

The nature of this modern social relation is part of the present history of Western philosophy whose truth is education. The social relation of self and other learns its truth in recollecting itself as the logic and content of this relation. As recollection it is a knowing that can only be sustained as learning, for learning is the ground of groundlessness. It is in such education that modernity is revealed to itself, and it is as this essence that it can now take the logic and content of its own metaphysical and social relation to relations with those who are other than modernity. Modernity, open to its self-re-formation in learning about itself from its Kantian and Hegelian experiences, is also a modernity open to learning about how this learning is also re-formed in relation to its non-Kantian and non-Hegelian others. In this re-forming, to which we will now turn our attention, the present history of Western philosophy can retrieve the aporetic modern truth of the idea that has become infused with implications of Western power and imperialism, namely, that of a common humanity. We will see how the modern mind, having retrieved its own groundlessness in the posited relation of life and death, and experienced as master and slave, is now open to other shapes of this groundlessness, and as such offers new opportunities for life and death to learn of themselves across cultures, and across the world.

## The West and its others

### Exporting education

Globalization, or the westernizing of the world, is the extension of the freedom of the master over the rest of the world. But, as we will see in a moment this freedom and its extension are grounded in a re-formative illusion. Similarly, Western critics of globalization suffer their own Kantian experience in that the conditions of the possibility of their critique are likewise the conditions of the possibility of the object of their critique. The critique of globalization – where globalization is seen as the mastery of the West over its others – is also a form of globalization, imposing the master/slave dialectic as explanation on precisely those it aims to protect from such imposition. As such, the critique of globalization is complicit with globalization. If critics of westernization want to comprehend this totality which is false, then such comprehension is within the Hegelian experience of the Kantian experience of the groundlessness of both globalization and its critique.

Some of the contradictions of the independence of the Western master in global relations are becoming increasingly apparent. For example, the freedom of the master requires others to work for him so that he is not corrupted with any negativity or dependence. He needs new markets for a constant supply of cheap commodities so that he can practise his freedom in ownership of objects. He needs security from those who would undermine freedom or launch attacks on its symbols. He needs to be self-sufficient in energy supplies, particularly in the fossil fuels that shape his culture, and he needs a sustainable environment. And, as is now apparent, he needs a regulated free market to protect him from himself.

Each of these needs exposes the master to the illusion of his independence. We have already seen these contradictions to be the modern Kantian experience of groundlessness. Their immediate effect in the master is the fear and trembling that he will lose all that he is and be turned into his antithesis, dependent, needy, vulnerable, and insecure. But the master can avoid both the Kantian and Hegelian experience by continuing to eschew fear and negation as error, and by continuing to posit them as other to his own self-certainty. He currently practises this eschewal by exporting fear, negation, vulnerability, and death to parts of the world that are other. This has become the single most important way in which the West refuses to learn from its experiences. It outsources the wage slavery required for a continuous supply of cheap commodities. It outsources fear, insecurity, and death by exporting them as conflict and war to foreign soil. It uses all means to control the supply of fossil fuels in particular, and the world market in general. It exports the pollution that is endemic to its freedom. Indeed, it does everything it can to keep its education in the groundlessness of fear, vulnerability, and uncertainty as far away as possible. Yet the fact the West works so hard to avoid the educative and self-reformative experience of modern groundlessness shows just how aware the West is of the education that it carries, and threatens.

## Culture of multiculturalism

Issues in the West around multiculturalism also concern reason's self-education. Within the limits of modernity they have their truth in the recollection that I am already other and the other is not me. When reason meets traditions within the West that are other than its own, it invariably does so as master. Modernity is not fully open to its truth when it creates spaces for the voices of other traditions – although learning requires service to such opportunities. The problem is that giving space only reaffirms the power of the giver. This is the Kantian experience of multiculturalism, that the conditions of the possibility of openness are likewise the conditions of the possibility of power and sovereignty. This is the dialectic of enlightenment in multiculturalism.

In addition here, it is the Hegelian experience of the Kantian experience that is openness to the autoimmunity of openness in multiculturalism. This Hegelian openness has its truth in the vulnerability of the master even to the closure that pertains in openness. This is the logic and content that has its truth where I am already other and the other is not me. The melting pot of modernity commends this aporia as the logic and content of multicultural education, for in the aporia modernity relates to the other truthfully, that is, with integrity rather than with intrigue, and in comprehending itself to be the totality that is false. Again, here, it is in learning of its positing of life and death that modernity opens itself up to new ways for others to begin to see their own vulnerabilities in the master.

There is a second point to make briefly here. When the history of Western philosophy is comprehended as the domination of rational culture over all other cultures, to the point where the voices of the latter are delegitimized and even silenced, the charges against it are of imperialism, racism, and ethnocentrism. The truth of these charges is unavoidable. For as long as the West has eschewed the truth of its otherness to itself, so too it has not understood its own truth in its others. Western life has protected itself against death in the form of these others. Its self-affirmation is the shape that the road of independence and dependence takes when its dialectic is comprehended as life without its truth in its other.[5] However, present recollection has to be clear about the present shapes of such misrecognition. For example, Hegel makes demeaning remarks about various cultures, including African slaves, Native Americans, Asians, and Jews. He is accused here of recollecting earlier and other cultures as unenlightened and inadequate. Critics who see racism here are, however, also recollecting Hegel's time and its judgements as unenlightened and inadequate. What will future recollections make of such judgements that accuse past imperialism by practising present imperialisms? It is for present recollection to know itself as the past of this future, and to know the imperialism of the critique of imperialism, and to comprehend this aporia as an invitation to the openness of the truth of the modern mind in its philosophical re-education and self-re-formation.

### World spirit

World spirit, too, has its truth in education. It is not a thing, although it is often criticized as if it were. It is that in which humanity learns of itself through its oppositions and contradictions. Recent Western philosophy has been sceptical of the rational imperialism implied by the concept of world spirit, and sceptical too of the idea of a common humanity, fearing that it is being defined in terms that are predominantly, if not exclusively, Western. This scepticism is warranted as a critique of the master. But in relation to the slave in the master it is a crisis of educational nerve. Humanity can be thought from within Western reason as a totality that is false, and such thinking is part of the present history of Western philosophy.

As with self and other, so with the West and its others, the relation has a logic and content of its own in the Hegelian experience of the Kantian experience. Where in the former this logic and content expresses itself in the learning that 'I am already other and the other is not me', so, in world spirit, 'the West is already other and the other is not the West'.

That the West is already other refers to its Kantian experience of itself in which its independence as master is negated by its needs and dependencies and collapses into its antithesis. That the other is not the West carries the duality of its Hegelian experience and its triadic significance. It means that the West recollects itself as itself, and it recollects that this recollection is not otherness *per se*. The result is an education in which the relation of the West to itself and its others is re-formed. The openness of the West to its truth in being so re-formed is how the West can have a spiritual relation to itself and to the world. This openness is world spirit, or the notion of the West in global relations.

A critic might say here that this account of world spirit is still too Western and ethnocentric. It is still world spirit seen from the perspective of the Western paradigm of consciousness and spirit. There are two responses to this, and both concern the complicity of thought in what it thinks. The Kantian experience trumps all other non-foundational thinking because it concerns the conditions of the possibility of their being known, and Hegel finds in this its own logic and content. Second, world spirit has to be explained from the Western point of view if it is to be educative of the West. Western domination is the condition of the possibility of the West being educated about itself in and by world spirit. Neither can the West duck its complicity here as the dominant force in the totality which is false.

We will make two final observations here about the educative significance of world spirit. First, it is during times of the greatest excesses of the master that his standpoint is most vulnerable to education. In the philosophy of history it is the case that education regarding freedom emerges most powerfully from negative experiences of universality. Christianity emerged from the tyranny of the Roman Empire, communal spirit from barbarian violence, conscience from heteronomous imposition, and modern social freedom from slavery.[6] In each case, freedom recollects its own development in the immanent educative force of such opposi-tions. Its most dramatic lessons are learned at times of greatest upheaval. The Kantian experiences of the autoimmunity of Western sovereignty explored in the present chapter are some of the present oppositions car-rying immanent educative logic and content.

Second, such an education brings an openness to learning in global relations which in itself makes a difference. This openness commends that the master learn of himself in the world from the ways in which the world learns of itself through the master. It holds the West open to being re-formed in this education. It knows the illusion of mastery and sovereignty, and educates against them when they are abstracted from their substance in fear and vulnerability. The more it is open to fear and vulnerability the less it needs to export them. In addition, this openness recognizes world spirit or humanity to be known as the education of the West rather than as the identity of the West. Most importantly, perhaps, it does not avoid the fact that the imperialism of the West is the deter-mining feature of this education in global relations. It is, rather, the condition of the possibility of its being open to its re-education. World spirit emerges now for the West in the openness of the master to learn-ing of his dependence. As a culture of the world the West is re-formed. As the notion, this is self-re-forming. And as self-re-forming, the notion is itself in the otherness that constitutes world spirit.

We cannot predict what will happen if the West brings its truth as education in life and death to its relations with its non-Western others, be they in the West or beyond. No one can know how a self-re-forming West might change global relations. It is possible that some traditions will be able to identify with this newfound integrity, and be able for the first time to find themselves present in the openness of the West to learning of itself from its own otherness. It is also possible that some traditions will not trust this truth, having witnessed previous Western intrigue and self-interest. It is possible too that some traditions will view this openness as weakness and as a time to strike hard at the enemy. In such circumstances the West needs to be as strong in its vulnerability as it has previously been in its power and autonomy. The need here is to pursue life and death in education with the same vigour that it is pur-sued in military campaigns. Wars may still occur, for in wars the truth of the life and death struggle speaks clearly. Wars unite the combatants in the struggle. But philosophical education can do the same when the modern mind, instead of exporting this struggle to its others, is re-formed in learning of death as its own truth in life. There may be times when even this education has to defend itself against an externally imposed truth in life and death. The just war sees vulnerability protect itself from the certainty of another that would impose upon it. Too often, however, the West has been this certainty in global relations.

## The history of Western philosophy and its other

The final manifestation of self and other we will look at is that of the relation between the history of Western philosophy and its others. In the modern mind of Kantian and Hegelian experience, the history of Western philosophy recollects its development to the point of this recollection. Herein its content becomes a subject in its own right. This is both the condition of the possibility of the history of Western philosophy as imperialism and of its self-critique of being such. In this aporetic education the history of Western philosophy learns of its own truth in recollective self-re-formation.

The history of Western philosophy fell into disrepute when Hegel also defined it as a content and a subject in its own right. In recollecting its beginning in Socratic self-consciousness he eschewed the Oriental worlds of China, India, and Persia as pre-philosophical, and as not driven by the vocation of consciousness for its subjective freedom. The criticism of this view as logocentric imperialism is justified. The history of Western philosophy evinces a mastery over cultures that are deemed to be outside of or which might prevent this development. But the truth of Western mastery is autoimmune because it can only be recollected. It falls under the weight of its own contradiction in the recollective conditions of its possibility. Yet it also has within it the Hegelian experience of the truth of this unstable recollection. We will illustrate its significance now in the relation between West and East.

### West and East

Hegel enjoyed the idea that the light of freedom in the world rose in the East, travelled westwards across the earth, and set in the West, with the wisdom of the owl of Minerva flying at dusk to recall the path of its development. The implication here is that the East is politically, socially, and philosophically naïve, being left behind by reason's self-development. In fact, Hegel treats the relation of East and West as a dialectic of master and slave. He sees the East characterized by fear through the strength and power of one man over another. The West, by contrast, is characterized by the experience of fear as the beginning of subjective thought and freedom, the slave's mind of his own in the master. Fear in the West is deemed formative in a way that it is not in the East.

But rather than merely positing the separation of East and West as fear and freedom, the recollection of the history of Western philosophy also draws them together. Freedom has its negative universality in fear, for it is fear – fear of the master of losing his sovereignty and fear of the slave as the truth of his living death – that teaches reason the universality of (its) freedom. 'I am already other and the other is not me' refers to the notion recollecting itself in fear and freedom. Thus, the East – taken here as the concept of fear in relation to but also dominant over the concept of freedom – has always been a formative component of Western philosophical education. The extent to which the West now exports fear serves to mask this significance of the East in the West.[7]

To recollect the East in the history of Western philosophy in this way is to re-form the West's conception of itself, and of its truth in relation to its others. Such recollection sees the history of Western philosophy start again, by recollecting its origins and its development differently. This is a new education for the history of Western philosophy and, in effect, a new day. The light that rises in the East and begins this new day is unavoidably Western, for it is still the West that is recollecting itself. But this imperial light is now of a different quality. It knows the East within itself, and recollects the future as the past that will have been present in this new day. The future is not a tense. It is rather a state of mind, one where the present is open to itself as the present future of a past, open, that is, to its educative truth in and as recollection. If this is the West's point of view, then the West is now in formative relation to itself and to the East. Even as the owl of Minerva recollects backwards she also recollects forwards in her openness to comprehend her re-formation in the day. It remains, of course, an open question as to how the East will find itself in the West. But formative relation is the risk that education demands – that the West practise its truth in education. Perhaps education here will be able to speak its own truth, that dawn and dusk, East and West, yield the new day to each other even in their opposition.

## God and man

A second significance of the Hegelian notion as the modern metaphysical and social relation is that it is the way in which God is known to the modern mind. Here, the logic and content of aporetic education is where 'God is already other and the other is not man'. It is in this education that the positing of God as other and unknowable becomes the condition of the possibility of knowing God.

As we saw earlier, the history of Western philosophy derived within Neoplatonic principles could prove that God existed, but not what

God is. From Stoicism to Locke Neoplatonic principles posited God as absolutely other to the thought that thinks him. Further, in and for life that posited itself as what is, the thought of God that produced infinite regression and contradiction proved also the need for the existence of God to lie beyond such contradiction and negation. It proved that the finite and negative thought of God must be in error. To be the truth of what is, it followed that God must be everything that finite thought is not. He must exist as first cause, he must not negate or contradict himself, and he must be unchangeable substance. We saw God known in this way in the history of Western philosophy in and as the cultures of error.

But the revolution of the modern mind re-educates thought about its own complicity in judging God other than his being known. Kantian experience recognizes that the conditions of the possibility of the proof of God's existence are likewise the conditions of the possibility of knowing what God is. The Hegelian experience of this experience knows this groundlessness to be its own logic and content. God here is the ground of groundlessness, or the truth of his being posited and recollected as such. This amounts to no more or less than the education of thought recognizing that in positing itself as error in relation to truth, it was itself the condition of the possibility of God being known in this way. The modern mind is modern in learning to recollect truth within and not without its being posited.

Recollection is the only way in which positing can know itself, and it does so now in two ways. It recollects the beginning of its becoming recollection in the intellectual template of God in the dialectic of universal and particular in the Ancient world, and in the separation of universal and particular in the mediaeval unhappy consciousness, to the point where it can recollect this as its own development. As the modern mind, recollection is positing recognized as misrecognition. It is the mind of the slave in the master. Thus, recollection holds the truth of the condition of the possibility of experience – positing – knowing itself.

In this unstable and restless education, there is formed the modern conception of God. This is no longer merely the proof that God exists as the condition of the possibility of his being posited as unknowable. It is rather the proof of what God is, namely, learning, and specifically aporetic learning. This is perhaps the most fundamental re-forming that emerges from the modern Kantian and Hegelian revolution. The oppositions and contradictions that made God unknowable, from Stoicism to Locke, are now experienced in the modern mind as the character of God. The absolute education here of the modern Kantian and Hegelian mind, in learning of contradiction as the groundless truth of self-re-formative learning, comes to know God in and as this restless self-re-formation. To know this modern God, then, is to know his strength in vulnerability, his ground in groundlessness, and his substance in subjectivity. It is also to find the slave in the master, the student in the teacher, dependence in independence, spirit in reason, death in life, and negation in certainty. Each of these knows God in man. Love of the difficulty of learning is love of God, and teaching is prayer.

The logical expression of this truth of God in learning has its own content where 'God is already other and the other is not man'. As we will see now, this severely tests the resistance of the modern mind against retreating into a more comfortable Neoplatonic view of God.

The Kantian revolution, as we saw earlier, is where reason learns of its universality and complicity in the unhappy consciousness, and has to recognize that it is not only the negation of irrational or superstitious assertions of God's existence, but also that these negations provide no positive standpoints that are immune from such negation. Thus, when the conditions of the possibility of experience *per se* are known to be the conditions of the possibility of God as an object of experience, this is also to realize that religion is already philosophy and that philosophy returns to religion. The knowledge of God, grounded in experience, is groundless because the conditions of the possibility of experience, in being recollected, are also groundless. God, even in being thought of, is other than himself, because his being thought is recollected as having been posited. There is no immediate originary knowledge of God for the modern mind. God is always (already) known in the conditions of the possibility that make him an object of experience. To know this, is to realize that the Neoplatonic God was posited as unknowable, but was not also recognized as being posited. But in the Kantian revolution where positing meets itself, so the conditions of the possibility of God also meet themselves. Positing, known to itself as positing, is a lost beginning. In this modern recollection, then, God is already other. Mediaeval cultures of error posited this condition of the possibility of knowing God in thought as error. The Kantian revolution recognizes the positing of thought in this way as groundless in its conditions of possibility.

The Hegelian experience of this Kantian experience learns that the other which God is, is not man. This has a dual significance. It means that God is not man, but it also means that God is the man who is other than himself, or not himself. For the man who knows himself in the Hegelian experience – where he is other to himself as to his others – to say that God is not man is to also say that God is this man. Thus, God is already other, and the other that God is to himself *is* the man who is other to God and to himself. Jesus carries the ambiguity of this truth where God is not man and yet is the man who is other to himself. His ground as God and man is itself groundless.

The difficulty that the Hegelian experience of the Kantian experience of the groundlessness of God presents for the modern mind is that it appears to ground God in how he is known by man. That God is already other refers specifically to our recollecting him as being posited by us. But this is not only an appearance. It is also exactly what the mind cannot avoid and is therein the substance of appearance. That it looks as if God is dependent upon how he is known will only be perceived as error if the condition of the possibility of knowing God, that is, thought, is posited as error. Kant shows that such positing is a misrecognition of the condition of possibility by itself, by thought, and Hegel shows how the learning of this misrecognition as recollection, or how thought as the truth of error, can be known in and for itself.

Thus, when the modern mind knows that man is the truth of God, it is to say that God is always of the idea that man has of himself. Freedom and God are two sides of the same comprehension or lack of comprehension. God is man's thought of himself. To interpret this as an affront to God's sovereignty is again to posit thought in a culture of error. This piety is no longer available to the modern mind, except insofar as it practises *ressentiment* against its own positing or will to power. The pre-judgement that God is unknowable led to intense struggles between the mind and the body, but in reality mediaeval man was excused from the hardest struggle of all, to know not just that God is, but what God is. The modern mind grants itself no such relief, for it is the recollection of the totality that is false, or the ground of groundlessness. Indeed, the modern mind is educated in the opposite direction to the mediaeval mind. The modern mind is first taught what God is by learning of the aporetic totality of the conditions of the possibility of knowing truth. God is lost before he is retrieved. Whereas, in the culture of error, God was assumed before he was learned about. The modern mind, in losing God, learns that truth is total, false, aporetic, difficult, and yet unavoidable because what is posited is recollected. From knowing what God is, only then does it also know that God is. Modernity is open to learning that God is from what God is. It is antithetical, then, to the Neoplatonic fundamentalisms of God's unknowability.

It is both controversial and counter-intuitive to argue that God, as truth, can be known and comprehended. But the recoil from such a claim shows the continuing influence of Neoplatonic principles. From the perspective of thought as error, the Hegelian experience of Kantian experience opens the modern mind up to charges of absolutism, that is, of the dogmatic assertion of a view of what truth is over any and all other such claims. But absolutism can be thought of differently here. If the 'ism' of absolutism refers to the thinking of truth in the modern mind as a culture, and if culture is understood as self-re-formation in opposition and contradiction, then absolutism can describe the self-re-formative experience of the totality that is false. The experience of truth is the experience of its opposition to itself. Such learning does not overcome assertion *per se*, for that is the nature of modern abstract positing. But it does understand the nature of the truth within it.

### Death and Life

The history of Western philosophy begins as a posited shape of the relation between life and death. Our study of the history of Western philosophy as the recollection of the modern mind now ends by returning to this relation, that is, by returning to its beginning.

Life is always a relation to death. But the relation is often hidden by the way life expresses its own certainty. The shape of life that is immediately *what is*, or is living, is already a positing of its relation to death. But life will not recall itself as this positing or this relation to death until it has a negative experience. This negative experience comes about when that which is alive becomes aware that it can die, that it contains nothing that cannot also absolutely melt away. This negative experience is the experience in life of death, and of the possibility of *its* death in particular. It is also the beginning of the recollection of positing, as it is of self-consciousness, reason, spirit, freedom, God, and truth. This is how and why fear is the beginning of wisdom. The negation of life by death is the beginning of life that, aware of itself, also seeks the truth of itself. Without death, life would not know to seek its own truth.

The modern mind is that which knows this seeking for truth as its own self-re-formative education. It comes to know death differently, not as an error, as it is in the cultures of error, but as the substance of that which knows itself in loss and recollection. The modern mind knows death as the introduction to freedom in life. It recollects how the search for its truth began without knowing that it had begun. The beginning was already a shape of the relation of life and death, but one in which the role played by negation and death as formative of this beginning is hidden by the certainty of life that it – life – is that which defines *what is*. Life carries death here as its own education and development, but does not understand that its definition of what is, is already formed in relation to death. As such, life is defined without death, and death and negation become other to life. This defines the shape of the history of Western philosophy which in searching for the truth of self-conscious life, eschews negation, contradiction, and death as other. In doing so, it rejects the most important part of itself, the part with the greatest educational significance.

The history of Western philosophy begins in misrecognition and continues in misrecognition, returned to the truth of itself in contradiction and self-opposition but lacking the recollective logic of itself *as* contradiction and opposition. Ancient philosophy knew life and death as the template but not as the actuality of life and death. Neoplatonic philosophy separated life and death such that the truth of what is could not also be that which is contradictory and changeable. The modern mind of Kantian and Hegelian experience returns death and negation to life, and therein returns the history of Western philosophy to its own beginning in the life and death relation, or the life and death struggle as Hegel calls it. We have followed the history of Western philosophy as the misrecognition by life of death. We have argued that life posits itself without death in different ways at different times, and that it is only in the modern mind that life as positing is recollected as negative and groundless. The modern mind speaks the truth of the recognition of death in life as the groundlessness of life, and speaks the truth of this groundlessness as recollection or education. Thus we have presented the history of Western philosophy as a history of the education of the master in trying and failing to think his own truth; or, the same, as the history of Western self-conscious life slowly learning of its truth in learning.

The modern mind, then, returns the history of Western philosophy to its original positing of itself in the Ancient World and finds there, Socrates trying to think the logic of the relation of life and death as its own educative content in recollection. In the *Phaedo*, which records Socrates's last dialogue before his death, he is to be found discussing the life and death relation as the truth of philosophy and the philosopher. He argues that life and death are related dialectically, in that one is always defined in relation to its opposite. The relation is also seen as formative in that less life generates more death, and *vice versa*. Socrates holds life and death together here not only as proof of each other but as proof that one is in the other. Death is in life in the way life moves towards death. Equally, life must be in death in the way that death becomes life again. It is the logic of their dialectical relation that underpins Plato's argument for the after life, the immortality of the soul, recollection, and the transmigration of souls. Dialectical logic makes their existence necessary. The soul must be immortal because there is life in death, and it must move from one body to another because the body turns to dust. Recollection proves the life of the soul in death because the soul is born knowing things that it cannot yet have learned in its present (re-)incarnation.

The dialectical relation that holds life and death together in this way does not apply to the body. The body is finite. It is of the earth and returns to the earth. Only the soul can hold life and death together, and is therefore not finite. It is this shape of life and death as body and soul that, as we saw earlier, becomes the dominant shape of Western Neoplatonic philosophy where the soul is unchangeable and eternal and the body is compound, changeable, and destructible. Nevertheless, this distinction between soul and body enables Socrates to argue that the significance of death does not apply to the body but to the soul, and further that the philosophical life is a life of death in life. 'Those who pursue philosophy aright study nothing but dying and being dead' (Plato, 1982, 223). His case here is that since philosophers prize the soul over the body, and since in death the soul is finally freed from corruption in the body, it follows that true philosophers are always aiming for death in life. Life is in death in the transmigration of souls, and death is in life in philosophical struggles. In this sense, 'the true philosophers practise dying' (1982, 235). Death provides that which the philosopher is always seeking, that is, to terminate the life of the intellect spent in service to the body. Since the soul 'never willingly associated with the body in life, but avoided it and gathered itself into itself alone, since this has always been its constant study . . . this means nothing else than that it pursued philosophy rightly and really practised being in a state of death' (1982, 281).

The Neoplatonic cultures of error struggled to hold on to the idea of philosophy as death in life. They saw death in life in relation to the finite body, and life in death related to the soul. Thought was judged from the posited standpoint of life to be in error because it dealt with what is not, by way of negation and contradiction. Thus the soul would only be redeemed of error in life after the death of the body. As such, philosophy at best could demonstrate the need for truth, that is, for a first cause and for the unchangeability of divine substance, but could not achieve it.

In the modern mind the relation of life and death learns of itself from itself. In the *Republic* such a relation belonged to the sun which, although not sight in itself, was the condition of the possibility of sight, and of its being seen. Now, in the modern mind, it is life and death that are the condition of the possibility of their being known. Both the sun and life and death have their truth posited in the shapes of thought that are this positing. Truth is the light that shines so that it might be seen, and life and death are experienced so that their truth might be understood. Life and death are the actuality of truth. When the modern mind knows of reason as actual, that is, as the positing of life and death, then it knows its truth within the light, within its conditions of possibility. Life and death are God's pedagogy, and are God as pedagogy. Neoplatonic logic, even in understanding the wisdom of negative teaching, found only infinite regression in actuality in this pedagogy because what was actual was mediated by thought, repeatedly. But the modern mind is based on a different logic, a logic that recognizes *itself* as pedagogical. In its aporetic logic it can hold infinite mediation as its own notion and as the truth of Neoplatonic cultures of error. It is in the modern mind, then, that life and death are recollected as the actuality of truth.

The modern mind is also a re-education regarding the relation of body and soul. Their absolute distinction as error and truth is negated in the Kantian experience of their shared conditions of possibility. A soul without a body is blind, and a body without a soul is empty. Their relation is their groundlessness. The logic of this groundlessness is its own content when it is recollected by itself. Body and soul are no longer the representation of the separation of life and death. In the modern mind, instead, they are the actuality of life and death. Their relation to each other is in the actuality of death in life and life in death. Choosing between them can only be grounded within a Neoplatonic culture of error.

The present history of Western philosophy, then, is returned to its own beginning in the life and death relation, and to its development in the way life posits negation as its absolute other. In the Ancient world it finds Socrates thinking the logic of life and death – and therefore the philosophy of any self-conscious beginning – as recollection. But Socrates does not have, available to him, the experience of the loss of death in life in the misrecognition of thought as error. It is therefore the modern mind that is able to recollect – undermine and retrieve – Socratic recollection as its own logic and content. This is the same as to say that the modern mind has the question of freedom and subjectivity determinative of it in a way that Socrates did not. The modern mind knows the abolition of slavery, or of living death, to be grounded in the universality of reason as its own condition of possibility. It knows too that this is the ground of modern bourgeois freedom. But death in life returns again to re-educate the modern master regarding the aporias of his identity and freedom. The philosophical truth of the modern mind here is where 'life is already other and death is not life'. This carries the truth of all previous misrecognitions of death in and by life.

Life and death have been and continue to be the totality that is false in and as the history of Western philosophy. In their relation as the modern mind they are perhaps ready now to carry their own truth in education beyond the cultures of the Abrahamic tradition, and to those cultures labelled as pre-philosophical by Hegel. A return to these pre-philosophical beginnings educates the modern mind about how to recognize itself even in cultures without reason, both on earth and, who knows, perhaps from beyond this earth. The shapes of life and death are the culture of culture and are the common language of mankind. As we mentioned earlier, war knows this common language well. Education, as yet, less well.

# Notes

## Introduction

1. Something like the recent collapse of banks who sold financial commodities whose claims for value were groundless.
2. Attempts at consistency regarding capitalization have proved fruitless. I have retained upper case where it is in a direct quotation, but dropped it elsewhere wherever I felt it possible to do so.
3. More on this concept of recollection later and in Chapter 7.
4. This is not to say that the modern illusions and appearances of the natural relation do not merit greater attention in their own right. In fact, given current ecological concerns, the contrary is the case.
5. We will see later that both sides here have supporters who attempt ingenious accounts for such contradictions.
6. Psalm 111: 10 states that 'the fear of the Lord is the beginning of wisdom'. Aquinas discusses this Psalm in the *Summa Theologica* (1920: 229; vol. 9, Part II, 2nd Part, 19.7) and, with the wisdom of Ben Sira (1916, Book I and Book XXV. 12), argues that although fear is appropriate in knowing God, faith is the beginning of wisdom regarding first principles and essence. Descartes' earliest known notebook, since lost, begins with the quotation that 'fear of the Lord is the beginning of wisdom' (1985, 1). The Islamic scholar al-Ghazali also refers to the fear of God being the beginning of wisdom in his autobiography *Deliverance from Error* (1980, 36).

## 1 Naming the Beginning

1. The nature of recollection as we are presenting it here disrupts a straight chronology. The recall of the past is a present recollection, and the present tense is used in the text to emphasize this. In educative terms, the past here is both negated and preserved.
2. See Heraclitus, 1987, fragment 51.
3. *Phaedo*, 66d.
4. See here Hegel, 1974, 77; 1970, 92, and Rose, 1996, 26–35.
5. Fragments 8–16, Aristotle, 1984b, 2390–3.
6. As Jaeger notes, this juxtaposition of space and human awe resembles the famous observation made 2000 years later by Kant in the conclusion to the *Critique of Practical Reason*, that 'two things fill the mind with ever new and increasing admiration and awe, the oftener and more steadily we reflect on them: the starry heavens above me and the moral law within me' (Kant, 1956, 166).
7. Using Jaeger's translation here of fragment 15.
8. One can note here that Aristotle distinguishes between Socrates, who never kept universals apart from their being known, and his Platonic successors who did give them a separate existence as ideas or forms (see Aristotle,

*Metaphysics*, 1078b 30–2; 1984b, 1705). That Aristotle seeks to establish the experience of reality against merely formal transcendental contemplation should not mask the ambivalence of this middle period, looking backwards to the idea and forward to the later period of empirical science.

9. Using Jaeger's translation of the *Metaphysics* here for emphasis; 1086b 18; 1984b, 1717; italics removed.

10. Jaeger finds the beginning of this reconstruction in books A–E. A and B are written earlier and in Assos. But the plan for the work outlined as a whole in B is itself abandoned, again due to developments in Aristotle's philosophizing. Jaeger says here, 'the sketch of the problems of metaphysics in B does not envisage the excursus into the general theory of substance and actuality in ZHΘ' (1962, 198). E 2–4 acts as a bridge to this later metaphysics of ZHΘ and I, texts that enable the transition from the ideas to substance as actual sensible material. These are, then, the main body of Aristotle's final version of the *Metaphysics*. Λ also deserves special mention here. This book is often referred to as Aristotle's theology and there seems to be general agreement that it is an independent work separate from the rest of the *Metaphysics* in which, nevertheless, it has been handed down. It is a document that gives the clearest possible evidence for the early Platonic and middle theological periods of Aristotle's thinking that Jaeger is reconstructing. Λ shows the relationship between substance and God in its totality. It represents, says Jaeger, 'the stage that we have discovered to come before the traditional metaphysics, a stage that was purely Platonic and did not recognize the doctrine of sensible substance as an integral part of first philosophy' (1962, 221). Λ then is a statement of Platonic theology and, as such, still represents the thinking of the aporias that arose within Platonism for Platonists. The later metaphysics may also show that Aristotle found it impossible to suppress the actual in order to prioritize the transcendent and in this sense his later metaphysics is also a response to this same aporia. Δ is another independent work, possibly the lecture on *Various Senses of Words*, while ά is a postscript that Aristotle's editors did not know where to assign in the book (see Jaeger, 1962, p. 169).

11. Jaeger also explores the place of the other key Aristotelian texts within this development. Among those that belong to the late period are *The Constitution of Athens*, the *History, Parts and Movement of Animals*, *Meteorology*, *On The Soul*, and *On The Interpretation Of Dreams*.

12. For example in Λ 8 of the *Metaphysics* around the issue of whether there is one or many prime-movers. Jaeger takes this as evidence that even in his late period Aristotle was 'wrestling with these problems anew and failing to solve them' (1962, 354). Aristotle here lives out in his own thinking the aporias that he experienced in trying to work with and against the universal forms. So, again, for example, Λ 8 of the *Metaphysics* contradicts Λ 7 and 9. The later work contradicts the early work on many key issues, not least in conceding *phronesis* to animals in the *Nichomachean Ethics* which directly opposes *phronesis* in the *Protrepticus*. Some works, such as the *Physics* and *On the Soul* contain evidence of both early and late periods. At times Aristotle expresses the doubts that accompany these contradictions, proceeding in his reasoning only by cautioning that he is working in the absence of certainty.

13. The *Organon* is held to be the *Categories*, *On Interpretation*, *Prior Analytics*, *Posterior Analytics*, *Topics*, and *On Sophistical Refutations*, though it is not a

term used by Aristotle. Jaeger argues that the logic of the *Categories* came early in Aristotle's life and from a time when he was still dependent on Plato for his view of the world, but that the text was not written by Aristotle. If true, then the principles of Neoplatonism that spring from the *Categories* have never faithfully carried at all the ambivalence of Aristotle's thinking.

14. Something Aristotle does also with rhetoric.
15. See *Sophistical Refutations*, 11. 172a, 13; 1984a, 292.

## 2   Hellenic and Alexandrian Philosophy

1. The latter wrote some 70 books at the rate of 500 words each day. See Diogenes Laertius, 2005, 180–1.
2. But this historical stoicism is very different from modern subjectivity.
3. Edwyn Bevan argues that Stoicism offered control over the only thing that could be brought under control, namely, the will, by the rational judgements open to the trained thinker. Stoicism offered protection against the chaos of the external world. See Bevan, 1913.
4. Or, for Copleston, the Middle Academy. Arcesilaus built on the scepticism of Pyrrho of Ellis.
5. This is the principle of *isostheneia*.
6. On the differences between the Cyrenaics and Epicurus on whether pleasure is motion (Cyrenaics) or not (Epicurus) see Diogenes Laertius, (2005) 136–9 and Epicurus's 'Letter to Menoeceus' in Epicurus, 1993, 61–8.
7. For a discussion of this see Hegel, 1974, 300–11; 1970, 322–36.
8. Edwyn Bevan (1913) argues that Poseidonius (c. 135–51 BC) may have been the chief source of ideas from which Philo drew.
9. It is a feature of Philo's philosophy that man is seen as a copy of God, just as the scriptures are allegorical and figurative.
10. Plotinus refers to the rituals of purification for those who wish to approach the 'Holy Celebrations of the Mysteries' (1991, 52). His first translator, Stephen MacKenna, notes that there is in Plotinus the 'desperate effort to express a combined idea that seems to be instinctive in the mind of man' (1991, xxxviii), namely that the good is universal and eternal yet is so little realized in the finite mind.
11. Porphyry notes that Plotinus seemed to be ashamed of being in his own body, seeking only to live a life in pure reason, and sharing in the divine intellect.

## 3   Mediaeval Christian Philosophy

1. The work of this author was mistaken for that of the Athenian convert Dionysius the Areopagite because the author used the pseudonym Dionysius the Presbyter. The authorship of these works remains unknown and they are dated as being written around the end of the 5th century AD.
2. See here, Augustine (1993) *On Free Choice Of The Will*, 118.
3. In *On Free Choice Of The Will*, he notes the perfect ambivalence of human and temporal education: 'the very thing by which man begins to be capable of receiving a commandment is that by which he begins to be able to sin'

(1993, 119). This is made clear in *Of True Religion*, where Augustine states that sin, by free will, is the way man 'learns by suffering to know the evil it did not learn to know by avoiding it. By making comparison between its former and its present state it loves more earnestly the good which it loved too little, as is seen from its failure to obey' (1959, 34).

4. Having established the pedagogical import of antithesis in man's divine education, Augustine is able to argue for the good that emerged from the sacking of Rome; for the paradox of a humility which exalts the mind (1972, 573); for God's being all-powerful yet creating men as self-pleasing (1972, 592); for the good that flows from grief; and for God's foreknowledge and man's freedom of the will.

5. See also Plato's *Gorgias*, 492e.

6. Augustine opposes Stoicism, arguing that those who remain unmoved by any emotions or feelings, have in fact 'lost every shred of humanity' (1972, 566).

7. See also *Of True Religion*, 1959, 41 and *Confessions*, 1991, 3 v. 9.

8. In Latin, the seven stages are *animatio, sensus, ars, virtus, tranquillitas, ingressio, and contemplatio*. For alternative translations see 2002b, 137n. Although Augustine here reads these stages around the idea of beauty, it is instructive in exploring the culture of error to do so strictly in terms of the soul's education.

9. See Psalm 72: 26; and Plotinus, *Enneads* 6.5.21.

10. *Enneads* 5.1.1.

11. Eriugena later reduces the four divisions to two – creator and created – and again from two to an indivisible one.

12. Excluding grammar and rhetoric.

13. Aristotle, *Metaphysics*, I. 3. 983a 25.

14. 'Remotion' is the term assigned to the negative education in which man learns of the things that God is not.

15. Cor. 1, 13:12.

16. Italics removed here.

17. I am working here with the 22-volume translation by the Fathers of the English Dominican Province (1920). As such, the style of referencing here is slightly different to elsewhere in the book. 'I.2.3' refers to Part I, question 2, article 3, and II.I.91.2 refers to Part II, first part, question 91, article 2.

18. On predestination Aquinas argues that some are saved and some are damned because this makes manifest God's goodness and justice.

19. See Copleston, (1962) *Mediaeval Philosophy* 2. II. p. 248.

20. Italics removed.

21. Italics removed.

# 4    Mediaeval Islamic and Judaic Philosophy

1. This is *nus, noesis, noeseos* in Aristotle; see *Metaphysics*, XII 1074b 34.

2. This is *aql, aqil, ma'qul*; see Fakhry, 2002, 28.

3. After the One, the heaven and the stars, come Saturn, Jupiter, Mars, Sun, Venus, Mercury, and the Moon.

4. We should note here that Henry Corbin warns against any westernizing of this cosmology in terms of a schema which seeks to reconcile thought and object. Primarily, this is because al-Farabi removes any dependence here upon

the object in favour of the role of the imagination within a prophetology. Corbin argues that al-Farabi exceeds any Hellenistic model that makes divine knowledge dependent upon the senses. We will return to this point later.

5. Corbin argues that al-Farabi deviates from pure Aristotelianism here in the role played by the acquired intellect, which can receive forms 'without passing through the intermediary of the senses' (2006, 162).

6. Against this, one might mention Richard Walzer who argues that revelation in al-Farabi is interpreted in 'the time-honoured fashion of Greek rationalism as established by Plato' (Walzer, 1962, 218).

7. Or self-apprehender.

8. Al-Ghazali here believes that Avicenna means that God can only know particulars in a universal way.

9. We note here that Avicenna, like al-Farabi, separates the active intellect from the human intellect, while Aquinas denies this separation as making any attempt to know God, to be futile. Corbin argues too that it was the role of the active angel that brought Avicennism in the West to a halt, particularly with regard to how it lifted the philosopher beyond established doctrine and away from earthly authority. It survived however in the East, not least in the school of Isfahan after the sixteenth century.

10. On the governing of the city Avicenna argues for three classes: the administrators, the artisans, and the guardians. All must perform socially useful tasks and idleness and unemployment are to be prohibited. There will be a common fund used to help the sick and to pay for the guardians. Gambling and usury are to be prohibited for they involve exchanges that are not grounded in socially beneficial trades or activities. Marriage is to be the bedrock of society and effort must be made to assure the permanence of the union, because love is the most important component of the general good. 'Love is achieved only through friendship, friendship through habit, and habit is only produced through long association' (2005, 372). Nevertheless a path to separation must be kept open because some natures will be unable to adapt to other natures. Women must be veiled and must not be the breadwinners, again in the name of social cohesion. In sum, 'whoever combines theoretical wisdom with justice is indeed the happy man. And whoever, in addition to this, wins the prophetic qualities becomes almost a human god' (2005, 378).

11. He promises a more positive doctrine in *The Principles of Belief*, which appeared in his *Revival of the Religious Sciences*. Marmura argues that it is in *Moderation of Belief* that al-Ghazali deals with true belief.

12. It may be appropriate here to see this difference in a way that is more commonly ascribed to Averroes. Corbin argues that the Islamic tradition of *ta'wil* or interpretation can hold one truth in what seems to the West to be a double truth.

13. Fakhry translates this as 'whoever repudiates cause actually repudiates reason' (2001, 27).

14. Averroes points out the logical paradox that the man who denies the intellect is of course using the intellect, and the logic of necessity within cause and effect to do so.

15. Fakhry notes here that Averroes has gone beyond Aristotle who nowhere argues that the unmoved mover has a creative function. In *De Coelo* Aristotle explicitly argues against the universe as created (*De Coelo*, 279b 12, 279b 18, and 3013b 1).

16. See Fakhry 2001, 157–8.
17. In his Introduction to the *Guide*, Shlomo Pines notes the subtleties of Maimonides's method of exposition. He is deliberately unsystematic because of the dangers of philosophy to the average reader. He employs here 'deliberate self-contradiction' (1963a, xciv). Leo Strauss notes something similar, finding the structure of the *Guide* 'neither entirely obscure nor entirely clear' (1963a, xvi). This enables the *Guide* to tell its secrets privately rather than publicly. It is private through contradiction, through being inaccessible, and through its unsystematic structure, for example, withholding a preface until a little way into Volume III. The *Guide*, that is for the trained reader, is the secret guide to the secret *Guide*.
18. One could compare this, for example, with Locke's concerns in *An Essay concerning Human Understanding*, at the way language causes obscurity and confusion in ideas and the way they are employed (Locke, 2004, 326–34).
19. *Ehyeh-Asher-Ehyeh*.
20. Maimonides uses the stories of Job and Abraham to illustrate these points.


## 5   Rationalist Philosophy

1. As for Aquinas, *Summa Theologica*, II. I. 29.3.
2. A symptom of this culture of error is that *conatus* – the motivation for self-preservation – thinks 'death least of all things' (1992, 192). Nevertheless, it is what leads Spinoza to conclude that each man should 'aim at the common advantage of all' (1992, 164).
3. Here Spinoza allows himself a moment of culture in arguing that when we know God to be the cause of pain, 'to that extent we feel pleasure' (1992, 211). Equally, death is less fearful 'the more the mind loves God' (1992, 220).
4. Written in 1686 but published only in 1846.
5. Its full title is *New System of the Nature of Substances and their Communication, and of the Union which Exists between the Soul and the Body*.
6. In the *Monadology*, Leibniz says that monads could be called 'entelechies'.
7. Even revelation must conform to this intuited knowledge.
8. In the intuitive knowledge of our own existence we have, says Locke, the 'highest degree of certainty' (2004, 547, italics removed).
9. Virgil, *Aeneid*, IV 175.


## 6   The Modern Mind

1. The logic of 'absurdity' here will unfold shortly.
2. Hegel refers here to the antiquarian logic as a 'heap of dead bones' (1969, 31), as 'dull and spiritless' (1969, 52), and as mere 'mechanical calculation' (1969, 52).
3. As such, the *Science of Logic* is the phenomenology of modern social and political experience. We return to this later.
4. These relations are explored as the present history of Western philosophy in the final chapter.
5. As it has in missing the ways in which the concept of ideology is itself ideological.

6. As elsewhere in this chapter, Kantian modernity refers to the aporetic relation of the conditions of the possibility of experience and of objects of experience, and not to Kant's transcendental method.
7. From *Beyond Good and Evil*, para. 36.

## 7   Present History of Western Philosophy

1. As Kant does, against himself, with the unknowable thing in itself.
2. See Nietzsche, *Twilight of the Idols*, Chapter 9.
3. As I write, the truth of the vulnerability harboured in the illusions of the master is illustrated by the collapse of banks in America, Britain, and Europe.
4. This is wonderfully illustrated, for example, in Ralph Ellison's novel *Invisible Man*.
5. Its others, too, had their own self-certainties that were also protected against negation by the West. These self-certainties lie outside the scope of this book.
6. I have expanded on this reading of the philosophy of history in the Appendix later.
7. Fear and freedom are similarly related and formative in the East, but the shapes it takes there are not part of the present study.

## Appendix

1. The Roman Empire spread from Britain across Europe to Africa and Asia. The final time that the Empire was ruled by one Emperor was just before the turn of the fifth century AD under Theodosius. It was he who declared Christianity to be the legitimate religion of the Empire, although he had himself been excommunicated by Ambrose in 390 AD for atrocities in Thessalonia. At his death in 395AD the Empire was divided into East and West, and ruled over by his two sons, Arcadius ruling the East and Honorius the West. This marked the beginning of a period of barbarian invasions in the West. In the East the Byzantine Empire centred on Constantinople, only falling to the Ottoman Turks some 1000 years later. It was in the context of the decline and fall of the Roman Empire that Christianity developed as a political power, seeking as we saw to establish divine freedom on earth. The histories of the West and the East differ greatly from this period on. The Patriarchs ensured that obedience rather than freedom remained the divine principle, and inwardness and subjectivity were not made a principle of the free revelation of truth. However, Western freedom can only recollect its own development and so we must turn our attention away from the Byzantine Empire and back to Europe in the so-called Dark and Middle Ages.

# Appendix

## Hegel's philosophy of history

A history of Western philosophy understood and presented, as above, as the recollection of the modern mind is unavoidably a philosophy of the history of Western philosophy. A philosophy of Western history – and Hegel's is at once both the most famous and the most infamous – is a philosophical autobiography. This means three things. First, it presupposes the identity of the writer who undertakes the enquiry. Second, the enquiry negates this identity and the enquirer becomes the enquiry. This means, and third, that the enquirer and the enquiry are complicit in the one relation of their – albeit aporetic – self-determination. A philosophy of Western history then, is hardly the magisterial rational teleological imperialism that is so often its image. Rather, a philosophy of history is a dialectic of enlightenment where negation is already certainty and certainty is returned to negation. This is why it is a *philosophy* of history; because it is grounded in the enquiry that repeatedly renders it groundless. Put differently, this is to say that the philosophy of the history of Western philosophy is the recollection of the conditions of the possibility of this recollection carried out by those same conditions of possibility.

The philosophy of Western history, in fact, is freedom recollecting itself. Freedom is both the beginning and the end of this education that seeks to Know Thyself. As the child, here, is father to the man, so too, the history of Western philosophy is the philosophy of the history. Freedom is not completed by this autobiography, nor is it exhausted by it. Instead, it is re-born, again, as the child of its own comprehension, which is to say, it is open, once again, to itself.

The history of Western philosophy, then, as we have presented it above, is also a philosophy of history. Two relations – the relation of the metaphysical and the social relations, and the relation of Neoplatonic and aporetic logic – have, together and apart, been shown as the form and content of the history of Western philosophy. These relations come to know themselves as the conditions of the possibility of that history. As such, and in this education, they learn of themselves as the philosophy of this history.

This reading of the history of Western philosophy as the philosophy of the history of Western philosophy opens up a way of re-reading and retrieving Hegel's philosophy of history. It has all three features of philosophical autobiography. It has Western freedom posit itself as the author and enquirer. The enquirer is negated by the enquiry just as the content of the enquiry is negated by the enquirer. They are complicit in the one relation of their being determined in and by the dialectic of positing and negation. Nothing is left stable or fixed. Indeed, the fundamental character of Hegel's philosophy of history is the groundlessness of both the enquirer and the enquiry. It is as education, as the struggle to Know Thyself, that this groundlessness is grounded. We will now present in brief this reading of Hegel's philosophy of history, up to the point where the social and metaphysical relations meet in the Kantian and Hegelian modern mind, which is examined in Part III. We will emphasize how, at certain moments, the dialectic of the groundlessness of freedom is its education and its development to a new stage of self-understanding.

## Recollecting the beginning

Part of the controversy regarding the philosophy of history concerns the judgements it makes on what marks the beginning of this history and what is cast aside as other to and not of this history. But the beginning of the recollection of the philosophy of history is not arbitrary. It begins in the present, which has its own becoming as an object for it. There is no philosophy of history without a beginning in the modern self-consciousness of the history of philosophy.

If Western freedom, thus aroused to account for itself in the history of Western thought, is to recollect its beginning, it will be where the simple opposition of life and death expressed itself in some kind of relation to itself. This abstract beginning can be found where life and death spoke of themselves as a third party, that is, as something in them but also of them at one and the same time. This third party is freedom's first voice, and in the recollection of life and death, or in the philosophy of history, freedom's first simple awareness of itself was heard at the Delphic oracle. Freedom recollects its beginning not in simple oppositions, but in knowing them to be posited. This is the voice that says Know Thyself. It speaks of a truth about freedom as education, as it does of how this education is most powerful at times of greatest vulnerability and doubt. The education of the West is not moved by victory but by loss, and the freedom it heralds is not grounded in sovereignty but in its vulnerability to itself.

## Ancient freedom

In Ancient Greece, and particularly in Ancient Athens, freedom has its form and content in the crumbling social relations of the city-state. It has its spokesman in Socrates, but it has its chronicler in Plato. Freedom of thought in the dialectic is essentially negative, and neither tradition nor custom can withstand its scepticism. In questioning the legitimacy of the whole that is taken for granted, the parts revolt against their master. As the unity of the *polis* falls apart into self-seeking groups and is divided into warring factions and interests, so freedom begins its ambivalent work, freeing the minds of men for the recollection of their determination in and by social relations that previously they were unaware of. The freedom to know and to recollect goes hand in hand with freedom from the social whole which preserved such ignorance. But, therefore, to become free to think for oneself also means to become free from an immediately unified ethical life. Freedom in this sense is tragic, and is founded upon destruction and corruption. This lesson will be repeated many times in the philosophy of history as freedom struggles to find its own truth in its mistakes.

## Roman freedom

Free thought opened up a gap – perhaps an abyss – between the social and the personal. Freedom found itself opposing the social in the name of the freedom of the thinker to think for himself. This expressed itself in an event of seminal importance for Western freedom when Roman power overcame the collapsing Greek states. When freedom recollects Rome and the Roman Empire it finds there a very different form of itself from Ancient Athens. In Rome, the havoc wrought by free thought becomes ordered in legislation. Freedom as the questioning mind has been unable to comprehend the role of the third party, or the role of recollection, that is the relation of the universal to the particular. As such, freedom becomes the lack of a middle between them, the lack of a relation that ties one to the other. Roman law is the actuality of this freedom that holds its moments apart. It grounds the abstract ego as legal personality defined by the right to own property, and it grounds the truth of this legal personality as a state and a political constitution. There is no recollection here, for there is no third party. The need to Know Thyself has been answered by legalism. The price for the independence of the person is independence from all persons. The only thing each person has in common is their indifference to each other. When freedom looks at this stage of its development it recognizes therein that life was self-certainty over the merely negative other, or was master over slave, and was the domination of the legal definition of what is over what is not. But it is from this absolute separation of life and death that freedom here is re-educated. There can be no return to an immediate ethical life for the genie is out of the bottle. Thus freedom has little choice but to turn inwards to try to find its principle and its universality within itself rather than external to it. As such, freedom as social relation becomes Neoplatonic Christian freedom.

## Christian freedom

It is in Christianity that death and nothingness are recollected as part of the principle of freedom, and this from what at first appears to be the antipathy of Christianity, namely the nature of the barbarians who invaded Europe and brought down the Roman Empire.

To begin with, when the son of God becomes man, divinity is found in subjectivity. The source of the pain of legal identity – the abstract ego or the legal person – now becomes the source of relief, namely, the individual subject. Moreover, there is a relation of subject and substance here, for God is now present in human form in real life. This unity now has a name. It is the holy spirit. This spirit is the duality of father and son known to itself as the thought of their relation. This is a new shape of freedom, because never before in the West has free thought known itself to be so close to the divine, or able to know that the divine was present in the thoughts of an individual mind. In both Alexandria and Rome spirit becomes the free intellectual life of God on earth. Freedom, now, is the site wherein love and not fear is the life of God. The witness of this freedom is to be visible in the practical sphere of the actual world, that is, in one's free actions. At a more general level, religion is the home of this free spiritual consciousness. It is reason as found in the inwardness of subjectivity, in the heart and the soul. The task now is to make external social relations comply with the strictures of this newly recognized inner freedom and truth. The principle of this religious freedom is that God's truth is within the self and that this self is responsible for creating a world in his own image. However, it is from an altogether unexpected source that Christianity finds the conditions under which it can enact its freedom as the truth of the social relation, and institute its principle in the correspondence of the free subjective thought (of God) and the free objective act (of God's will). This unexpected source is the negation of Roman law and the fall of the Empire to the barbarian invasions.[1]

## Barbarian education

It is from within the barbarian invaders of the West that the Christian population developed in Europe. Their barbarity is of central importance

in the development of freedom because out of their ferocious opposition comes a strong spirit of loyalty and community. Again, here, it is in
opposition, loss, and death that freedom moves forward.

Barbarian community is expressed through opposition, and the independence of each person shares the ambivalence of this opposition. In
addition, Christianity will suit those in whom opposition is a deeply
ingrained characteristic, setting as it does its own struggle for integrity
in the opposition of inner piety and outer external interest. It is in a
culture of such opposition that freedom begins to develop again into a
new form of itself, and this out of the great kingdoms of the Visigoths,
the Franks, the Ostrogoths, the Lombards, Burgundians, and the Angles
and Saxons, or, in Hegel's classification, the Romanic kingdoms and
the German-speaking nations which he distinguishes according to the
intermixing of culture of the former and the more settled blood lines of
the latter. These latter have a stronger sense of subjectivity or of 'heart'
than the former and are thus more significant in terms of the development of Western freedom becoming grounded in free subjectivities and
free thought. The principle of the heart here lies in the satisfaction of its
own desires. This too is the principle of Christianity in which the universal absolute is determinate only within the faithful individual. Both
the heart and Christianity are tied to the freedom of the subjective. This
plays itself out politically in that, unlike Greece or Rome, associations
are not made for external reasons but out of a free subjective choice
that is grounded precisely in the subject, that is, in the fidelity to the
association once made. This is the integrity of the subjective freedom of
political allegiances. It is from these two characteristics of freedom and
fidelity of association that the state as modern freedom understands it
will begin to develop. Nevertheless, at this early stage of the barbarian
cultures, freedom and fidelity make for an arbitrary patchwork of rights
and privileges, lacking, at all, any idea of a central legitimating and
universal authority.

## Mediaeval freedom

Freedom recollects its principle in the Middle Ages trapped within the
opposition between the inner and the outer worlds. Protection from
external threats requires allegiances and associations that corrupt the
integrity of these pacts. A similar fate befalls the Church and religion.
Working for the glory of God on earth, the Church intervenes in secular
life and works for external rather than internal ends. What ought to be
rendered to God was rendered instead to Caesar.

Freedom here is caught between obedience to external authority and the savagery of arbitrary political association. Most significantly the Church seeks inner truth from the actual aesthetic of occupying the land in which Christ was born and lived. The Crusades represent the Church's desperate desire for the highest possible form of sense-experience of God on earth, that is, to possess for its own pleasure the land on which divinity had actually come to earth. Yet the experience of the Crusades undermines the Church for the sensuous experience of liberating the Holy Land is one of blood, vice, and barbarity. What freedom experiences here is the absolute opposition of inner piety and outer atrocity. It learns that it cannot find itself, its own principle, in such campaigns for the internal by means of the external. It learns too that the Church distorts the principle of freedom, of religion, in its corruption in the world of externality, and turns religion/freedom into the slavery of men's souls. It learns, in short, that it had undermined its own standpoint by employing violence to serve its own ecclesiastical ends. When freedom hits rock bottom here in terms of its despair at ever realizing itself, it has already learned something new. The despair of freedom returns to it as an education in how it can only determine itself internally. It must be accountable and answerable to itself by way of its own subjectivity. It must choose this integrity freely and then be responsible for that integrity in the external world. The inner unites with the outer here in the form of chivalric codes and monastic orders. But, crucially, this brings to an end the period of freedom's self-incurred alienation from itself. This does not mean that inner and outer are finally reconciled, but it does mean that freedom has returned to the vocation to know Thyself by way of reason, rather than by thoughts aimed at other merely external ends. Scholasticism is the name given to the activity of free thought in mediaeval times attempting therein to justify faith by thought. The state is the name given to the principle of freedom that breaks the hard heart of isolation in favour of free associations under universal laws. Now freedom includes the freedom to restrict itself on behalf of the rational principle of its universality. Against slavery, freedom now extends its principle to all subjectivity. But it is not so much from slavery as through slavery that freedom has become emancipated from its own alienation and slavery to the external.

It takes the complete separation of inner and outer, in the Crusades and elsewhere, for freedom to learn that it cannot be established by conquest or imposed from without, or gained by way of territory. Freedom is driven to the point where it realizes that such negation contains a deeply important political education, namely that the external can be imbued with the freedom of subjectivity only freely, that is, by the consent of those who find their truth in freedom. The Christian principle of divinity in subjectivity is now ready to take a new religious and political form, the form of freedom as spirit.

## Spiritual freedom

The fall of the Byzantine Empire returns ancient literature from the East to the West and contributes to the renaissance of humanistic learning and to the learning of freedom in subjectivity as of universal and political significance. But the education that freedom receives from its period of self-alienation culminates in the European Reformation. The principle of that alienation, carried by the Church, is that the truth of the deity is sensuous and external. All of its corruptions are made possible by this belief or this dogma. It is Luther who publically opposes this dogma and who, in doing so, undermines all of the practices and policies based around it, most notably that of indulgences.

His own search was for God within free thought in spiritual form and not in external form. He opposes the spiritual vacuity of works performed in the world as merely observances of external authority or of purely earthly ends. Instead, Luther finds the truth of God lying within the subjective and therefore within freedom. This belongs to the subjective heart but also has an objective truth in that it re-casts the authority of Christian doctrine according to personal conviction. If it were restricted to feeling then freedom and truth would belong to a natural will and not to thought at all.

Post-Reformation Europe is therefore given its primary task of bringing together the inner and the outer, religion and the state, into the unity of subjective freedom. Culture is given the responsibility of reproducing the form of this universality in thought, educating in such a way as to show how the freedom of the will manifests itself in social reality. As such, culture is the process by which thought is educated to know that the state and its laws are religion or freedom manifested in the actual world. But this is not the end of freedom's becoming. Culture is experienced as opposition even in representing the truth of religion and the state as freedom. This is no longer experienced in the way that oppositions were experienced in the period of alienation, because now freedom knows such oppositions to be its own formative significance. They are, after all, what has taught freedom about itself. The advance here is that freedom can know its culture, its education, to lie in opposition and not somehow to lie outside it. Another way of saying this is that now thought can speak of its freedom as spirit, as the free thought that knows God within itself. But there are illusions present here which determine how modern thought will misrecognize itself again.

Nevertheless, the task for post-Reformation Europe is to realize the truth of religion, of subjectivity, and of freedom, in the secular, that is, in the state. How can the divine, known in subjective freedom, be made actual and present in social relations? The answer is, through rational principles. When law no longer conflicts with religious conscience, and when man's accountability to himself for his actions in the world is extended to all men, then reason becomes universal freedom. Duty and conscience are the names of this universal expression of rational freedom as spirit. However, freedom now has to learn of new atrocities in its recent history. Freedom seeks spirit as the unity of religion and the state, or of subjective disposition and rational exposition. Thought cannot have this unity immediately, else it is natural law and not free or of thought at all. In the gap, then, in spirit between subjective disposition and objective compliance there grows the terror of mistrust and confusion. The attempted reunion of these opposites takes spiritual form as the terror of the French Revolution.

Taken together, however, reformation and enlightened revolution are the totality of freedom, the former emancipating conscience from external dogma, the latter instituting the constitution of free citizens under the rational principle of subjective freedom and duty. When reformation and revolution do not act together, however, religion and the state are held apart in opposition with one side imposing its will on the other. It still lies ahead for freedom to comprehend reformation and enlightenment as sharing the same foundation and speaking the same truth.

## Freedom's education

So, when freedom looks back at its history in the West, it finds its development punctuated with fine ideals and horrendous practices. But it also sees that its development is one of learning about itself from its most difficult oppositions, contradictions, and failures. Indeed, what the social relation learns is that its truth already lies in that which opposes it. It is now able to recollect that freedom, when posited as the life that is not death, eschews negation as its other. As such, since loss is not part of its identity, when truth is lost to it, it is a self-fulfilling tautology that truth cannot be thought because truth cannot have loss as its own truth. Contradiction is the cause and effect of truth separated from thought. From here, freedom, in the education of the philosophy of history, experiences contradictions in two ways. First, as that which means that thought cannot know truth because thought's relation to the true is always one of opposition and negation. Second, however, contradiction acts as an education about universality that lies within the identity of thought, a universality that contradiction teaches thought to be true. It is in negative experiences that thought develops new understandings about itself. It is where it learns to recognize itself in loss and loss in itself. This recollection, known as the modern mind, as well as some of the shapes in which it presents itself, has already been discussed in Part III, where the social and metaphysical relations are recollected as speaking with one aporetic voice.

# References

Adorno, T. W. (1973) *Negative Dialectics*, trans. E. B. Ashton, London: RKP.

Adorno, T. W. (1991a) 'Why Philosophy?' in D. Ingram and J. Simon-Ingram (eds) *Critical Theory, The Essential Readings*, NY: Paragon House.

Adorno, T. W. (1991b) *The Culture Industry*, ed. J. M. Bernstein, London: Routledge.

Adorno, T. W. (2000) *Metaphysics*, trans. E. Jephcott, Cambridge: Polity Press.

al Farabi, A. N. (1998) *On The Perfect State*, trans. R. Walzer, Great Books of the Islamic World, Inc.

al-Farabi, A. N. (2001a) *Alfarabi: The Political Writings*, trans. C. E. Butterworth, Ithaca and London: Cornell University Press.

al-Farabi, A. N. (2001b) *Alfarabi: Philosophy of Plato and Aristotle*, trans. M. Mahdi, Ithaca: Cornell University Press.

al Ghazali, A. H. M. (1980) *Deliverance from Error*, trans. R. J. McCarthy, Louisville: Fons Vitae.

al-Ghazali, A. H. M. (2000) *The Incoherence of the Philosophers*, trans. M. E. Marmura, UT: Brigham Young University Press.

al-Ghazali, A. H. M. (2005) *Letter to a Disciple*, trans. T. Mayer, Cambridge: The Islamic Texts Society.

Aquinas, T. (1920) *Summa Theologica 22 volumes*, trans. Fathers of the English Dominican Province, London: Burns Oats and Washbourne Ltd.

Aquinas, T. (1975a) *Summa Contra Gentiles Book 1: God*, trans. A. C. Pegis, Notre Dame: University of Notre Dame Press.

Aquinas, T. (1975b) *Summa Contra Gentiles Book 2: Creation*, trans. J. F. Anderson, Notre Dame: University of Notre Dame Press.

Aquinas, T. (1975c) *Summa Contra Gentiles Book 3: Providence Part I*, trans. V. J. Bourke, Notre Dame: University of Notre Dame Press.

Aquinas, T. (1975d) *Summa Contra Gentiles Book 3: Providence Part II*, trans. V. J. Bourke, Notre Dame: University of Notre Dame Press.

Aquinas, T. (1975e) *Summa Contra Gentiles Book 4: Salvation*, trans. C. J. O'Neil, Notre Dame: University of Notre Dame Press.

Aquinas, T. (1998) *Selected Writings*, trans. R. McInerny, London: Penguin.

Aristotle (1984a) *The Complete Works of Aristotle volume 1*, ed. J. Barnes.

Aristotle (1984b) *The Complete Works of Aristotle volume 2*, ed. J. Barnes.

Augustine (1942) *Divine Providence and The Problem of Evil*, trans. F. E. Tourscher & R. P. Russell, NY: Helenson Press.

Augustine (1957) *Against the Academicians*, trans. Sister M. P. Garvey, Milwaukee: Marquette University Press.

Augustine (1959) *Of True Religion*, trans. J. H. S. Burleigh, Indiana: Regnery/Gateway Inc.

Augustine (1972) *City of God*, trans. H. Bettenson, Harmondsworth: Penguin.

Augustine (1991) *Confessions*, trans. H. Chadwick, Oxford: Oxford University Press.

Augustine (1993) *On Free Choice of the Will*, Indianapolis: Hackett Publishing Co.

Augustine (2000) *Soliloquies*, trans. K. Paffenroth, NY: New City Press.

Augustine (2002a) On the Trinity, trans. S. MacKenna, Cambridge: Cambridge University Press.

Augustine (2002b) *On The Magnitude of the Soul*, trans. J. J. McMahon, in *The Fathers of the Church, volume 4*, WA: The Catholic University of America Press.

Aurelius, M. (1945) *Marcus Aurelius and His Times*, trans. G. Long, NY: Walter J. Black Inc.

Aurelius, M. (1964) *Meditations*, trans. M. Staniforth, Harmondsworth: Penguin.

Averroes (1987) *The Incoherence of the Incoherence*, trans. S. Van den Bergh, E. J. Gibb Memorial Trust, reprinted Cambridge: Cambridge University Press.

Averroes (2001) *Decisive Treatise and Epistle Dedicatory*, trans. C. E. Butterworth, UT: Brigham Young University Press.

Avicenna (1952) *Avicenna's Psychology*, trans. F. Rahman, London: Oxford University Press.

Avicenna (1984) *Remarks and Admonitions: Part One, Logic*, trans. S. C. Inati, Toronto: Pontifical Institute of Mediaeval Studies.

Avicenna (2005) *The Metaphysics of The Healing*, trans. M. Marmura, UT: Brigham Young University Press.

Bacon, F. (1952) *Advancement of Learning, Novum Organum, New Atlantis*, Chicago: Encyclopaedia Britannica, Inc.

Bevan, E. (1913) *Stoics and Sceptics*, Oxford: Oxford Clarendon Press.

Copleston, F. (1962–5) *A History of Philosophy volumes 1–7*, NY: Image Books.

Corbin, H. (2006) *History of Islamic Philosophy*, London: Kegan Paul.

Derrida, J. (1986) *Glas*, Lincoln and London: University of Nebraska Press.

Derrida, J. (1987) *Of Spirit*, Chicago: University of Chicago Press.

Derrida, J. (2005) *Rogues*, CA: Stanford University Press.

Descartes, R. (1984) *The Philosophical Writings of Descartes, volume 2*, trans. J. Cottingham et al., Cambridge: Cambridge University Press.

Descartes, R. (1985) *The Philosophical Writings of Descartes, volume 1*, trans. J. Cottingham et al., Cambridge: Cambridge University Press.

Dews, P. (1992) *Autonomy and Solidarity*, London: Verso.

Laertius, D. (2005) *Lives of Eminent Philosophers Books VI–X*, trans. R. D. Hicks, MA and London: Loeb Classical Library.

Duns Scotus, J. (1987) *Philosophical Writings*, trans. A. Wolter, Indianapolis: Hackett Publishing Co.

Jesus, Son of Sirach (1916) *The Wisdom of Ben Sira*, London: SPCK, reprinted Kessinger 2004.

Ellison, R. (1952, 2001) *Invisible Man*, London: Penguin.

Epicurus (1993) *The Essential Epicurus*, trans. E. O'Connor, NY: Prometheus Books.

Epicurus (1994) The Epicurus Reader: Selected *Writings and Testimonia*, trans. B. Inwood, Indianapolis: Hackett Publishing Co.

Epictetus (1983) *The Handbook*, trans. N. P. White, Indianapolis: Hackett Publishing Co.

Epictetus (2004) *The Discourses Books 1 and 2*, trans. P. Matheson, NY: Dover Publications Inc.

Eriugena, J. S. (1987) *Periphyseon (The Division of Nature)*, trans. I. P. Sheldon-Williams, WA: Dumbarton Oaks.

Fakhry, M. (2001) *Averroes, His Life, Works and Influence*, Oxford: Oneworld Publications.

Fakhry, M. (2002) *Al-Farabi: Founder of Islamic Neoplatonism*, Oxford: Oneworld Publications.

Habermas, J. (1987) *The Philosophical Discourse of Modernity*, Cambridge: Polity Press.

Hegel, G. W. F. (1969) *Science of Logic*, trans. A. V. Miller, London: George Allen and Unwin.

Hegel, G. W. F. (1974) *Lectures on the History of Philosophy, volume 2*, trans. E. S. Haldane and F. H. Simson, London: RKP, (Werke 19, *Vorlesungen über die Geschichte der Philosophie* II, Frankfurt, Suhrkamp Verlag, 1970).

Hegel, G. W. F. (1975) *Hegel's Logic*, trans. W. Wallace, Oxford: Clarendon Press.

Hegel, G. W. F. (1977) *Phenomenology of Spirit,* Oxford: Oxford University Press, (*Sämtliche Werke; Bd. II, Phänomenologie des Geistes*, Leipzig, Meiner, 1949).

Hegel, G. W. F. (1987) *Introduction to the Lectures on the History of Philosophy*, trans. T. M. Knox and A. V. Miller, Oxford: Clarendon Press, (Sämtliche Werke, Vol. 15a: *Vorlesungen über die Geschichte der Philosophie. Einleitung: System und Geschichte der Philosophie*. Vollstandig neu nach den Quellen hrsg. V. Johannes Hoffmeister, Leipzig, 1940).

Heidegger, M. (1992) *Being and Time*, trans. J. Macquarrie and E. Robinson, Oxford: Blackwell.

Heraclitus, (1987) *Fragments*, trans. T. M. Robinson, Toronto: University of Toronto Press.

Jaeger, W. (1962) *Aristotle*, Oxford: Oxford University Press.

Kant, I. (1956) *Critique of Practical Reason*, trans. L. W. Beck, NY and London: Macmillan.

Kant, I. (1968) *Critique of Pure Reason*, trans. N. Kemp Smith, London: Macmillan.

Kant, I. (1989) *The Critique of Judgement*, trans. J. C. Meredith, Oxford: Clarendon Press.

Kierkegaard, S. (1985) *Philosophical Fragments/Johannes Climacus*, trans. H. V. Hong and E. H. Hong, Princeton: Princeton University Press.

Kierkegaard, S. (1989) *The Concept of Irony*, trans. H. V. Hong and E. H. Hong, Princeton: Princeton University Press.

Leibniz, G. W. (1998) *Philosophical Texts*, trans. R. S. Woolhouse and R. Francks, Oxford: Oxford University Press.

Locke, J. (1996) *Some Thoughts Concerning Education and Of The Conduct of the Understanding*, Indianapolis: Hackett Publishing Co.

Locke, J. (2004) *An Essay Concerning Human Understanding*, London: Penguin.

Maimonides (1963a) *The Guide of the Perplexed Volume One*, trans. S. Pines, Chicago: The University of Chicago Press.

Maimonides (1963b) *The Guide of the Perplexed Volume Two*, trans. S. Pines, Chicago: The University of Chicago Press.

Marx, K. (1975) *Early Writings*, trans. R. Livingstone, London: Penguin.

Nietzsche, F. (1968) *Basic Writings of Nietzsche*, trans. W. Kaufmann, NY: The Modern Library.

Nietzsche, F. (1982) *The Portable Nietzsche*, trans. W. Kaufmann, NY: The Viking Press.

Origen (1979) *Origen*, NJ: Paulist Press, The Classics of Western Spirituality.

Philo (2006) *The Works of Philo*, trans. C. D. Yonge, MA: Hendrickson Publishers.

Plato (1982) *Plato I Euthyphro, Apology, Crito, Phaedo, Phaedrus*, trans. H. N. Fowler, Harvard and London: Loeb Classical Library.

Plotinus (1991) *The Enneads*, trans. S. MacKenna, London: Penguin.
Proclus (1995) *The Theology of Plato*, trans. T. Taylor, Frome: The Prometheus Trust.
Pseudo-Dionysius (1987) *Pseudo-Dionysius: The Complete Works*, NY: Paulist Press, Classics of Western Spirituality.
Rose, G. (1996) *Mourning Becomes the Law*, Cambridge: Cambridge University Press.
Seneca (1997) *On the Shortness of Life*, trans. C. D. N. Costa, London: Penguin.
Empiricus, S. (2000) *Outlines of Scepticism*, eds J. Annas and J. Barnes, Cambridge: Cambridge University Press.
Spinoza, B. (1889) *The Chief Works of Benedict De Spinoza Volume I*, trans. R. H. M. Elwes, London: George Bell and Sons.
Spinoza, B. (1992) *Ethics, Treatise on the Emendation of the Intellect and Selected Letters*, trans. S. Shirley, Indianapolis: Hackett Publishing Co.
Virgil, (1990) The Aeneid, London: Penguin.
Walzer, R. (1962) *Greek into Arabic*, MA: Harvard University Press.

## Additional Bibliography

Abelard, P. (1974) *The Letters of Abelard and Heloise*, trans. B. Radice, London: Penguin.
Abelard, P. (1995) *Ethical Writings*, trans. P. V. Spade, Indianapolis: Hackett Publishing Co.
Abelard, P. (2005) *The Story of My Misfortune*, NY: Dover Publications Inc.
Al-Kindi (1974) *Al-Kindi's Metaphysics*, trans. A. L. Ivry, Albany: State University of New York Press.
Anselm of Canterbury (1998) *Anselm of Canterbury: The Major Works*, Oxford: Oxford University Press.
Aquinas, T. (1993) *Aquinas Selected Philosophical Writings*, trans. T. McDermott, Oxford: Oxford University Press.
Aquinas, T. (2002) *Aquinas Political Writings*, trans. R. W. Dyson, Cambridge: Cambridge University Press.
Augustine (1938) *Concerning the Teacher and On the Immortality of the Soul*, trans. G. C. Leckie, NY: Appleton-Century-Crofts Inc.
Augustine (1944) *The Happy Life (De Beata Vita)*, trans. R. A. Brown, WA: The Catholic University of America.
Augustine (1968) *The Retractions*, trans. Sister M. I. Bogan, *The Fathers of the Church, volume 60*, WA: Catholic University of America Press.
Augustine (1996) *Enchiridion on Faith, Hope and Love*, trans. J. B. Shaw, WA: Regnery Publishing Inc.
Augustine (2001) *Augustine Political Writings*, trans. E. M. Atkins, Cambridge: Cambridge University Press.
Boethius (2000) *The Consolation of Philosophy*, trans. P. G. Walsh, Oxford: Oxford University Press.
Bonaventure (1993) *The Journey of the Mind to God*, trans. P. Boehner, Indianapolis: Hackett Publishing Co.
Copleston, F. (2004) A History of Medieval Philosophy, Notre Dame: University of Notre Dame Press.
Derrida, J. (1978) *Writing and Difference*, London: Routledge.
Derrida, J. (1988) *Limited Inc.*, Evanston: Northwestern University Press.
Derrida, J. (1995) *Points ... Interviews 1974–1994*, CA: Stanford University Press.
Dunlop, D. M. (1971) *Arab Civilization to AD 1500*, London: Longman.

Eusebius (2005) The History of *the Church*, trans. A. C. McGiffert, Stilwell: Digireads.com Publishing.

Fakhry, M. (1997) *Islamic Philosophy, Theology and Mysticism*, Oxford: Oneworld Publications.

Fakhry, M. (2004) *A History of Islamic Philosophy*, Third Edition, NY: Columbia University Press.

Farias, V. (1989) *Heidegger and Nazism*, Philadelphia: Temple University Press.

Hegel, G. W. F. (1956) *The Philosophy of History*, trans. J. Sibree, NY: Dover Publications; (Werke 12 *Vorlesungen über die Philosophie der Geschichte*, Frankfurt, Suhrkamp Verlag, 1970).

Hegel, G. W. F. (1967) *Philosophy of Right*, trans. T. M. Knox, Oxford: Oxford University Press.

Hegel, G. W. F. (1970, 2004) *Philosophy of Nature*, trans. A. V. Miller, Oxford: The Clarendon Press.

Hegel, G. W. F. (1990) *Lectures on the History of Philosophy: Volume III Mediaeval and Modern Philosophy*, trans. R. F. Brown, J. M. Stewart, and H. S. Harris, Berkeley: University of California Press.

Heidegger, M. (1969) *Identity and Difference*, NY: Harper Torchbooks.

Heidegger, M. (1987) *Introduction to Metaphysics*, Newhaven: Yale University Press.

Heidegger, M. (1988) *The Basic Problems of Phenomenology*, Bloomington: Indiana University Press.

Hyman, A. and Walsh, J. J. (eds) (1973) *Philosophy in the Middle Ages*, Indianapolis: Hackett Publishing Co.

Kierkegaard, S. (1973) *The Concept of Dread*, trans. W. Lowrie, Princeton: Princeton University Press.

Kierkegaard, S. (1983) *Fear and Trembling/Repetition*, trans. H. V. Hong and E. H. Hong, Princeton: Princeton University Press.

Kierkegaard, S. (1988) *Stages on Life's Way*, trans. H. V. Hong and E. H. Hong, Princeton: Princeton University Press.

Krell, D. F. (1993) *Basic Writings: Martin Heidegger*, London: Routledge.

Leibniz, G. W. (1968) *Basic Writings*, trans. G. R. Montgomery, Illinois: The Open Court Publishing Co.

Netton, I. R. (1992) *Al-Farabi and his School*, Richmond: Curzon Press.

Parmenides (1991) *Fragments*, Toronto: University of Toronto Press.

Plato (1956) *Protagoras and Meno*, London: Penguin.

Plato (1960) *Gorgias*, London: Penguin.

Plato (1977) *Plato IV Cratylus Parmenides Greater Hippias Lesser Hippias*, trans. H. N. Fowler, Harvard and London: Loeb Classical Library.

Plato (1987) *Plato VII Theaetetus/Sophist*, trans. H. N. Fowler, Harvard and London: Loeb Classical Library.

Plato (1993) *Philebus*, trans. D. Frede, Indianapolis: Hackett Publishing Co.

Plato (1994) *The Republic*, London: Everyman.

Plato (2005) *Plato IX Timaeus Critias Cleitophon Menexenus Epistles*, trans. H. N. Fowler, Loeb Classical Library.

J. B. Ross and M. M. McLaughlin (eds), (1977) *The Portable Medieval Reader*, NY and London: Penguin.

Seneca (1968) *The Stoic Philosophy of Seneca: Essays and Letters*, trans. M. Hadas, NY and London: W. W. Norton and Co.

Spinoza, B. (1955) *Works of Spinoza*, trans. R. H. M. Elwes, NY: Dover Publications.

Wolin, R. (1993) *The Heidegger Controversy*, Cambridge MA: The MIT Press.

# Index